History and Nature of Science [HNS]

CONTENT STANDARD G: As a result of the activities in grades K–4, all students should develop an understanding of

- Science as a human endeavor [HNS 1]

Content Standards: Grades 5–8

Science as Inquiry

CONTENT STANDARD A: As a result of their activities in grades 5–8, all students should develop

- Abilities necessary to do scientific inquiry
- Understanding about scientific inquiry

Physical Science [PS]

CONTENT STANDARD B: As a result of their activities in grades 5–8, all students should develop an understanding of

- Properties and changes of properties in matter [PS 4]
- Motion and forces [PS 5]
- Transfer of energy [PS 6]

Life Science [LS]

CONTENT STANDARD C: As a result of their activities in grades 5–8, all students should develop an understanding of

- Structure and function in living systems [LS 4]
- Reproduction and heredity [LS 5]
- Regulation and behavior [LS 6]
- Population and ecosystems [LS 7]
- Diversity and adaptations of organisms [LS 8]

Earth and Space Sciences [ESS]

CONTENT STANDARD D: As a result of their activities in grades 5–8, all students should develop an understanding of

- Structure of the earth system [ESS 4]
- Earth's history [ESS 5]
- Earth in the solar system [ESS 6]

Science and Technology [S&T]

CONTENT STANDARD E: As a result of the activities in grades 5–8, all students should develop an understanding of

- Abilities of technological design [S&T 4]
- Understanding about science and technology [S&T 5]

Science in Personal and Social Perspectives [SPSP]

CONTENT STANDARD F: As a result of the activities in grades 5–8, all students should develop an understanding of

- Personal health [SPSP 6]
- Populations, resources, and environments [SPSP 7]
- Natural hazards [SPSP 8]
- Risks and benefits [SPSP 9]
- Changes in environments [SPSP 10]
- Science and technology in society [SPSP 11]

History and Nature of Science [HNS]

CONTENT STANDARD G: As a result of the activities in grades 5–8, all students should develop an understanding of

- Science as a human endeavor [HNS 2]
- Nature of science [HNS 3]
- History of science [HNS 4]

Teaching Children Science

Discovery Activities and Demonstrations for the Elementary and Middle Grades

Teaching Children Science

Discovery Activities and Demonstrations for the Elementary and Middle Grades

SECOND EDITION

Joseph Abruscato

University of Vermont

PEARSON
AB

Boston   New York   San Francisco
Mexico City   Montreal   Toronto   London   Madrid   Munich   Paris
Hong Kong   Singapore   Tokyo   Cape Town   Sydney

Series Editor: *Traci Mueller*
Editorial Assistant: *Krista E. Price*
Senior Marketing Manager: *Elizabeth Fogarty*
Editorial-Production Administrator: *Annette Joseph*
Editorial-Production Service: *Susan Freese, Communicáto, Ltd.*
Text Designer and Electronic Composition: *Denise Hoffman*
Composition Buyer: *Linda Cox*
Manufacturing Buyer: *Andrew Turso*
Cover Administrator: *Joel Gendron*
Cover Designer: *Suzanne Harbison*

For related titles and support materials, visit our online catalog at www.ablongman.com.

Between the time Website information is gathered and then published, it is not unusual for some sites to have closed. Also, the transcription of URLs can result in typographical errors. The publisher would appreciate notification where these errors occur so that they may be corrected in subsequent editions.

Many of the designations used by manufacturers and sellers to distinguish their products are claimed as trademarks. Where those designations appear in this book and Allyn and Bacon was aware of a trademark claim, the designations have been printed in caps or initial caps.

Library of Congress Cataloging-in-Publication Data

Abruscato, Joseph.
    Teaching children science : discovery activities and demonstrations
for the elementary and middle grades / Joseph Abruscato.—2nd ed.
      p. cm.
    Includes bibliographical references and index.
    ISBN 0–205–40262–3
    1. Science—Study and teaching (Elementary)—Activity programs.
    2. Science—Study and teaching (Middle school)—Activity programs. I. Title.

LB1585.A3 2004
372.3'5044–dc21

                                           2003052435

Printed in the United States of America

10 9 8 7 6 5 4 3 2 1   RRD-VA   08 07 06 05 04 03

For my mother
who showered me with hugs and love
and filled my young life with books

Contents

3A The Cosmos: Content   63

3B The Cosmos: Attention Getters, Discovery Activities, and Demonstrations   81

PART TWO

The Life Sciences and Technology   101

4 The Life Sciences and Technology:
Unit, Lesson, and Enrichment Starter Ideas   109

5A Living Things: Content   133

5B Living Things: Attention Getters, Discovery Activities, and Demonstrations   147

PART THREE

The Physical Sciences and Technology   195

7 The Physical Sciences and Technology:
Unit, Lesson, and Enrichment Starter Ideas   203

Welcome to *Discovery Activities and Demonstrations for the Elementary and Middle Grades*

You are going to find this book a wonderful resource, now and in the future! It provides what I call *starter ideas* for planning science units and lessons, a wide range of activities and projects for children of all grade levels, and the actual background content you will need to know as you teach children science. Given this wealth of information, you will probably want to keep this book right on your desk!

Another reason you will find this book helpful is that it is easy to use. *Discovery Activities and Demonstrations* is organized into three parts, each of which covers one of the major fields of science:

- Part One: The Earth/Space Sciences and Technology
- Part Two: The Life Sciences and Technology
- Part Three: The Physical Sciences and Technology

New in this edition, each part opens with an introduction that provides background information about the field of science at hand. In each introduction, a section called *History and Nature* looks at careers in science, key events in the development of the field, and the lives of real women and men who helped shape that development. Another section called *Personal and Social Implications* reviews issues of personal and community health as well as the hazards, risks, and benefits that go along with scientific development. A final section, *Technology: Its Nature and Impact,* discusses and illustrates specific developments and considers the long-term implications of technology for our world.

As in previous editions, the first chapter in each part—Chapter 1, 4, or 7, respectively—provides a variety of practical starter ideas to help you plan and teach the science units and lessons related to the topic of focus. A chapter-ending section of *Resources for Discovery Learning* provides a variety of new source materials, including lists of related articles from the journals *Science and Children* and *Science Scope* and an assortment of current websites and their URLs (uniform resource locators).

These part-opening chapters are followed by two pairs of "A" and "B" chapters. Each "A" chapter contains science content, and the corresponding "B" chapter provides science activities for children that pertain to that content. These activities are grouped by grade level (that is, young learners and middle-level learners) and activity type (Attention Getters, Discovery Activities, and Demonstrations).

Here is an example of how each part is organized:

Part One   The Earth/Space Sciences and Technology

Chapter 1   The Earth/Space Sciences and Technology:
              Unit, Lesson, and Enrichment Starter Ideas

Chapter 2A   The Earth's Surface, Atmosphere, and Weather: Content

Chapter 2B   The Earth's Surface, Atmosphere, and Weather:
              Attention Getters, Discovery Activities, and Demonstrations

Chapter 3A   The Cosmos: Content

Chapter 3B   The Cosmos: Attention Getters, Discovery Activities,
              and Demonstrations

Parts Two and Three follow the same structure but deal with the life sciences and the physical sciences, respectively. So, look for a chapter of starter ideas followed by alternating content chapters and activities chapters. It's all here, no matter what the subject!

As you read and work with *Discovery Activities and Demonstrations,* you will also become familiar with some of the current developments in the science-teaching field and learn how to apply them in your own classroom. Today's science teachers need to know about these developments:

1. *Constructivism.* There is little question that we create much of our own reality. One way of looking at how we integrate life experiences into our mental processes is provided by the theory of *constructivism.* This theory is addressed early in each part of the book—namely, in Chapters, 1, 4, and 7 in a section called *Assessing Prior Knowledge and Conceptions.* When applied in the classroom, constructivist theory guides teachers in thinking about what they are doing to help children get beyond scientific misconceptions and acquire more appropriate knowledge, skills, and values.

2. *The National Science Education (NSE) Standards.* All of us who teach children science need some direction, and the best current direction is provided by the NSE Standards. As indicated by the icon shown in the margin, the NSE Standards for grades K–8 are addressed at relevant points throughout the book. Specifically, the part-opening sections include content about the nature and development of the sciences, which correlates directly to recommendations of the standards; Chapters 1, 4, and 7 use the standards as organizers for lesson and unit planning; and in the "B" chapters, every activity references one or more relevant standards. Finally, the complete NSE Standards for grades K–8 are reprinted just inside the front cover of this book, providing easy access to this useful information.

3. *The Internet.* As incredible as it may seem, teachers and students today have almost instant access to much of the recorded information of humankind. The Internet is now ubiquitous in U.S. classrooms, from kindergartens through the primary grades and on up. But applying this technology in useful and productive

ways remains a challenge for many teachers. This text will provide guidance for doing so in several ways:

- Each of Chapters 1, 4, and 7 ends with a section called *Resources for Discovery Learning,* which includes a section of valuable websites that pertain to the topic at hand: the earth/space sciences, the life sciences, or the physical sciences. A brief description is given of each site as well as the URL.

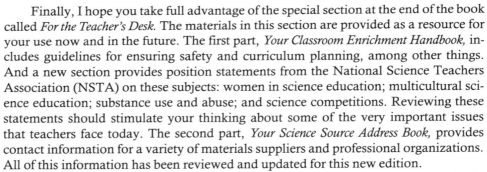

- Each of these chapters also contains a section called *WebQuest Starter Ideas,* which provides specific ideas for creating Internet-based, science-related experiences for children. By reviewing these ideas, you will come to understand what's involved in creating good Internet activities for children.

- Internet-related content is identified throughout the text using the icon shown in the margin.

Finally, I hope you take full advantage of the special section at the end of the book called *For the Teacher's Desk.* The materials in this section are provided as a resource for your use now and in the future. The first part, *Your Classroom Enrichment Handbook,* includes guidelines for ensuring safety and curriculum planning, among other things. And a new section provides position statements from the National Science Teachers Association (NSTA) on these subjects: women in science education; multicultural science education; substance use and abuse; and science competitions. Reviewing these statements should stimulate your thinking about some of the very important issues that teachers face today. The second part, *Your Science Source Address Book,* provides contact information for a variety of materials suppliers and professional organizations. All of this information has been reviewed and updated for this new edition.

I'm sure that you will enjoy reading *Discovery Activities and Demonstrations for the Elementary and Middle Grades* and that you will learn much from it. Use it to help create a classroom in which children look forward to science time as a wonderful opportunity to learn from and be with *you!*

Acknowledgments

Many people have shaped the content of this book, directly and indirectly. I would like to thank a few of my dearest friends and colleagues for their continued support and encouragement: Lowell J. Bethel at the University of Texas; Jack Hassard at Georgia State University; Russell Agne, Susan Baker, and Joyce Morris at the University of Vermont; Rod Peturson of the Windsor Schools, Ontario, Canada; Marlene Nachbar Hapai at the University of Hawaii, Manoa; William Ritz at California State University, Long Beach; Larry Schaeffer at Syracuse University; and the public school teachers I work with every week at Orchard Elementary School and Malletts Bay School.

J. A.

The Earth/Space Sciences and Technology

History and Nature of the Earth/Space Sciences

Tonight, and every night, *you* have the chance to see a wondrous puzzle exactly as generations of humans before you have seen it. Tiny objects will begin to emerge, gleaming and glimmering, and darkness will envelop everything around you. This great and glorious puzzle is the night sky.

Trying to make sense of what lies above us is a mark of our humanity. Likewise, the mysteries of the earth below make us wonder. We ask "What?" and "How?" and "Why?"

These are the same questions that guide what earth and space scientists do. They search for answers to the puzzles of our world, so we will eventually understand what really lies above and below. The earth/space sciences include the fields of astronomy, geology, oceanography, meteorology, and astronomy. Each requires people who wonder.

Careers in the Earth/Space Sciences

Many career paths exist for those women and men who have the required motivation, knowledge, and skills to formally explore the sky above and the earth below. Here are a few of the wide range of possibilities:

- *Geologist*. I love to tease my geologist friends by calling them "rock watchers." Of course, they tell me with great gusto that they do much more than watch rocks—and of course, they do. Geology includes the study of the origin of the earth, the history of the earth, and the external and internal structure and movements of the earth.

- *Oceanographer*. Not all oceanographers spend the day scuba diving in warm tropical waters, but some do! In fact, the work done by oceanographers takes them to oceans all over the world. That work might involve study of the characteristics of the seafloor, the ocean water itself, and the forms of life in, on, and under the ocean.

■ *Meteorologist.*   The constantly smiling and sometimes overly excited weather people you watch on local news shows may be meteorologists or newscasters acting as if they are meteorologists! A real meteorologist has taken courses dealing with atmospheric phenomena and how various weather systems affect life on earth.

■ *Astronomer.*   If you've looked at the night sky and been enthralled by the amazing display of objects above your head, you have taken the first step that all astronomers take: to think beyond the boundaries of Earth and its atmosphere. Modern astronomers have excellent backgrounds in physics and mathematics as well as considerable computer expertise.

Key Events in the Development of the Earth/Space Sciences

610–425 B.C.E.	Philosophers Anaximander, Pythagoras, Xenophanes, and Herodotus propose that fossils found inland once lived in the sea.
140	Ptolemy incorrectly concludes that the earth is at the center of the solar system.
1797–1726	James Hutton concludes that processes that were constantly occurring—such as erosion, deposition, earthquakes, and volcanic eruptions—produced the rocks of Scotland. These ideas are the foundation for the principle of uniformitarianism.
1781	William Herschel discovers the planet Uranus, the first such discovery since ancient times.
1804	Georges Cuvier studies fossils found around Paris and suggests that they are thousands of centuries old. This meant that the earth was much older than people thought at the time.
1820–1821	Mary Anning excavates the world's first fossil plesiosaur.
1830	Charles Lyell publishes *Principles of Geology*, a book that Charles Darwin took along on his explorations.
1847	Maria Mitchell, an American astronomer and professor, discovers a comet whose path took it near the star Polaris.
1856	The first recognized fossil human, a Neanderthal, is discovered in Düsseldorf, Germany.
1912	Alfred Wegener proposes the theory of continental drift, suggesting that the individual continents were once part of one supercontinent.
1957	The Soviet Union launches *Sputnik,* the earth's first artificial space satellite.
1969	American astronaut Neil Armstrong walks on the surface of the moon.
1969	The American *Apollo* missions bring rocks home from the moon to the earth.
1971	Stephen Hawking poses the hypothesis that primordial black holes might have been created in the Big Bang: a theorized explosion that marked the origin of the universe billions of years ago.
1974	Stephen Hawking applies quantum field theory to black hole spacetime and shows that black holes radiate mass/energy that may result in their evaporating.
1980	Alan Guth proposes the inflationary Big Bang universe, which suggests that the universe expanded at a rate that kept doubling for a brief period of time after the Big Bang.
1980	Louis W. Alvarez, Walter Alvarez, Frank Asaro, and Helen V. Michel publish their asteroid impact theory of dinosaur extinction in *Science Magazine*.

1981   The United States launches the first space shuttle: the *Columbia.*

1990   The Hubble Space Telescope is placed in orbit; after its optical systems are improved, it sends back extraordinary pictures of the universe.

1990   The COBE (Cosmic Background Explorer) satellite transmits data that indicate that the background radiation of the universe is what would be expected if the universe originated in a manner consistent with the Big Bang theory.

1991   The Chicxulub crater is discovered in the Yucatán Peninsula, supporting the asteroid impact theory first suggested in 1980.

1993   J. William Schopf publishes a description of the oldest fossils known to science: 3.5 billion-year-old microfossils from the Apex Basalt in Australia.

1995   Michael Mayor and Didier Queloz identify the first planet outside our solar system.

1997   The Mars probe *Sojourner* lands and transmits pictures of the planet's surface to Earth.

1998   The moon probe *Lunar Prospector* sends back data that indicate that some water in the form of ice lies beneath its surface.

1998   Construction begins on the *International Space Station.*

2001   The *Mars Global Surveyor* probe completes its primary mapping study of the Martian surface and reveals that there once was and now may be liquid water near the surface.

Women and Men Who Have Shaped the Development of the Earth/Space Sciences

PTOLEMY (87–150 B.C.E) was an astronomer, mathematician, and geographer. He proposed that the earth was at the center of the universe and that the other heavenly bodies—such as the sun and planets—moved in orbits around it. He was, of course, incorrect.

TYCHO BRAHE (1546–1601), a Danish astronomer, gathered data that were eventually used to predict the motion and orbits of the planets. These data quashed any remaining support for the Ptolemaic, or Earth-centered, view of the universe.

SOPHIA BRAHE (1556–1643), the younger sister of Tycho Brahe, gathered and contributed data used to predict planetary orbits. In addition to her astronomical work, she was also a well-known horticulturalist and historian.

NICOLAUS COPERNICUS (1473–1543) was a mathematician, physician, lawyer, and perhaps priest who became known for suggesting that the sun was at rest in the center of the universe. This is now know as the heliocentric theory.

GALILEO GALILEI (1564–1642) is credited with many discoveries related to the motion of the pendulum, the construction of compasses and telescopes, and observations of the satellites of Jupiter and the phases of Venus. He espoused Copernicus's view that the planets revolved around the sun and was accused of being a heretic.

ISAAC NEWTON (1642–1727) provided the foundation for modern physics and mathematics. His studies of the natural world led to the development of the law of inertia, the law of action and reaction, and the relationship of force to the acceleration of a mass. He proposed the universal law of gravitation and is credited as being the co-inventor of calculus.

CAROLINE LUCRETIA HERSCHEL (1750–1848) and her brother William gathered data on astronomical objects. After William's death, Caroline completed their work on the creation of astronomy data sources, which were called *catalogs*.

MARY ANNING (1799–1847), a self-taught paleontologist, became known for excavating the fossil remains of an icthyosaurus, a plesisaur, and a pterodactyl.

MARIA MITCHELL (1818–1889), an American astronomer, discovered a comet whose path took it near the star Polaris; she was also known for her analysis of sunspots.

CHARLES D. WALCOTT (1850–1827) was a geologist and paleontologist who made a number of discoveries related to ancient animal and plant life. The most important of these was his study of the Middle Cambrian Burgess Shale, which had an extraordinary range of fossils.

ANDRIJA MOHOROVICIC (1857–1936), a Croatian geologist and meteorologist, made extraordinary discoveries related to weather and seismology. The Mohorovicic discontinuity, the boundary between the crust and the mantle of the earth, was eventually named in his honor.

ALBERT EINSTEIN (1879–1955) was a German-born physicist whose special theory of relativity and general theory of relativity provided the basis for much of what is known about the nature of time, space, and matter.

ALFRED WEGENER (1880–1930) was trained in astronomy but pursued meteorology as his profession. Curiously, he eventually became world famous for work in yet another field: geology. He first proposed the theory of plate tectonics, which is the foundation for modern ideas about continental drift.

CHARLES FRANCIS RICHTER (1900–1985) carried out work on the classification of earthquakes based on energy release. The Richter scale was developed from his careful analysis of data acquired at the Caltech Seismological Laboratory.

LUIS ALVAREZ (1911–) received the Nobel Prize for physics in 1968 for his study of subatomic particles. He became even more famous for his study of a thin, clay layer under the earth's surface that contains large amounts of iridium. This discovery lent support to the theory that dinosaur extinction was caused by an asteroid crashing into the earth and releasing the iridium-containing material.

WALTER ALVAREZ (1940–), the son of Luis Alvarez, discovered a thin, clay layer of soil that had high concentrations of iridium and also marked the end of the Cretaceous period and the dinosaurs. This research gave credence to the asteroid impact theory as the explanation for dinosaur extinction.

VERA COOPER RUBIN (1928–) has studied the orbital velocities of hydrogen clouds, and her results support the belief that there are large amounts of dark matter in the universe. (Dark matter is matter that cannot be seen or measured directly.)

STEPHEN HAWKING (1942–), an English physicist, has emerged as one of the most inventive scientific geniuses since Einstein. His theories about black holes and the origin of the universe guide what today's cosmologists explore. His ideas may ultimately provide physicists with a grand unified theory: one equation that will encompass all of the other equations that describe interactions in the universe.

Personal and Social Implications of the Earth/Space Sciences

The quality of the air we breathe and the water we drink, the safety of the structures in which we work and live, and the protection of our natural resources can all be influenced by knowledge gained through the earth/space sciences. This knowledge affects us as individuals and as members of the communities in which we live.

Personal and Community Health

The work done in the earth/space sciences affects our well-being in many ways. For instance, geologists gather information about the quality of agricultural soils and the safety of recreational areas such as ski slopes and reservoirs formed behind earthen dams. The safety of our transportation system, including roads, tunnels, and bridge supports, all depends on geologists' knowledge of the rocks and rock layers underneath them.

We count on the forecasting capabilities of meteorologists to tell us how to dress for personal comfort and to provide us with a timeline for the pending arrival of violent weather. And the knowledge of the night skies provided by astronomers permits us to navigate the earth safely and even guides farmers and fishermen in their food production efforts.

Hazards, Risks, and Benefits

Today, earthquakes, volcanic eruptions, violent weather, tsunamis, and the like can all be forecast using the predictive capacities of the earth/space sciences. Given these predictions, individuals and societies can make important health- and safety-related decisions, often saving lives. In the developed nations of the world, personal housing, civic structures, and commercial buildings are all built to withstand disasters of all kinds.

Earth/Space Science Technology: Its Nature and Impact

The women and men who explore the earth/space sciences solve the mysteries of nature by observing, poking at, and prodding it with *technology.* That technology is sometimes as simple as a compass and sometimes as complex as a radiotelescope. Whether simple or complex, the technology used by earth/space scientists is always designed for a very specific purpose.

The Design of Earth/Space Science Technology

Astronomy, geology, meteorology, oceanography, and the other subdisciplines of the earth/space sciences depend on *instrumentation:* radiotelescopes that "listen" to the stars, seismographs that reveal movements within the earth, weather instruments that gather

data about the atmosphere, and underwater microphones that track migration
patterns of sea life. All of these instruments are designed to meet the following criteria:

1. The problem addressed with the technology has been clearly specified and is one
   for which data can be expected to be obtained.
2. The technology itself can reliably gather, display, and transmit data.
3. The data gathered are presented in a manner that can be easily interpreted.
4. The device or instrument provides researchers with constant feedback about the accuracy of the data being represented, errors that may have occurred in the gathering
   and processing of the data, and suggestions for troubleshooting malfunctions.

Examples of Earth/Space Science Technology

A variety of instruments are used to gather information about the earth, the oceans, the
atmosphere, and outer space:

Hand lenses (magnifying glasses)   Seismographs
Microscopes   The global position system (GPS)
Optical telescopes   Weather maps
Radiotelescopes   Anemometers
The Hubble Space Telescope   Barometers
High-resolution cameras   Thermometers
Satellites   Scuba equipment
The orbiting space station   Bathyscaphe (self-propelled underwater
Radar   observatory)
Sonar   Computers

Long-Term Implications of Earth/Space Science Technology

Earth/space scientists seek to provide answers to basic questions about the earth—our
home. Some of the data they acquire will eventually be used to improve our quality of life
in ways large and small. However, earth/space scientists generally do not focus on the immediate application of new knowledge and skills to human problems. That is the work of
engineers and technicians.

   Engineers, who search for solutions to human problems, understand that their work
has real limitations. For instance, their solutions are usually temporary, since the frontiers
of scientific knowledge are constantly expanding. Their solutions may also be too be
costly and carry risks. For example, the use of movement-sensitive underwater microphones may disrupt whale migration patterns.

   Some technological solutions may even have harmful consequences. For example, an
imperfect or malfunctioning earthquake or tsunami warning device might produce information that causes people to panic—triggering the hording of food and water and producing
evacuation problems—when there was really no cause for alarm in the first place. So, not
all technological solutions are successful.

1

The Earth Space/Sciences and Technology

Unit, Lesson, and Enrichment Starter Ideas

Kelly's Gift

Kelly was in such a rush to get into the school that she bumped into the big, brown trash can by the front door and dropped her lunch box. She picked it up, walked through the doorway, and raced down the hallway to her classroom. The door was open and the lights were on, which meant that her teacher was somewhere in the building. She pulled a chair to the side of her teacher's desk, sat down holding her lunch box on her lap, and patiently waited.

In Kelly's lunch box was a present that Aunt Nicole had brought back from vacation. Kelly had wrapped it carefully in foil before putting it next to her sandwich. It was a very special rock, a rock filled with holes, a rock that would float!

"Good morning, Kelly. You certainly are an early bird today," her teacher said, entering the classroom.

"I've got a surprise for you," said Kelly, placing the shiny object at the front of the teacher's desk. "You can show it during science, but I wanted you to see it first."

"That's wonderful. I'll do that, but right now, I have to get the model volcano from Mr. Johnson's room." Kelly's teacher turned and hurried out the door.

Kelly went to her own desk and stared at the foil-wrapped rock. "Oh well," she thought to herself, "I guess it's OK if everybody sees it at the same time."

Science time was right after lunch. The lesson was about the earth's crust. Kelly's teacher forgot about the rock, and Kelly was too shy to mention it.

When Kelly got to school the next day, she went right to the teacher's desk, picked up the foil-wrapped object, looked at it, and without a word handed it to her teacher.

"Thanks, Kelly. I'm so sorry I forgot this yesterday. We'll unwrap it during science time today. I can't wait to see what it is."

Science time finally arrived, but just as the teacher was reaching for the foil-wrapped rock, the school fire alarm went off. There wasn't a fire, but everyone had to stay outside until someone fixed the alarm, which wouldn't stop ringing. By the time the children were able to enter the school, science time was over.

At the end of the day, Kelly quietly walked up to the teacher's desk, picked up the magic floating rock, and a minute later dropped it in the big, brown trash can just outside the school.

As you plan earth/space science and technology units and lessons, think about Kelly's magic floating rock and all of the children for whom rocks and oceans and outer space are sources of wonder. Once you have done this, begin to think of your plans as starting places, not ending places. You do need to plan well and to plan ahead, but you also need to be flexible enough to receive and incorporate the gifts that children bring. What are these gifts? They are the children's ideas about the natural world, their questions about things they observe that don't make sense—and of course, the occasional foil-wrapped floating rock.

Assessing Prior Knowledge and Conceptions

"But we learned all that in Mr. Greeley's class last year."

Have you ever been in a classroom and observed a teacher getting "ambushed"? That's what happens when teachers assume that children know little or nothing about a topic, only to discover too late that they know a lot. The results are also disastrous when teachers assume that children know a lot about a topic and, in fact, know very little. (Plus, valuable lesson-planning time will have been wasted.) Even assumptions about children's beliefs about phenomena in the natural world can stop teachers in their tracks. Children may have very strongly held beliefs that are totally incorrect, and that may not be discovered until the class is deep in a lesson or unit.

So, as a teacher in the real world of schools and classrooms, how can you quickly get a sense of what the children know, what skills they possess, and what they believe? Part of the answer is to use *probes:* basic questions and simple activities that get children thinking and talking about particular topics. The answers children give will provide very direct guidance about what you should include in science units and lessons.

The probes and sample responses that follow come from informal interviews that I or my students have done with children. I think you'll be amazed at some of the responses and motivated to develop probes that you can use *before* planning units and lessons.

Probe	Responses That Reveal Prior Knowledge and Conceptions
■ After giving a young child an assortment of rocks, leaves, and twigs: *Would you please put these into groups and then tell me how you made your choices.*	"I wanted to get three in each group." "I put the big rock with these because it was lonely."
■ After showing a fossil: *How do you think this fossil was made?*	"The animal touched the mud and it hardened. Then the bones were left behind." "When the rock was made, the object was touching it."
■ *Why is it light outside during the day and dark outside during the night?*	"Because a different part of the country faces the sun." "Because the sun isn't around during the night-time. The moon is there instead."
■ *How do you think the earth began?*	"The Big Bang. We learned about it last year." "I don't know. I wish Adam and Eve didn't take the apple of knowledge; then we wouldn't have to go to school."

(continued)

Probe	Responses That Reveal Prior Knowledge and Conceptions
■ *Where do you think soil comes from?*	"It doesn't come from anything. It was always here." "Well, some of it comes from leaves." "I think it's from under the rocks and then the rocks get moved by the glaciers and the soil is left."
■ *What are the stars?*	"They are reflections from the moon." "They are little balls of light."
■ *Some people think we should send astronauts to explore Mars, and some people think doing that would be a waste of money. What do you think?*	"Well, it depends if it's safe or not. If it's safe to go, we should go to see what is there. But if it wasn't safe, we could just send more rockets with TV cameras." "We should send people there to see if anything there is alive. There might be some things there we could get, like metals and gold."

Unit Plan Starter Ideas

That great idea for a science-teaching unit may come from deep within your brain, your school curriculum guide, a state science curriculum framework, a science resource book, a course, a workshop, a discussion you have with children, or some other source. Unfortunately, a great idea (like a friend, an umbrella, and a good restaurant with cheap food) is sometimes hard to find when you really need one.

To make it easier for you to come up with great ideas for science units, I have prepared two different sources of unit starter ideas:

1. The first is based on the National Science Education (NSE) Standards for science content. I created these starter ideas for standards related to grades K–4 and 5–8.

2. The second source of starter ideas is based on my study of earth/space science topics that commonly appear in school curriculum guides. These are shown by grade level.

I am certain that the unique compilation of starter ideas that follows will help you plan and create wonderful discovery-based teaching units.

Ideas Based on the NSE K–8 Content Standards

> **CONTENT STANDARD K–4: Earth and Space Sciences [ESS]**
> As a result of their activities in grades K–4, all students should develop an understanding of:
> Properties of earth materials
> Objects in the sky
> Changes in earth and sky[1]

■ Starter Ideas for the Properties of Earth Materials

UNIT TITLE: *My Rock Collection*

UNIT GOAL: Students gather rocks outdoors, observe them, learn that they are made of different substances, and classify them.

UNIT TITLE: *Soils Here/Soils There*

UNIT GOAL: Students collect soil samples from various locations, observe them, and classify them on the basis of color, particle size, texture, and how they react with water.

■ Starter Ideas for Objects in the Sky

UNIT TITLE: *The Sun and the Moon*

UNIT GOAL: Through class discussions and reading, students describe the general characteristics and relationships among the sun, planets, moon, and stars.

UNIT TITLE: *The Planets and the Stars*

UNIT GOAL: Through class discussions and reading, students describe the general characteristics of the planets and the stars.

■ Starter Ideas for Changes in the Earth and Sky

UNIT TITLE: *Our Earth Changes*

UNIT GOAL: Students use their memories, interviews with adults, and daily weather and climate observations to identify observable changes that occur on the earth, including the yearly changes in seasons.

UNIT TITLE: *Our Moon*

UNIT GOAL: Students observe the moon, keep track of its apparent change in shape, draw its changing appearance, and search for patterns in the observations they have collected.

As a result of the activities in grades 5–8, all students should develop an understanding of:

Structure of the earth system

Earth's history

Earth in the solar system

■ Starter Ideas for the Structure of the Earth's System

UNIT TITLE: *The Earth Is a System*

UNIT GOAL: Students describe the layers of the earth, its core, and how the core and layers interact.

UNIT TITLE: *Solid or Not?*

UNIT GOAL: Students give descriptions of the evidence that supports the hypothesis that the solid earth beneath their feet is constantly changing. Their descriptions will include references to the movements of plates, constructive and destructive forces, and the rock cycle (i.e., the change of old rocks to particles and their eventual reformation into rocks).

■ Starter Ideas for the Earth's History

UNIT TITLE: *Yesterday and Today*

UNIT GOAL: Students identify modern earth processes—such as plate movement, erosion, and atmospheric changes—and make hypotheses about whether these processes have also occurred in the past.

UNIT TITLE: *Surprising Events*

UNIT GOAL: Students create written research reports using information from reference books and Internet searches that describe the characteristics of possible catastrophic events in the earth's history, including asteroid or comet collisions.

■ Starter Ideas for the Earth in the Solar System

UNIT TITLE: *Where Are We, Really?*

UNIT GOAL: Students create charts, graphs, and drawings that demonstrate their knowledge of the position of the earth in the solar system and the locations of the other eight planets, moons, asteroids, and comets.

UNIT TITLE: *The Sun Does It All*

UNIT GOAL: Students give evidence that supports the hypothesis that the sun is the major source of energy for phenomena such as plant growth, winds, ocean currents, and the water cycle.

CONTENT STANDARDS K–8 RELATED TO:
Science and Technology [S&T]
Science in Personal and Social Perspectives [SPSP]
History and Nature of Science [HNS][2]

UNIT TITLE: *How Do They Know?*

UNIT GOAL: Students identify the forms of technology used by meteorologists and build a model of at least one instrument used to gather weather observations.

UNIT TITLE: *Protect Yourself*

UNIT GOAL: Students identify natural hazards that might affect them or others, their frequency of occurrence, and the protective steps individuals can take when specific hazards such as violent storms and earthquakes occur.

UNIT TITLE: *Who Are They?*

UNIT GOAL: Students do library and Internet research to prepare brief biographies of Ptolemy, Tycho Brahe, Johannes Kepler, and Alfred Wegener that focus on their contributions to our understanding of the earth and its systems.

Ideas Based on Typical Grade-Level Content

■ Starter Ideas for Kindergarten

UNIT TITLE: *The Same and Different*

UNIT GOAL: Children compare a variety of rocks in terms of size, shape, form, color, texture, and density and create a set of rocks that each share at least two characteristics.

UNIT TITLE: *What Is the Weather?*

UNIT GOAL: Children observe the daily weather, tell about it, and make note of any changes from the previous day's weather.

UNIT TITLE: *What Is under Your Feet?*

UNIT GOAL: Children observe that rocks and soil are under their feet when they are outdoors and use a colander to sort rocks, pebbles, and soil.

■ Starter Ideas for First Grade

UNIT TITLE: *The Sun, the Moon, and the Stars*

UNIT GOAL: Children compare the relative sizes and changing positions of the sun, moon, and stars.

UNIT TITLE: *Water Everywhere and in the Air*

UNIT GOAL: Children compare various forms of precipitation and clouds and learn that water evaporates from water sources on the earth, condenses in the air, and eventually returns to the earth.

■ Starter Ideas for Second Grade

UNIT TITLE: *Lakes and Oceans*

UNIT GOAL: Children discover that freshwater and saltwater have different characteristics, learn how beaches are made, and discover the origins of sand.

UNIT TITLE: *The Reasons for Seasons*

UNIT GOAL: Children compare the four seasons and learn that they result from the position and tilt of the earth in its path around the sun.

UNIT TITLE: *Climate Here, Climate There*

UNIT GOAL: Children describe the different climate zones of the world and the types of plants and animals found in them.

■ Starter Ideas for Third Grade

UNIT TITLE: *A Visit to the Planets*

UNIT GOAL: Children learn the names of the planets, their characteristics, and their distances from the sun.

UNIT TITLE: *Group the Rocks*

UNIT GOAL: Children learn that rocks can be classified into three major groups on the basis of their characteristics and origins.

■ Starter Ideas for Fourth Grade

UNIT TITLE: *Earth Layers and Changes*

UNIT GOAL: Children learn that the earth consists of various rock layers and that changes are occurring continually in its crust.

UNIT TITLE: *Star Search*

UNIT GOAL: Children learn that the sun is one of a multitude of stars in the Milky Way and learn to recognize the major constellations in the night sky.

UNIT TITLE: *Weather Today, Weather Tomorrow*

UNIT GOAL: Children construct and use simple weather instruments and then use the data they have gathered to forecast the weather for the next day.

■ Starter Ideas for Fifth Grade

UNIT TITLE: *The Earth Long Ago*

UNIT GOAL: Children learn the clues that scientists use to determine the ages of rocks, the major time periods of the earth's geologic history, and the types of living things that existed during each time period.

UNIT TITLE: *Earth Treasures: How to Find and Use Them Carefully*

UNIT GOAL: Children learn how humans locate and use the earth's mineral resources and the possible environmental problems associated with the acquisition and use of these resources.

■ Starter Ideas for Sixth Grade

UNIT TITLE: *Mapping the Weather*

UNIT GOAL: Students learn the meanings of the principal symbols used on a weather map and how to use a succession of daily weather maps to predict tomorrow's weather.

UNIT TITLE: *Voyaging around the Earth to the Moon and Planets*

UNIT GOAL: Students learn how the space shuttle operates and how future space explorers will travel, work, and live in space.

■ Starter Ideas for Seventh Grade

UNIT TITLE: *Making Maps*

UNIT GOAL: Students learn how to represent topographic features on a map.

UNIT TITLE: *Faults and Folds*

UNIT GOAL: Students learn the causes and characteristics of normal faults, thrust faults, upward rock folds, and downward rock folds.

■ Starter Ideas for Eighth Grade

UNIT TITLE: *Moving Plates*

UNIT GOAL: Students learn the basic theory of plate tectonics and the associated effects of crustal movements, including continental drift, earthquakes, and volcanoes.

UNIT TITLE: *The Universe*

UNIT GOAL: Students learn the relationship between the solar system and the Milky Way and the galaxies and the universe.

Lesson Plan Starter Ideas for Common Curriculum Topics

Sometimes, you will be responsible for teaching lessons that are part of units prepared by committees of teachers in your school district or units that are commercially available. You may wonder how to break these units into lessons. To help you come up with lesson ideas for the earth/space sciences, I have analyzed a variety of teaching units and prepared a list of lesson plan starter ideas based on topics usually covered in these units. The lesson descriptions are very specific, so each description may also be viewed as the lesson's principal objective.

■ Starter Ideas for Characteristics of the Earth, Its Atmosphere, and the Oceans

- Make a labeled drawing that shows that the earth consists of rock layers.
- Draw clouds child have observed, and then classify each cloud into one of the following categories: cumulus, cirrus, or stratus.
- Predict tomorrow's weather based on today's weather, write a script for a weather forecast, and videotape the forecast.
- Evaluate the accuracy of a television weather forecast.
- Use a stopwatch to find the time interval between lightning and thunder.
- Calculate the distance from a thunderstorm using the time interval between lightning and thunder.
- Judge how well children could follow safety precautions if they were playing outside and thought that a thunderstorm or tornado was coming.
- Prepare a weather chart that identifies temperature, wind speed, wind direction, cloud cover, and precipitation every day for one week.

■ Starter Ideas for the Water Cycle

- Describe and diagram the water cycle, and then make a presentation to a class of children at an earlier grade level.
- Write a story that includes a prediction of how life in school would change if the water supply to the school was cut in half.
- Count the number of times a water fountain is used in an hour, and estimate the water usage for one day.
- Observe and collect data related to the impact of people on the water cycle.
- Evaluate local streams, rivers, ponds, lakes, or ocean beaches to decide which would pose the least pollution hazard for swimmers, using newspaper articles gathered by the teacher as the basis for their evaluations.
- Make a hypothesis about how weather affects daily life, and carry out a survey to test the hypothesis.
- Create labeled drawings that show the characteristics of three different climate zones.

■ Starter Ideas for Rocks and Minerals and the Earth's Crust

- Compare and contrast the characteristics of the earth's crust, mantle, and core.
- Make a chart that compares the characteristics of rocks and minerals.
- Classify rocks by their characteristics and the processes by which they were formed.
- Make a cartoon in which each frame shows a stage in the process by which rock is broken down to produce soil.
- Analyze soil samples using a hand lens, and separate rock and mineral particles from organic matter.
- Describe how fossils are formed and how they are used to determine the relative ages of rocks.

■ Starter Ideas for Space

- Identify the major objects seen in the sky—such as the sun, moon, stars, and planets—from pictures and through direct observation.
- Infer the relative positions of the sun, earth, and moon from a list of observations made during an annular eclipse.
- Write a poem that includes the idea that the sun is the source of the earth's energy.
- Make a chart that compares the sun and the earth in terms of size, shape, color, state of matter, and temperature.
- Use an orange and a flashlight to show how the rotation of the earth determines night and day and how the earth's revolution and tilt determine the seasons.
- Create a sequence of drawings that shows how the moon appears to change shape as it revolves around the earth.
- Make a labeled diagram that shows the relative positions of the nine planets of the solar system.
- Make a chart that compares the other eight planets with the earth in terms of physical characteristics.
- Create an illustration on chartpaper that shows the orbits of planets, moons, asteroids, and comets.
- Make a hypothesis to explain what motivated humans to view groupings of stars as constellations.
- Write a poem that includes the idea that a star changes size and color and goes through a life cycle.
- Describe the relative locations of the planets with respect to the sun and our solar system within the Milky Way.
- Predict what humankind will do to survive when the sun ceases to shine.

WebQuest Starter Ideas

Imagine the WebQuest possibilities for your students when you teach the earth/space sciences! They'll be able to use the vast resources of the Internet to discover fascinating information about the galaxies, the stars, the sun, the planets, and the earth, their home.

The starter ideas in this section will help you plan your own earth/space science WebQuests. As you study the ideas, please keep the following in mind:

1. The WebQuests are correlated with the NSE Standards for grades K–8 (which are reprinted inside the front cover).
2. In the WebQuest context, the term *reports* has a very broad meaning and includes poster preparation, skits, dance, video presentations, labeled diagrams, and, of course, traditional written reports, if and when appropriate.

■ Starter Ideas for WebQuests

WEBQUEST TITLE: *Your Home on the Moon*

SUGGESTED GRADE LEVELS: 2, 3, 4

NSE CONTENT STANDARDS: ESS 3; S&T 1 and 3; SPSP 3

CHALLENGE—MOTIVATION: You wake from a deep sleep. Your mother enters your room and says, "Dear, pack your favorite things. Our neighborhood has been picked to move to the moon. You'll be able to bring . . ."

CHALLENGE—REPORTS: Do Internet research to discover what your *new* neighborhood will be like. Then write a letter to your grandmother that has drawings that show your home on the moon, breathing equipment, and even your pets.

KEY TERMS FOR SEARCH ENGINES: Moon, Moon Base, Moon Colony, Living on the Moon

WEBQUEST TITLE: *Learn About Volcanoes*

SUGGESTED GRADE LEVELS: 2, 3, 4

NSE CONTENT STANDARD: ESS 3

CHALLENGE—MOTIVATION: You and your family have won an all-expense-paid trip to the "big island" of Hawaii.

CHALLENGE—REPORTS: Make a travel guide that your family can use when they visit Kilauea. The travel guide should include pictures, a map, and . . .

KEY TERMS FOR SEARCH ENGINES: Hawaiian Volcanoes, Eruptions, Lava, Volcano Model, Kilauea

WEBQUEST TITLE: *Your Trip through the Solar System*

SUGGESTED GRADE LEVELS: 3, 4, 5

NSE CONTENT STANDARDS: ESS 5 and 6; SPSP 1

CHALLENGE—MOTIVATION: You have just won a contest that provides enough prize money to make a 20-minute film for children called *Your Solar System Neighbors.*

CHALLENGE—REPORTS: Plan the film, showing how much time you would spend on each object in our solar system, what you would tell about each, and . . .

KEY TERMS FOR SEARCH ENGINES: Astronaut, Cosmonaut, Solar System, Asteroid Belt

WEBQUEST TITLE: *The Dinosaur Discovery*

SUGGESTED GRADE LEVELS: 3, 4, 5

NSE CONTENT STANDARDS: ESS 1; SPSP 4; LS 8

CHALLENGE—MOTIVATION: You wake up perspiring with your hands shaking. You have had bad dream about a dinosaur trying to get into your house. It had a very large head, small front legs, and . . .

CHALLENGE—REPORTS: Do Internet research to find out what dinosaurs lived near your house. Then make a poster that shows what they looked like, what they ate, and . . .

KEY TERMS FOR SEARCH ENGINES: Prehistoric, Dinosaur, Extinct, Fossil

WEBQUEST TITLE: *Tracking the "Twisters"*

SUGGESTED GRADE LEVELS: 3, 4, 5

NSE CONTENT STANDARDS: ESS 3; S&T 1 and 2

CHALLENGE—MOTIVATION: You were just given the job of "Chief Tornado Tracker." You must be able to tell where tornadoes will most likely strike this year and . . .

CHALLENGE—REPORTS: Prepare a pamphlet (a small booklet) for people to read that has a map, tornado danger zones, safety precautions, and . . .

KEY TERMS FOR SEARCH ENGINES: Tornadoes, Twisters, Tracking Tornadoes, Tornado Safety

WEBQUEST TITLE: *Rocks under Your Feet*

SUGGESTED GRADE LEVELS: 3, 4, 5

NSE CONTENT STANDARDS: ESS 1 and 3; SPSP 3

CHALLENGE—MOTIVATION: Your teacher wants your group to make a presentation about the rocks in your state or province, but he or she wants you to do it in a very interesting way.

CHALLENGE—REPORTS: Write a skit (a short play) in which the characters are all different rocks that have entered a "Rock Beauty Contest." In the play, each rock must . . .

KEY TERMS FOR SEARCH ENGINES: (Your State or Province), Geology (Your State or Province), Rocks, U.S. Geological Survey

WEBQUEST TITLE: *The Message in the Bottle*

SUGGESTED GRADE LEVELS: 5, 6, 7

NSE CONTENT STANDARD: ESS 3

CHALLENGE—MOTIVATION: While walking along a beach on the eastern coast of North America, you see a bottle that has just been trapped against a rock. As you get closer, you can see that there is a message . . .

CHALLENGE—REPORTS: Write a two-page story that tells what the message said, where it was put in the ocean, and the path it probably took. Be sure to include . . .

KEY TERMS FOR SEARCH ENGINES: Gulf Stream, Ocean Currents, Atlantic Ocean

WEBQUEST TITLE: *The Ozone Layer—What Is It?*

SUGGESTED GRADE LEVELS: 5, 6, 7

NSE CONTENT STANDARDS: ESS 3; SPSP 1, 5, and 8

CHALLENGE—MOTIVATION: Here is a mystery: Having ozone in the stratosphere is a good thing, but it's dangerous at ground level. Why is there such a difference?

CHALLENGE—REPORTS: Prepare charts and diagrams to explain the mystery. Be sure to show what ozone is, why its location is important to the health and lives of . . .

KEY TERMS FOR SEARCH ENGINES: Ozone, Pollution, Smog, Stratosphere Ozone, Ground-Level Ozone

Classroom Enrichment Starter Ideas

In-Class Learning Centers

A well-prepared in-class learning center offers children many opportunities to make their own discoveries. In order to be well prepared, such a center must provide a wide range of materials that encourage hands-on, discovery-based learning, ranging from print and audiovisual resources to art supplies and games. In addition, the learning center must be located where children have ready access to it yet can also be somewhat removed from the larger classroom setting while doing independent activities.

The following starter ideas for in-class learning centers should get you thinking about how to create centers in your own classroom. Note that the relevant NSE Standard is identified for each starter idea and that asterisks indicate those that are particularly suited for young children.

■ Starter Idea for a Learning Center

CENTER TITLE: *Spaceship Earth*

NSE CONTENT STANDARD: ESS 6

IDEA: Place this center in a location where students can turn out the lights when necessary. Also make available space for working with clay, assembling models, and making large murals. In the center, arrange a library section containing books

This learning center—Spaceship Earth—provides enough activities and materials to hold the children's interest throughout the unit.

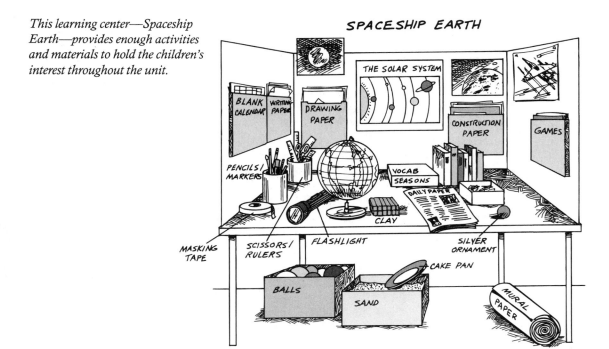

SPACESHIP EARTH

about the sun, earth, seasons, stars, planets, and solar system. Ideally, if you have a computer with relevant software and Internet access, place it in or near the center, as well.

So that students will know what to do in this center, provide activity cards or guide sheets that give directions for activities based on the following ideas:

- *Globe Explorations* Children locate where they live on the globe along with nearby bodies of water and one place to which they have traveled.
- *Seasons Murals** Children draw or paint murals that show seasonal changes.
- *Phases of the Moon* Children take home calendars and draw the nightly shape of the moon for the course of 4 weeks.
- *Clay Planets* Children make labeled models of the sun and planets.
- *Reflection** Children observe how the visibility of a ball of foil or silver ornament changes when light from a flashlight strikes the surface of the ball or ornament in bright light and in total darkness.
- *Surface of the Moon** Children model the moon's surface by shaping sand in a pie plate.

■ Additional Starter Ideas for Learning Centers

CENTER TITLE: *Wild Weather*

NSE CONTENT STANDARD: ESS 3

IDEA: Identify characteristics of violent weather phenomena, make related drawings, and illustrate the safety precautions to be followed for each.

CENTER TITLE: *Wet and Wonderful**

NSE CONTENT STANDARD: ESS 4

IDEA: Make models of mountains and river beds with sand and soil, and observe how water poured on each model travels through and changes it.

CENTER TITLE: *What's a Land Form?**

NSE CONTENT STANDARD: ESS 4

IDEA: Use art materials to create various landscapes and then label mountains, hills, plateaus, and valleys.

CENTER TITLE: *Constellation Celebration*

NSE CONTENT STANDARD: ESS 6

IDEA: Use art materials to make diagrams of the major constellations; label the key stars in each and do research to find if, when, and where it will be visible.

Bulletin Boards

Good bulletin boards have the potential to be something that children can both look at and learn from. There are many ways to use classroom bulletin boards to enhance earth/space science units and to extend your teaching to nonscience areas. The following list offers a few starter ideas for you. Again, asterisks indicate ideas that may be particularly appropriate for young children.

■ Starter Ideas for Bulletin Boards

BULLETIN BOARD TITLE: *The Air—Who Needs It?*

IDEA: Divide the bulletin board into two categories: one labeled "Needs Air to Work" and one labeled "Doesn't Need Air to Work." Show students a jar filled with air and ask, "What is inside this jar?" Pour the air out of the jar by placing it under a water-filled jar and bubbling air up into it. Then discuss the question "What can air be used for?" with the class. Provide the children with magazines and scissors, and have them cut out pictures for each category and then staple each picture on the board to form a collage.

BULLETIN BOARD TITLE: *Wind**

IDEA: How do we know the air is there? Provide and display various photographs and pictures illustrating the effects of wind (e.g., a collapsed umbrella, tree leaves blowing, and kites flying). Have the children make drawings of their observations of the presence of wind, and include their drawings in the bulletin board display. Children may wish to write stories to accompany their pictures.

Bulletin boards can draw children into the science topic you wish to introduce.

BULLETIN BOARD TITLE: *Save Water**

IDEA: Design a bulletin board showing a cutaway view of a typical house. Include in the diagram a bathroom, kitchen, laundry room, and outdoor hose. Prepare a set of cards listing various ideas for saving water. (Examples: "Take a short shower." "Don't leave the water running." "Don't play with the hose.") Using yarn and push pins, have children connect these ideas to the places in the house where they should be carried out.

BULLETIN BOARD TITLE: *Shadows on the Moon*

IDEA: Use cutouts representing the earth, moon, and sun to depict why the moon appears crescent shaped. Prepare other cutouts to represent the various phases of the moon, and have the children arrange them on the bulletin board in proper sequence.

BULLETIN BOARD TITLE: *Natural Features*

IDEA: Provide a set of labels for land types, including grasslands, mountains, hills, lakes, rivers, and so on. Attach pictures showing examples of each land type to the board. Challenge the children to attach the pictures under the correct headings.

BULLETIN BOARD TITLE: *Land Shapes*

IDEA: Place on the bulletin board a large topographical map that includes a key. Then place cards on the board representing different physical features that can be found on the map. Have the children attach the cards to the proper locations on the map.

BULLETIN BOARD TITLE: *Our Changing Earth*

IDEA: Prepare a bulletin board so it has two distinct halves. Title one side "Changes Caused by Humans" and the other "Changes Caused by Nature." Attach an envelope containing a random assortment of pictures that depict an example for one half or the other. Have the children attach each picture to the proper half.

Field Trips

Field trips provide amazing opportunities for discovery learning, as they take children out of the classroom and immerse them in the real world. Whether you teach in a city, suburban, or small-town school, you can find ideas for field trips all around you. To understand just how true that is, think about how you could tailor each of these topics to the resources of the community in which you teach:

Weather reporting
Pollution prevention
Water quality
Recycling

The field trip may be to the regional meteorological center or the park down the street, but either way, children will be eager to see what the day will hold. After all, children *love* field trips!

Here are starter ideas for field trips for all schools. Note that asterisks indicate activities that may be particularly appropriate for young children.

■ Starter Ideas for Field Trips

FIELD TRIP TITLE: *The Weather Station**

IDEA: Even the smallest communities have locations where you can observe the operation of weather measurement and forecasting equipment. Be sure to find out ahead of time what equipment is used so you can familiarize your class with it. Contact the person who will be showing you around to let him or her know the abilities and interests of your students. Prior to the trip, discuss or review topics such as cloud types, precipitation, violent weather, and weather forecasting. During the visit, be sure that you or the guide explains the purpose of the weather station. Also discuss the instruments and procedures used in long-range forecasting. There are many follow-up activities for this trip, including the construction of simple instruments for a classroom weather station, the giving of daily weather reports, and long-range forecasting.

FIELD TRIP TITLE: *Touch the Earth*

IDEA: This field trip would be helpful any time your class is studying changes in the earth's surface. The destination should be any place where the surface of the land is being disturbed, such as a construction site, beach, or the edge of a stream or river. Institute appropriate safety procedures depending on the location. Students should have notebooks, magnifying glasses, and something to use to carry samples. Follow-up activities could include presenting topic reports, making displays of collected items, and preparing charts showing the results of soil and water testing.

FIELD TRIP TITLE: *Visit a Potter**

IDEA: A visit to a potter's or sculptor's studio can be a fascinating way for children to observe the relationship between art and earth science. At these sites, the children will be able to learn about the earth materials in use, techniques for shaping the materials, how the finished product is preserved, and how the artist thinks about the materials used as well as the origin of the design for the finished product.

FIELD TRIP TITLE: *Pollution Prevention Location!*

IDEA: Many factories have added pollution controls to smokestacks and have taken other measures to reduce air pollution. Contact the public relations officer of any large company in your region to arrange for a visit. Consider a visit to a garage to see automobile air pollution devices being repaired, cleaned, or installed. Finally, many states and cities have installed pollution-monitoring stations to measure air quality. If your state has a mobile monitoring station, you might arrange for it to be brought to your school.

MAKE THE CASE   *An Individual or Group Challenge*

■ **The Problem**   Children need science experiences that range across the earth/space, life, and physical sciences. Teachers may tend to emphasize those topics they feel most comfortable with and thus inadvertently limit the scope of children's learning.

■ **Assess Your Prior Knowledge and Beliefs**

1. When you compare your knowledge of the earth/space sciences to your knowledge of the life sciences and physical sciences, do you believe you have acquired more, less, or the same amount of basic science content in each?

	More	*Less*	*Same*
Physical sciences	_____	_____	_____
Life sciences	_____	_____	_____

2. When you were a student in grades K–8, were you exposed to more, less, or the same amount of earth/space science content as you were to life science content and physical science content?

	More	*Less*	*Same*
Life sciences	_____	_____	_____
Physical sciences	_____	_____	_____

3. Dinosaurs are an ever-popular earth/space science topic for children. Identify five discrete items of knowledge that you have about dinosaurs.

   _____

   _____

   _____

   _____

   _____

4. Now identify five things about dinosaurs that you think you should know but do not.

   _____

   _____

   _____

   _____

   _____

■ **The Challenge**   You are part of a team of teachers planning a unit on dinosaurs. Give examples of earth/space science activities you might include.

Many of the factors that make the city an interesting and exciting place to live also make it a place that overflows with field trip possibilities. Here are additional starter ideas that should stimulate your thinking about field trips for children in city schools:

■ Starter Ideas for Field Trips

FIELD TRIP TITLE: *What Cracks the Sidewalks?*

IDEA: Children survey the sidewalks on the school grounds to find large and small cracks and make hypotheses about what causes the cracks.

FIELD TRIP TITLE: *What Happens to the Rain (Snow)?*

IDEA: Children search for evidence that will tell how rain or melted snow is absorbed by the soil or carried off.

FIELD TRIP TITLE: *What Clouds Are Those?*

IDEA: Children go outside to draw clouds, classify them, and track their movements.

FIELD TRIP TITLE: *Which Way Is North?*

IDEA: Children use compasses to identify north, south, east, and west on their playground.

FIELD TRIP TITLE: *Map Our Block*

IDEA: Children estimate distances to key buildings, count steps between landmarks, and gather related information to create a map of their block.

FIELD TRIP TITLE: *Earth Resources in the School Building*

IDEA: Children walk through and around the school to locate earth resources that are part of their building.

FIELD TRIP TITLE: *Trash and Treasure*

IDEA: Children walk around the block on recycling day (i.e., the day in which households and businesses are to use special blue or green plastic boxes to dispose of materials that may be recycled) to determine the extent to which apartment houses, homes, and businesses participate in recycling.

Additional Field Trip Destinations

Archaeological dig
Astronomy department at a local college
Building site with foundation excavation
Geology department at a local college
Gravel or sand pit
Hot-air balloon festival or exposition
Lakeshore or seashore
Museum with geological display
Road cut where rock layers can be safely observed

Stone quarry
Water reservoir
Water treatment plant

Cooperative Learning Projects

As you consider the following starter ideas for cooperative learning projects, keep in mind the importance of stressing the three key aspects of cooperative learning:

1. Positive interdependence
2. Individual accountability
3. Development of group process skills

■ Starter Ideas for Cooperative Learning Projects

PROJECT TITLE: *Planet X*

IDEA: Provide each cooperative learning group with access to resource books containing descriptive information about each planet in the solar system. After the students have had an opportunity to skim through the books, give each group an envelope with the words *Planet X* written on it. Inside each envelope will be an index card with the name of a planet. The groups are not to divulge the names of the planets. Provide all groups with art materials, including pâpier-maché, paint, and posterboard. Give each the goal of creating a model of the planet that fits the descriptive information in the resource books and a poster that lists important information. Instruct the groups not to include the name of their planet on the poster. After the groups have completed their work, organize the mystery planets and posters in a display. Encourage members of each learning group to work as a team as they study the other planets and posters and attempt to identify them.

PROJECT TITLE: *Mission Possible*

IDEA: Provide each learning group with resource materials describing the characteristics of the planets of the solar system. The materials should include some information on the distances of these planets from the sun. Also provide the groups with posterboard, drawing materials, and a pocket calculator. Challenge each group to select a planet, do additional library research, and prepare large drawings and charts that show the group's response to the following:

1. How far away is the planet from the earth?
2. Has the planet been explored with space probes?
3. How long would it take a spaceship to get to the planet?
4. What special features should a group of scientists exploring the planet be sure to observe?
5. Make a drawing showing the inside of an imagined spaceship sent to explore the planet. Be sure to include places for the crew to eat, exercise, rest, and so forth.

PROJECT TITLE: *Weather the Storm*

IDEA: Give each group the challenge of developing a skit about the approach of a violent storm and a group of people camping outdoors. The skit must include accurate scientific information about violent storms and the safety measures that should be taken. Write the name of a violent storm (e.g., blizzard, hurricane, thunderstorm, tornado) on an index card, and give each group a different storm. Warn the groups to do their work in a way that does not reveal the storm to other groups. Encourage the groups to make simple props out of art materials. Have each group present its skit to the class as a whole.

■ Additional Starter Ideas for Learning Groups

- Have groups create and update weather maps.
- Have each group make a weather forecast and broadcast it on the school public address system.
- Challenge groups to build model volcanoes.
- Have groups write and perform skits on earthquake safety.
- Have groups create displays of rocks found in the state or province.
- Have groups create a series of newsprint panels that illustrate the major events in a recent spaceflight.

RESOURCES FOR DISCOVERY LEARNING

Internet Resources
Websites for Earth/Space Science Units, Lessons, Activities, and Demonstrations

Sharing NASA

quest.arc.nasa.gov

This NASA site is dedicated to providing students and teachers with real-time experiences with ongoing NASA projects. As NASA initiates and carries out projects, students and teachers can connect to the projects and gather information about the explorations they unfold. For example, students can gather information about flying the shuttle, spacecraft explorations of distant planets, and space-based life sciences research.

NASA Space Image Libraries

www.okstate.edu/aesp/image.html

Finding current photographs and drawings related to the study of space is a particular problem, since ongoing developments often make the illustrations in textbooks and curriculum resource materials obsolete. This site solves that problem and more, providing graphics related to the earth, the planets, the universe, spacecraft, and almost anything else you can think of to support children's study of earth and space sciences.

CNN Interactive Weather Main Page

cnn.com/WEATHER/

This site will provide you and your children with a wide variety of weather resources that could serve as the basis for ongoing weather projects. Included are up-to-the-minute forecasts for every major city in the world, current weather maps, access to information about the locations and movements of major storms, and even allergy reports. This site is a gold mine of information for a creative teacher who wants to develop weather-related WebQuests for individual students or cooperative groups.

Volcano World

www.volcanoworld.org

This well-done site will provide you and your students with a wealth of information and graphics about volcanoes, including a "Volcano of the Week," video clips of volcanoes, and even "Volcanoes of Other Worlds," a presentation of volcanic activity on the moon and planets. If you enter the "Kids Door," you will find stories, games, and other activities for young people. As a teacher, you will be most interested in this site's "Lesson Plan" section.

Earth/Space Science Lesson Plans

ericir.syr.edu/Virtual/Lessons

When you reach this site, select "Science" from the introductory page. Doing so will take you to an extensive collection of lessons, each identified by title as well as suggested grade level. The lessons originate from a wide variety of sources and cover a broad range of topics. Some effort has been made to put them in a consistent format; however, the fact that they come from different sources has resulted in format variations. Nevertheless, this is one of the most comprehensive sources of earth and space science-related lessons you are likely to find on the Internet.

The Jason Project

seawifs.gsfc.nasangov/

This award-winning site will be of great interest to you if you teach in the upper-elementary grades. It provides an extraordinary array of enrichment materials that will help your students carry out inquiry experiences that will answer such questions as, What are the earth's dynamic systems? How do these systems affect life on our planet? How do humans study these systems? You'll be amazed to discover the resources available to teachers and students who participate in the project.

Print Resources
Articles from Science and Children and Science Scope

Ashby, Suzanne. "NASA Quest." *Science Scope* 33, no. 1 (September 2000): 40–43.

Barker, Marianne. "Student Centered Seismology Activities." *Science Scope* 23, no. 4 (January 2000): 12–18.

Booth, Bibi, et al. "Energy: Fuel for Thought." *Science and Children* 39, no. 8 (May 2002): 35–42.

Corder, Greg, and Darren Reed. "It's Raining Micrometeorites." *Science Scope* 26, no. 5 (February 2003): 23–25.

Danaher, Edwin. "Science 101: How Do Snowflakes Form?" *Science and Children* 40, no. 1 (January 2003): 53.

Giacalone, Valerie. "How to Plan, Survive, and Even Enjoy an Overnight Field Trip with 200 Students." *Science Scope* 26, no. 4 (January 2003): 22–26.

Gibb, Lori. "Second Grade Soil Scientists." *Science and Children* 38, no. 3 (November/December 2000): 24–26.

Hemmenway, Mary Kay. "Our Star, the Sun." *Science and Children* 38, no. 1 (September 2000): 48–51.

Lester, Dan, et al. "The Sun Tower." *Science and Children* 38, no. 3 (November/December 2000): 14–17.

Lucking, Robert A., and Edwin P. Christmann. "Tech Trek: Technology in the Classroom." *Science Scope* 26, no. 4 (January 2003): 54–57.

Mohler, Robert J. "More Space Shuttle Experiments Take Flight." *Science and Children* 38, no. 2 (October 2000): 38–43.

Newhouse, Kay Berglund. "What Lies in the Stars?" *Science and Children* 39, no. 6 (March 2002): 16–21.

Paty, Alma Hale. "Rocks and Minerals: Foundations of Society." *Science Scope* 23, no. 8 (May 2000): 30–31.

Riddle, Bob. "Scope on the Skies: The Brightest Stars in the Sky." Science Scope 26, no. 4 (January 2003): 60.

Riddle, Bob. "Scope on the Skies: Scintillating Stars." *Science Scope* 26, no. 5 (February 2003): 56–57.

Smith, Shaw. "Turning Bread into Rocks." *Science Scope* 24, no. 2 (October 2000): 20–23.

Sorel, Katherine. "Rock Solid." *Science and Children* 40, no. 5 (January 2003): 24–29.

Wiig, Diana. "A Week with the Stars." *Science and Children* 39, no. 7 (April 2002): 22–25.

Wiley, David, and Christine Anne Royce. "Crash into Meteorite Learning." *Science and Children* 37, no. 8 (May 2000): 16–19.

NOTES

1. This standard, as well as the others identified in later sections, are excerpted with permission from the National Research Council, *National Science Education Standards* (Washington, DC: National Academy Press, 1996), pp. 104–171. Note that the bracketed symbol to the right of each standard was prepared by this author. See also the list of all the K–8 content standards inside the front cover of this book.

2. Note that I have related this sampling of NSE Standards E, F, and G to the earth/space sciences.

2A The Earth's Surface, Atmosphere, and Weather

Content

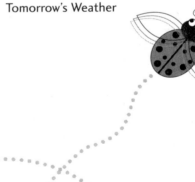

Spaceship Earth: What Is It Made Of?

You don't have to hitch a ride on the next space shuttle to treat yourself to a high-speed space adventure. You are having one right now! All living things—including you and me—are passengers on the most elaborate and marvelous spaceship that will ever hurl through space and time. It's the top-of-the-line luxury model, fully equipped with water, oxygen, and abundant food. And best of all, each and every seat has a fantastic view!

We can become so comfortable riding along on *Spaceship Earth* (otherwise known as the "third rock from the sun") that we take its very existence and nature for granted. If you take the time to learn more about the earth, you will discover that it's just as fascinating as the moon, planets, stars, and mysteries that lie at the far reaches of the universe.

The Earth beneath Your Feet

The earth, our personal spaceship, is full of surprises. One of the most extraordinary findings actually comes from the common misconception that we're walking around on some enormous, solid ball of rock. In fact, the earth is a giant, layered sphere made of materials that are as different as oil and water and rock and diamonds. Even more surprising is that at the center of the earth lies something completely unexpected—a liquid.

To understand the makeup of the earth, we need to figuratively peel off layers and work our way to its center. The first layer is a thin shell that ranges from 11 kilometers (about 7 miles) to 32 kilometers (about 20 miles) in thickness. This crust is thought to be divided into seven major sections called *crustal plates*. These plates are interesting for many reasons, including the fact that they are slowly moving and carrying oceans and continents along with them.

Under this first layer, we find the *mantle*, which is about 2,870 kilometers (1,780 miles) deep. Figure 2A.1 shows the crust and the mantle. Earthquake waves move faster in the upper mantle than in the crust. Knowing the rates at which earthquake waves travel through the different layers gives geologists important clues about the nature of the rock layers themselves.

Under the mantle, we find the *core*. Although no one is exactly sure of its composition, we do have an important clue: The fact that the earth has a magnetic field strong enough to turn a compass needle is evidence that a mass of molten metal exists at the center. The movement of this hot liquid metal, which is likely a mixture of iron and nickel, may create electric currents that produce the magnetic field.

Gradual Changes in the Earth's Surface

If you look outside your window, you may see mountains, prairies, a desert, a lake, or maybe just other buildings. Whatever the case, the view you see creates an illusion—an illusion of permanence. In fact, all of our surroundings are in the process of gradual

FIGURE 2A.1   The upper mantle lies between Hawaii and California.

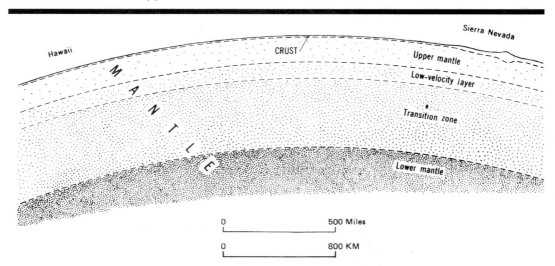

change, including the walls of the buildings you may see. More startling yet is the idea that even the enormous continents are in constant motion.

Most geologists now believe that all the continents were once joined into a single, large land mass. Alfred Wegener, who proposed this theory in 1912, named this land mass *Pangaea*. He believed that it broke apart and the pieces slowly drifted to where they are now. They are still moving but only very slowly at rates of between 1 and 5 centimeters per year. Australia and Africa are moving northward, so some time in the next 50 million years, Australia may strike Asia and Africa may strike Europe. Wegener's theory seems correct because geologists have discovered similar rock structures on the west coast of Africa and the east coast of South America. This similarity, along with the discovery of similar fossils in both locations, is strong evidence that the two continents were once part of the same land mass.

Continental drift is not the only cause of change in the earth's surface. External forces, such as weathering and erosion, constantly wear down the surface, and internal forces, which come from heat and pressure, push rock layers upward and sideways to form mountains and cause plate movement.

In order to keep track of when these various changes happened during the earth's history, scientists have created a geologic time scale. The largest division in the scale is the *era*. Each era is named for the type of life that existed then. Here are the four eras of geologic time and the approximate beginning of each:

Precambrian era	4,500,000,000 years ago
Paleozoic era	600,000,000 years ago
Mesozoic era	225,000,000 years ago
Cenozoic era	70,000,000 years ago

Table 2A.1 gives an overview some of the most important characteristics of each era.

TABLE 2A.1   The four eras

ERA	LIVING THINGS PRESENT	GENERAL CHARACTERISTICS
Precambrian: 4,500,000,000 years ago	Single-celled and multicelled life appear.	This era represents about 90% of all geologic time. The earliest rocks on Earth are found in Precambrian deposits. They are about 4.6 billion years old.
Paleozoic: 600,000,000 years ago	The first land plants, reptiles, fish, spiders, and insects appear.	This was a time of great change. Sheets of ice covered much of the land in the Southern Hemisphere. Seas and oceans formed in the Northern Hemisphere. In time, much of the ice melted and land masses emerged from the oceans.
Mesozoic: 225,000,000 years ago	The first mammals, frogs, flowering plants, and dinosaurs appear. The dinosaurs also become extinct.	The Appalachian Mountains, Rocky Mountains, and Sierra Nevada Mountains were all formed. Great seas in the middle of North America disappeared, and these areas formed plains. The levels of the oceans dropped, and the climate became colder.
Cenozoic: 70,000,000 years ago	Mammals flourish, including humans, dogs, horses, and cattle.	Movement of the seven crustal plates pushed up mountains and increased earthquakes and volcanic activity. Glaciers from both polar regions spread out toward the equator. At one point, glaciers covered North America between the Appalachian Mountains and the northern Rocky Mountains. Eventually, the glaciers receded into south central Canada.

Violent Changes in the Earth's Surface

If you stood between the railroad tracks in front of a freight train moving only 1 mile (less than 1 kilometer) an hour, you would gradually learn that powerful forces can have great consequences even though they are acting slowly. The same is true for the movement of crustal plates discussed earlier in this chapter. Violent changes happen where the plates meet, pushing and slowly grinding against one another.

Earthquakes

Imagine being sound asleep and being awakened by the feeling that your house was rocking back and forth. If you have actually had this experience, you know that this is what it's like to be in an earthquake.

This probably isn't news to you if you live in California, one part of North America where seismographs record a great deal of activity from the movement of plates. In western California, the Pacific plate is moving northwest and rubbing against the North American plate—the plate that North America rides on. Figure 2A.2 shows the location of the San Andreas fault, which runs from northern to southern California. This figure also shows the dates of major earthquakes in California and areas where rock layers are very slowly being pushed out of position.

Volcanoes

On August 24, in the year 79, the apparently extinct volcano Vesuvius suddenly exploded, destroying the cities of Pompeii and Herculaneum.[1] Vesuvius had been quiet for hundreds of years, its surface and crater were green and vine covered, and no one expected the explosion. Yet in a few hours, volcanic ash and dust buried the two cities so thoroughly that their ruins were not uncovered for more than 1,600 years!

Molten rock below the surface of the earth that rises in volcanic vents is known as *magma,* but after it erupts from a volcano, it is called *lava.* It is red hot when it pours out of the vent, but it slowly changes to dark red, gray, or black as it cools. If lava erupts in large volumes, it flows over the surface of the earth. Generally, very hot lava is fluid, like hot tar, whereas cooler lava flows more slowly, like thick honey.

FIGURE 2A.2

This map shows the San Andreas fault system and other geological faults in California.

All lava that comes to the surface of the earth contains dissolved gas. If the lava is a thin fluid, the gas escapes easily. But if the lava is thick and pasty, the gas escapes with explosive violence. The gas in lava may be compared with the gas in a bottle of soda pop. If you put your thumb over the top of the bottle and shake it, the gas separates from the liquid and forms bubbles. When you remove your thumb, there is a miniature explosion of gas and liquid. The gas in lava behaves in somewhat the same way; it causes the terrible explosions that throw out great masses of solid rock as well as lava, dust, and ashes.

The violent separation of gas from lava may produce rock froth, called *pumice.* Some of this froth is so light that it floats on water. In many eruptions, the froth is broken into small fragments that are hurled high into the air in the form of volcanic ash (gray), cinders (red or black), and dust.

The Earth's Land Surface

Rocks

A rock can be much more than what it seems at first glance. Indeed, rocks provide us with many of the things that make possible an enjoyable and productive life. From rocks come the soils that nourish plants; the minerals we use for nutrients, fertilizer, adornment, and raw materials for manufacture; and, of course, the special stones that skip across the surface of a quiet pond on a hot summer day.

Igneous rocks are formed from the heating or cooling of melted materials in the earth (see Figure 2A.3). The word *igneous* comes from a Latin word meaning "coming from fire." Igneous rocks on land are exposed to the elements of the hydrosphere and atmosphere. Water, wind, and temperature changes cause the chemical and physical breakdown of igneous rocks, a process known as *weathering.* The particles and pieces removed by weathering are moved from place to place by the wind, water, and, in some cases, glaciers. This movement results in *erosion,* or the wearing away of the land. Many of the particles and pieces are washed into streams and rivers and eventually transported to the oceans. Thus, matter that was originally inland igneous rock is washed up in layers at the water's edge to form beaches or, more commonly, settles in layers on the ocean floor.

FIGURE 2A.3
Igneous rocks are the result of volcanic activity.

Particles of rock transported to the oceans are called *sediment.* Over a long time, layers of sediment may become pressed together, eventually becoming *sedimentary rocks* (see Figure 2A.4). Sedimentary rocks are formed from particles that were originally part of any other type of rock, from chemical reactions that occur in the ocean and result in small crystals, and from organic matter.

When rocks are heated or pressed together for a long time, they can change. Rocks that have undergone this process are known as *metamorphic rocks* (see Figure 2A.5). Fashioned deep within the earth, metamorphic rocks are formed from igneous or sedimentary rocks. The term *metamorphic* comes from Greek words meaning "change" and "form."

Minerals

Rocks are combinations of *minerals,* naturally occurring chemical elements or compounds. Gold, silver, and platinum, for example, are well known and highly valued minerals found in rocks. Many mineral compounds include oxygen and another element found in abundance in the earth's crust: silicon. These compounds are known as *silicates.* Quartz, feldspar, and mica are all examples of silicates. Quartz consists of one silicon atom for every two oxygen atoms. Because its atoms are tightly joined, it is a very hard mineral. Feldspar commonly contains aluminum-oxygen and silicon-oxygen combinations of atoms. In some feldspars, however, sodium, calcium, or potassium replaces the aluminum. Feldspar is a softer mineral than quartz. Mica has

FIGURE 2A.4
Sedimentary rocks are formed in layers.

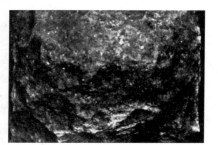

FIGURE 2A.5
Metamorphic rocks are the result of pressure, heat, and chemical action.

an atomic pattern that causes it to be easily separated into thin sheets. Biotite and muscovite are two minerals that are micas.

Ores (which are useful metals) and gems (which are crystals that have an unusual color and the ability to reflect light from their many faces, or facets) are also minerals, but they are not silicates. Other nonsilicate minerals are calcite, gypsum, halite, and fluorite. Sulfur, gold, and graphite are nonsilicate minerals that are elements. An *element* is a substance composed of just one type of atom.

Scientists are able to identify the minerals that make up rocks by performing laboratory tests. Each mineral has a variety of identifying characteristics, including color; streak (the color it leaves when it is rubbed against a piece of porcelain); luster (the property of reflecting, bending, or absorbing light); the form of its crystals; cleavage and fracture (how it splits or breaks apart); relative weight; and hardness (how easily it can be scratched). Figure 2A.6 shows the hardnesses of common minerals as determined by a measuring system known as *Mohs' hardness scale.* As you can see from these charts, if you know the Mohs' scale for some common materials, you can determine the hardness of another mineral by scratching it with the materials.

FIGURE 2A.6   These charts illustrate the Mohs' hardness scale and the places of some common materials in it.

Mohs' Hardness Scale

Hardness	Mineral
1	Talc
2	Gypsum
3	Calcite
4	Fluorite
5	Apatite
6	Feldspar
7	Quartz
8	Topaz
9	Corundum
10	Diamond

Explanation: A given mineral will scratch those minerals above it in the table and will be scratched by those below it.

Some Common Materials and Their Places in the Hardness Scale

Hardness	Common Material	Comment
about 2.5	Fingernail	Will scratch gypsum with difficulty but will not scratch calcite.
about 3	Copper	Scratches calcite; will also be scratched by calcite.
about 5 to 5.5	Glass	With difficulty scratches apatite; also scratched by apatite.
about 5.5 to 6	Knife blade	Will scratch feldspar with difficulty.
about 7	File	Will scratch quartz with difficulty.
about 9	Silicon carbide	With difficulty scratches corundum; also scratched by corundum.

In addition to the common characteristics noted in the previous paragraph, a mineral may display some special properties, such as magnetism (being attracted to a magnet); fluorescence (glowing under ultraviolet light); phosphorescence (glowing after an ultraviolet light that has been shining on it is turned off); and radioactivity (giving off rays that can be detected by a Geiger counter).

Fossils

The earth today contains billions of living things that display amazing variety in both appearance and behavior. However, life as we know it has changed a great deal over the 5 billion years in which the earth has existed. For example, dinosaurs once lived in Utah, great mammoths lived in Canada, and swampy forests once stretched across parts of Pennsylvania and Illinois. We know this, even though none of these things exist anymore, because we have found evidence of their existence in the form of fossils.

Fossils are created in a variety of ways. Since dead plants and animals usually decay quite rapidly, only the harder parts of their bodies are preserved. These parts are fossilized as a result of the presence of water containing mineral matter that replaces the hard portions of the animal. This explains why teeth, shells, bones, and woody tissues are all commonly found fossils. If plant or animal remains are covered by a protective material soon after death, the likelihood of fossilization increases. For example, the remains of creatures that live in the water fall to the bottom of the lake or seafloor, where soft mud and sand may bury them. Fossils that form in such environments are preserved in sedimentary rocks. Some fossils are found in the form of molds or casts. For example, seashells buried in mud and sand may eventually dissolve in the water. The cavity that is left may preserve the outline of the shell and its surface. Minerals from groundwater may settle in this mold and eventually form a cast of the original shell.

Fossils are seldom found in igneous rocks, since the process by which such rocks are formed would tend to destroy any remains of living things. However, wind-blown ash from volcanic activity may settle on animal or plant material and provide a protective covering that increases the likelihood of fossilization. Yellowstone National Park in Wyoming contains fossilized remains of forests that were covered by volcanic ash and dust.

Some unfossilized remains of plants and animals that lived millions of years ago have been found. At least one mammoth has been discovered preserved in ice. Natural mummies have also been found. Amber, a fossilized plant resin, has served as the final resting place for a variety of small plants and animals, and tar pits have been the source of beautifully preserved animal bones. The La Brea tar pits in the Los Angeles area are probably the best-known source of information about the plants and animals that lived thousands of years ago. Apparently, the animals became stuck in these natural tar pools. The tar has acted as a preservative and has provided scientists with excellent specimens of plant and animal life (see Figure 2A.7, page 40).

Fossils of the earliest humanlike creatures have been found in Africa and are approximately 2 to 3 million years old. Modern humans—that is, creatures that would appear to us to be very much like ourselves—have probably existed for about 100,000 years. Our present physical and mental capabilities make us a species with an enormous capacity to both adapt to diverse environments and change environments to fit our needs.

FIGURE 2A.7

This reconstruction of an American mastodon becoming entrapped in a La Brea tar pit captures the anguish of that moment in time. Fossilized remains found in the La Brea tar pits have provided a great deal of information about early life on North America.

Dinosaurs

Few members of the parade of life that has marched across the earth offer as much fascination to children and adults as the dinosaur. The dinosaur was an air-breathing animal that could be as small as a chicken or as large as a whale. Body forms varied considerably from species to species: Some dinosaurs walked on two feet, others on four; some had horns, others had talons, and still others had large teeth. Some dinosaurs were meat eaters, and others were vegetarians.

Tyrannosaurus was a dinosaur that reached a length of 14 meters (about 47 feet), weighed more than an elephant, had teeth that were 8 to 15 centimeters (about 3 to 6 inches) long, huge feet, powerful claws, and relatively small, grasping "animal hands." It spent most of its time on land, moved about on two legs, and was a meat eater.

Apatosaurus, a large amphibian, was probably a vegetarian. It walked on four legs and had a very large and long neck. Fossil evidence of an apatosaurus more than 21 meters (about 67 feet) long has been found in Colorado.

Stegosaurus was about 6.5 meters (21 feet) long, moved about on four limbs, and had a small head and brain and a large, curved, armor-plated back. The armor consisted of a double row of upstanding plates over the full arch of the back and two or more spikes on a powerful tail. The spikes on the tail were an effective weapon for warding off attackers. Although its brain was small, stegosaurus had a large nerve center in its pelvis that controlled the muscles of the tail and the rear legs.

Triceratops was one of a group of horned dinosaurs. Its huge head was approximately one-third its entire length. On its head were one small horn and two large ones. Its bony crest apparently protected its neck. This dinosaur was 7 meters (about 22 feet) long and was a vegetarian.

Fossil evidence reveals that the peak of the dinosaurs' development occurred near the end of the Cretaceous period in the Mesozoic era. However, no one is sure why the dinosaurs became extinct. Some scientists have suggested that a catastrophe such as an earthquake, volcano, or sunlight-blocking cloud resulting from a comet strike killed the dinosaurs. However, this theory does not explain why *only* the dinosaurs were destroyed, while other life forms survived. Scientists have also conjectured that the apatosaurus and its vegetarian relatives eventually became extinct because their huge bulk made it difficult for them to move to new environments as changes occurred in their natural habitat, but this does not explain the extinction of all the dinosaurs. Changes in climate may have changed the vegetable and animal life upon which dinosaurs fed, but there were places where such climatic changes did not occur, so some species of dinosaurs should have survived. Perhaps one of the children you teach will someday develop a theory that explains the extinction of the dinosaur satisfactorily.

The Earth's Oceans

When we look at the ocean, we see nothing but water. Imagine for a moment that the water disappeared. What would you expect the floor of the ocean to look like?

The Ocean Floor

With the water gone, you would see gently sloping areas, known as *continental shelves,* along the edges of the continents. These areas extend outward to a region of ocean floor that slopes steeply to a flatter part of the ocean floor called the *abyssal plain.* Not all continents have a gradually sloping continental shelf. In some places, the shelf extends hundreds of kilometers; in other places, the coastline drops immediately into deep water.

The continental shelf receives the sediment carried by rivers from the land surface. The material covering it is called the *continental deposit.* The edges of the continental shelf mark the beginning of a steeply sloping region known as the *continental slope.* The continental slope extends until it reaches the ocean floor, which is lined with ridges known as *midocean ridges.* Between the ridges lie the *abyssal plains.* The ridge that rises from the Atlantic Ocean floor is called the *Mid-Atlantic Ridge.* The islands known as the Azores are the peaks of the Mid-Atlantic Ridge that have risen above the water. Although there are ridges in the ocean floor beneath the Pacific Ocean, they are not as tall as the Mid-Atlantic Ridge.

The ridges on the ocean floor are made by molten rock from deep within the earth pushing upward and slowly spreading out to the east and west. Thus, the ridges indicate places where the ocean floor is actually expanding. The movement of continents away from these areas is known as *continental drift.* Since the earth is not becoming larger, there must be an explanation for what happens as new land is created at the ridges and pushed outward. The explanation can be found in *ocean trenches.* At other places on the ocean floor the earth's crust is being pushed downward, creating large trenches. Ocean trenches are the most striking feature of the Pacific Ocean floor. The trenches are thousands of kilometers long and hundreds of kilometers wide.

Ocean Currents

Throughout history, sailors have used their knowledge of the locations of ocean currents to move from place to place quickly and to avoid sailing against currents, but what causes the currents in the first place? The explanation must begin with sunlight. The equatorial regions of the earth receive more sunlight than other places on the planet's surface. Because they do, the oceans in the equatorial regions absorb an enormous amount of energy and become warm. The warmed waters have a tendency to move, and it is this moving of ocean water away from the equator that results in the major ocean currents. The earth's rotation turns these currents clockwise in the Northern Hemisphere and counterclockwise in the Southern Hemisphere. Along the eastern coast of North America, a powerful current called the *Gulf Stream* carries warm waters from the equator northward and then eastward toward England.

Although many people are familiar with the major ocean currents at the water's surface, few people realize that there are currents far beneath the surface. There is, for example, a deep current that flows out of the Mediterranean under the surface current that flows into the Mediterranean at the Straits of Gibraltar. It is said that ancient sailors familiar with this unseen current sometimes took advantage of it by putting weighted sails *into* the deep water.

Seasonal changes in the strength, direction, and temperature of currents produce a variety of effects. Fish dependent on the movement of currents to carry food to the area of the ocean in which they live may perish if the current changes. Variations in the temperature of a current can affect the hatching of fish eggs. These effects impact humans because humans depend on the ocean's resources.

Ocean Resources

The oceans of our planet are a source of food, minerals, water, and perhaps, if we discover how to convert ocean movements into a usable form, energy. The challenge we face is to harvest the ocean's resources without diminishing their richness.

The living resources of the ocean begin with *phytoplankton*—tiny, one-celled plants that carry out photosynthesis. Their capturing of sunlight is the first step in creating the food chains and webs found in the oceans. Phytoplankton serve as food for microscopic animals known as *zooplankton*. Zooplankton are then eaten by larger organisms, and these organisms are eaten by still larger organisms. Thus, the energy originally received by the phytoplankton is passed along through the ocean food chains and webs (see Figure 2A.8).

The food chains and webs of the oceans can be thought of as a vast repository of protein-rich foods, and many modern technologies are used to locate and acquire fish, mollusks, and crustaceans for human consumption. Hopefully, international agreements concerning overfishing and water pollution control measures will permit future generations to benefit from these food resources.

The adage "Water, water everywhere and not a drop to drink" may have been true once with respect to salty seawater, but it is not true any longer. One important ocean resource is the water itself. Modern desalinization plants make it possible for communities that do not have access to freshwater to get it from saltwater. This is accomplished by evaporating seawater, which yields freshwater as vapor. The water vapor then condenses to form liquid water, which can be used for drinking, farming, or industrial uses. Sodium chloride and other substances are left behind as solids. The process is somewhat costly in terms of the energy required to evaporate seawater; however, as the technology improves and becomes more efficient, more of the earth's population will get its freshwater from seawater.

FIGURE 2A.8

If you examine this ocean food chain closely, you will discover how the energy consumed by phytoplankton eventually sustains life for the shark.

The ocean is a vast resource for humankind. With technological advances and a sensitivity to maintaining the quality of the water in the earth's oceans, humans will no doubt find and use other valuable ocean resources.

The Earth's Atmosphere and Weather

The thin layer of air surrounding the earth—the *atmosphere*—changes continuously. When we use the term *weather,* we are describing the condition of the atmosphere at a given time. That condition may be hot, cold, windy, dry, wet, sunny, or cloudy. The term *climate* is used to describe the total effect of the day-to-day changes in the atmosphere.

Because the earth receives almost all its heat energy from the sun, we can say the sun is the principal cause for changes in the weather. Heat energy from the sun causes the air to warm and move upward, water to evaporate into the atmosphere, and the flow of air parallel to the earth, which we call *wind.* These changes play a part in determining the extent and type of *precipitation* (rain, snow, hail, sleet) that reaches the earth's surface.

Scientists who study the weather and predict weather changes are called *meteorologists.* Every country has meteorologists who gather weather data from a variety of sources, summarize it, record it using various symbols on a weather map, and then make predictions.

Water in the Atmosphere

The percentage a meteorologist finds when the amount of moisture in the air is compared to the amount of moisture the air could hold at a particular temperature is known as the *relative humidity.* When the relative humidity is high, the air contains a great amount of moisture and the evaporation of perspiration is slow, which makes us feel uncomfortably warm. When the temperature in the air drops to a certain point, the air can no longer hold the water vapor in it. The air at this temperature is *saturated.* The temperature at which a given body of air becomes saturated is called the *dew point*. As air rises in the atmosphere, it cools. When the rising air is cooled to its dew point, condensation may occur. Drops of water form when enough molecules of water vapor accumulate around and become attached to a particle of dust in the atmosphere. Billions of tiny droplets of water form a cloud.

There are two ways in which water exists in the atmosphere: as clouds and as precipitation. Table 2A.2 gives an overview of the characteristics of cloud and precipitation types.

Violent Weather

The earth is not always a peaceful place, and the same is true of its atmosphere. Under the right conditions, violent weather—including thunderstorms, tornadoes, winter storms, and hurricanes—can have a great impact on the surface of the earth and all of the life on it! Table 2A.3 describes some common violent weather phenomena.

TABLE 2A.2   Water in the atmosphere

WATER FORM	CHARACTERISTICS
Clouds	*Low clouds* include fog, stratus, stratocumulus, cumulus, and cumulonimbus. Their bases range from the surface up to 1,900 meters (about 6,500 feet). These clouds are usually made up entirely of water droples and are extremely dense.
	Middle clouds include both altocumulus and altostratus. The average heights of their bases range from 1,980 to 7,000 meters (about 6,500 to 23,000 feet). They are usually made of water droplets, ice crystals, or both and vary considerably in density.
	High clouds are cirrus, cirrocumulus, and cirrostratus. Their bases are generally above 5,030 meters (about 16,500 feet). They are always made of ice crystals and vary greatly in density.
	Cumulonimbus clouds are in a category by themselves. They may reach from the lowest to the highest atmospheric levels. During their life cycle, they may produce many of the other cloud types.
Precipitation	*Dew* is condensed water vapor that has formed tiny water droplets on cool objects.
	Frost forms when water vapor changes directly into ice crystals.
	Rain is condensed water vapor that falls as a liquid.
	Snowflakes are usually six-sided crystals formed by the direct change of water to a solid.
	Hail is round, hard pellets of ice associated with a thunderstorm. Hail pellets are concentric layers of ice formed as a result of the movement of the pellets in vertical cycles through thunderclouds.
	Sleet is small particles of clear ice that were originally raindrops. It results from raindrops passing through a layer of cold air.

Tomorrow's Weather

Because changes in the conditions of the atmosphere (the weather) tend to move in regular patterns above the earth's surface, the weather we will experience tomorrow will likely be much the same as the weather someplace else today. As a result, the most important tool that the weather forecaster has is the *weather map*. He or she studies the most recent weather map and tries to predict both the strength of the disturbances observed and their path. The forecaster also studies the map to see where and how new disturbances are being formed.

Meteorologists in North America know that in the middle latitudes, the upper air moves from west to east. Storms tend to enter from the west, pass across the middle of the continent, and move toward the North Atlantic. Thus, the weather that is likely to affect a local area is predicted on the basis of the larger-scale weather movement depicted on a weather map. The map is created by first recording symbols representing the data gathered at weather stations—pressure, temperature, humidity, wind direction, wind velocity, and cloud types.

TABLE 2A.3   Violent weather phenomena

PHENOMENON	CHARACTERISTICS
Thunderstorm	Upward and downward air movements (convection) produce a thunderstorm. Denser air sinks and warmer, less dense air rapidly rises. The down draft produces winds and heavy rain or hail. Some thunderstorms even produce tornadoes.
	Thunder is produced by the explosive expansion of air heated by a lightning bolt. The lightning is seen before the thunder is heard. The distance from lightning can be estimated by counting the time in seconds between seeing lightning and hearing thunder and then dividing by 5.
	Lightning is caused by the movement of charged particles in a thunderstorm that produces electric fields. These cause currents (lightning) to flow within a cloud, from cloud to cloud, from cloud to ground, and in some cases, from ground to cloud.
Tornado	This short-lived storm has high-speed winds that rotate counterclockwise. These winds may appear as a funnel attached to a thundercloud, which can pick up and move dust and debris if it nears or touches the ground.
Snowstorm	A storm in which snow falls for several hours without letting up.
Freezing rain, freezing drizzle, and ice storm	Freezing rain or freezing drizzle occurs when the surface temperature is below 0°C (32°F). The rain falls as a liquid but freezes in an ice glaze on objects. If the glaze is thick, it's called an ice storm.
Cold wave	A time period in which the temperature falls far below normal.
Hurricane	A violent rain and wind storm that gets energy from the heat of seawater. The quiet core, or eye, is surrounded by blowing winds. The thunderclouds of a hurricane sometimes cause tornadoes.

Meteorologists use a variety of instruments to collect this data. The pressure of the air above us is measured with a *barometer*. The *wind vane* is used to determine the direction of the wind at the earth's surface. Wind speed is measured with an *anemometer*, an instrument consisting of a set of cups mounted so that they can easily be rotated by the wind. The amount of moisture in the air is determined by a *hygrometer*. The amount of moisture that reaches the ground as precipitation is measured by *rain and snow gauges*.

The characteristics of the air high above the earth are commonly determined by the use of *radiosondes*. These are miniature radio transmitters to which are attached a variety of weather instruments. Radiosondes are carried aloft by balloons or small rockets. Data gathered by the instruments are transmitted back to earth by the radio transmitter.

In recent years, *weather satellites* have greatly improved the accuracy of weather forecasts. Their photographs of the clouds over the earth's surface reveal a great deal about weather phenomena. Such satellite photography, when used with information about air temperature, atmospheric pressure, and humidity, is of great assistance to meteorologists as they develop their weather forecasts for a particular area.

Summary Outline

I. The earth consists of various layers; the outermost layer is the crust, which is divided into seven crustal plates.
   A. The crust of the earth has undergone numerous gradual and violent changes during the earth's history.
   B. The land surface of the earth is composed of a variety of rocks, minerals, and soils.
   C. Fossil evidence of life forms that have existed in various periods of the earth's history has been found.
   D. The ocean floor has many features, including the continental shelf, continental slope, and ocean ridges.
   E. Ocean currents are the result of the sun warming the water and the earth's rotation.
   F. Humankind depends on the oceans as a source of food and other natural resources.

II. The atmosphere is a thin layer of constantly moving air that surrounds the earth.
   A. Water vapor in the atmosphere sometimes condenses to form clouds.
   B. Some water vapor in the atmosphere condenses and falls to earth as precipitation.
   C. Thunderstorms, tornadoes, winter storms, and hurricanes are examples of violent weather phenomena.
   D. Barometers, anemometers, and hygrometers are some of the instruments used to measure weather phenomena.
   E. Using information from these instruments and weather maps, scientists are able to make short-term and long-term weather forecasts.

NOTE

1. The discussion of volcanoes was excerpted with minor modifications from *Volcanoes*, a pamphlet prepared by the U.S. Geological Survey, U.S. Department of the Interior. This pamphlet is available for purchase from the Superintendent of Documents, Government Printing Office, Washington, DC 20402.

2B The Earth's Surface, Atmosphere, and Weather

Attention Getters, Discovery Activities, and Demonstrations

47

ATTENTION GETTERS

How Are Rocks the Same and Different?

Children can discover the similarities and differences among types of rocks by doing hands-on activities.

Materials	3 locally gathered rocks 1 large nail 3 sheets of white paper

Motivating Questions
- Do any of the rocks look or feel like any of the other rocks?
- How can we tell if one rock is harder or softer than the others?

Directions
1. Bring to class or take the class outside to find three rocks that look and feel different.
2. Display one rock on each sheet of paper, and have children come forward to make observations. As they do, write their observations on the board.
3. Scratch each rock with the nail, and have the children observe that some rocks are harder than others, that some rock particles scrape off, and that the scraped-off particles are of different sizes and colors.

Explanation/ Science Content for the Teacher
The earth's crust is made of different types of rocks. Rocks are different because of the materials within them and the ways in which they are formed. Wind, water, and ice break rocks into smaller pieces. Soil is made of small particles of rock as well as other material.

What Is in Soil?

Materials
1 cup of potting soil   3 sheets of white paper
1 cup of top soil from outdoors   3 hand lenses (magnifying glasses)
1 cup of sand (aquarium sand will do)

Place materials on a table so individual children can observe the soils.

Motivating Questions
- Will these soils look the same or different when we examine them with a hand lens?
- What do you think we will find in the soils?

Directions
1. Write the following terms on the board: *sand, outdoor soil, potting soil.* Read and pronounce each term with the class.
2. Sprinkle a small amount of each type of soil on a sheet of paper, and have the children use hand lenses to examine the soils.
3. As the children make observations, write them on the board under the appropriate term. *Note:* You may wish to sprinkle some soil particles on an overhead transparency and project the image.

Explanation/
Science Content
for the Teacher   Over long periods of time, rocks are broken into tiny particles. These particles, mixed with other materials, make up soil. Although sand gathered from a shoreline will contain pieces of shell and other debris, soil is mostly rock particles. Top soil contains amounts of sand, water, air, and decayed organic material. Potting soil usually contains less sand and more organic material than top soil. The organic material allows it to retain water for long periods of time.

For Young Learners [ESS 3]

How Does a Thermometer Change on Hot and Cold Days?

Materials   1 outdoor thermometer containing red liquid   1 glass of cool water
3 rubber bands   1 glass of hot water

Motivating
Questions   Display the thermometer and ask:
- What do we call this?
- Where have you seen thermometers?

Directions   1. Wrap a rubber band around the thermometer at the level of the liquid.
2. Put the base of the thermometer in cool water, and have volunteers observe the new level of the liquid. Put a second rubber band at this level.
3. Have the children predict how the level will change when the thermometer is placed in warm water; then place the thermometer in warm water and mark the level of the liquid with the third rubber band.
4. Discuss how looking at an outdoor thermometer might help people decide what to wear on hot and cold days.

Explanation/
Science Content
for the Teacher   A thermometer registers the temperature of its surroundings. The level of liquid rises or falls due to increases or decreases in its volume as a result of heating or cooling. The red liquid in a typical household thermometer is tinted alcohol. Some thermometers, however, contain mercury, a silvery liquid metal.

For Young Learners [HNS 2 and 3]

Weather Sayings: True or False?

Materials   Access to the Internet   Science resource books and encyclopedias
Posterpaper and markers

Motivating
Questions   - What does the word *superstition* mean?
- What are some of the superstitions you know about?
- What are some examples of weather superstitions?

Directions   1. Have the class vote on whether each of the following statements is true or false. Then ask them to give their reasons for voting as they did and to explain how each statement could be tested.

"Birds flying south means cold weather is coming."
"Squirrels gathering nuts means cold weather is coming."
"When the leaves on trees turn upside down, it's going to rain."
"A sunny shower won't last half an hour."
"If you wash your car, it's going to rain tomorrow."

2. Divide the class into cooperative groups and give them the task of discovering three weather sayings, deciding how each could be tested, and sharing their reasons for believing it to be true or false. Each group should write their sayings on posterpaper.

3. Bring the groups together, and ask for a class vote on whether each saying is true or false.

4. Finally, have the groups reveal the results of their research.

**Explanation/
Science Content
for the Teacher**

Here are some additional weather sayings you may wish to share:
"You can smell rain when it's coming."
"When your joints give you pain, it's going to rain."
"Red sky at night, sailor's delight. Red sky in the morning, sailors take warning."
"When smoke descends, good weather ends."

For Middle-Level Learners [ESS 4]

What Crushed the Can?

Materials

2 empty soda cans
Tongs or heat-resistant potholder mitts
Ice cubes in a bowl of water
Access to an alcohol burner, stove top, or electric hot plate

**Motivating
Questions**

- What do you think will happen if we put a little water in the can, heat the can, and plunge it into the ice water?
- What do you think causes this to happen?

Directions

1. Add about one-fourth of a cup of tap water to the empty can.
2. Heat the can over the heat source until the water boils and steam is visible.
3. Using tongs or mitts, drop the can into the ice water.

**Explanation/
Science Content
for the Teacher**

The heated water changes to steam. The steam forces some of the air out of the can. When the can is dropped into ice water, the steam in the can condenses and the pressure within the can is reduced. Atmospheric pressure (the pressure of the air outside the can) crushes the can.

For Middle-Level Learners [ESS 4]

What Pushed the Egg into the Bottle?

Materials

1 cooled, peeled, hard-boiled egg   Matches
1 sheet of paper about 8 cm square   Tongs
1 glass gallon jug or old-fashioned milk bottle

Motivating Questions
- What do you think will happen if we put the egg on the empty bottle?
- What do you think will happen if we put the egg on the bottle after we have burned some paper in the bottle?

Directions
1. Put the egg on the open bottle top with the narrow end down, and ask the second motivating question.
2. After listening to the predictions, remove the egg, light the paper with the match, drop it (using the tongs) into the bottle, and quickly replace the egg. The egg will be pushed into the bottle.

Explanation/ Science Content for the Teacher
The burning paper heats the air within the bottle, causing it to expand. The egg acts as a valve, allowing some but not all of the expanding air to leave the bottle around the narrow end of the egg. Thus, the air in the bottle is at a lower pressure than the air outside the bottle. The pressure of the air outside of the bottle (atmospheric pressure) slowly forces the egg into the bottle. *Safety Note:* Be sure to point out to the children the safety precautions you employ as you use a match and handle the burning paper. Explain that they should not try this activity at home without adult supervision.

For Middle-Level Learners [S&T 4]

Can We Make Fog?

Materials
2 resealable sandwich bags containing ice cubes
2 empty, clean plastic 2 liter soda bottles with labels removed
1 funnel
1 electric tea kettle or other source of very hot water
1 flashlight

Motivating Questions
- What do you think will happen when we put a bag of ice cubes on top of the bottle with cool water?
- What do you think will happen when we put a bag of ice cubes on top of the bottle of hot water?

Directions
1. Add cold water to one bottle until it is about four-fifths full. Fill the second bottle with hot water to the same level.
2. Cover the top of each bottle with a sandwich bag containing ice cubes, and have the children predict the changes that will occur within the bottle.
3. Use the flashlight to illuminate the inside of each bottle. The children should be able to observe fog above the surface of the hot water. You may wish to darken the room for this part of the demonstration.

Explanation/ Science Content for the Teacher
Some of the hot water evaporates into the air above it. When that air is cooled by the bag of ice cubes, the water vapor condenses into tiny droplets. These droplets are in fact a cloud. When a cloud is formed at the earth's surface above land or water, it is called *fog*. Depending on the room's temperature and other factors, the children may be able to see some fog above the hot water even without the use of the sandwich bag with ice cubes.

DISCOVERY ACTIVITIES

How to Make a Fossil

Objectives
- The children will create fossils from samples of plant material.
- The children will explain the process by which fossils are produced in nature.

Sciences Processes Emphasized
Hypothesizing   Communicating
Experimenting

Materials for Each Child or Group
Aluminum foil pie plate   Water   Plaster of paris
Plastic spoon   Vaseline
Assortment of plant materials, including portions of a carrot, a leaf, and a twig

Motivation
Be sure to have two or three real fossils on hand, if possible, or reference books with pictures of various fossils. Display the fossils or pictures of the fossils, and have children make observations about their characteristics. Encourage the children to discuss how the fossils may have been formed. Tell the children that they will create their own fossils during this activity.

Directions
1. Have the children coat each portion of the plants they are using with a thin layer of vaseline.
2. Have the children mix the plaster of paris with water in the bottom of the pie plate until they obtain a thick, smooth mixture.
3. Have the children gently press the plant material into the upper surface of the plaster of paris and set the plaster aside to harden.
4. Bring the children together for a group discussion. Emphasize that what they have done represents *one* way in which fossils are formed; that is, plant or animal material falls into sediment, making an imprint. If the sediment then hardens into rock, the imprint will remain even though the organic matter decays.
5. When the plaster is dry and they have removed the plant material, the children will be able to observe a permanent imprint.
6. Establish a display of reference books showing pictures of fossils. Have the children look at pictures of fossils and hypothesize about how they were formed.

Key Discussion Questions
1. Have you ever found any fossils or seen any fossils on display? If so, what were they like and where did you see them? *Answers will vary.*
2. The fossils you made are known as *molds*. How could a scientist use a mold fossil to make something that looked like the object that formed the mold? *He or she could use something like clay to press against the mold fossil. The surface of the clay would take the shape of the original material.*

Science Content for the Teacher
A fossil is any preserved part or trace of something that lived in the past. Leaves, stems, bones, and even footprints have been preserved as fossils. Some fossils are formed when water passing over and through portions of animal or plant remains deposits minerals that replace the original materials. In other cases, animal and plant remains are buried in sediment. An imprint of the shape is left in mud even

when the material decays, and if the mud hardens and turns to rock, the imprint is preserved. This type of impression, which the children have replicated in this activity, is known as a *mold.*

Extension   *Science:* You may wish to encourage some children to do an activity that will extend their knowledge of fossil molds to fossil casts. They can replicate the formation of a cast fossil by mixing plaster of paris outdoors and filling in animal tracks with it.

For Young Learners [ESS 3]

Weather or Not

Objectives
- The children will observe and record daily weather conditions.
- The children will compare their observations with information on weather maps.

Sciences Processes Emphasized   Observing   Comparing
Measuring

Materials for Each Child or Group   Outdoor thermometer marked in Celsius
Newspaper weather map for the days of the activity
Legend from weather map showing symbols and meanings

Motivation   Create a weather chart on the chalkboard that has columns for temperature, cloud, wind, and precipitation data. While the children watch, fill the columns of the chart with your personal observations of the present weather, using the appropriate symbols from a weather map. Challenge the children to guess what is meant by each symbol. After some discussion, explain what each symbol represents and indicate that the children will use these symbols on the charts they make.

Directions   1. After giving the children some time to practice drawing each weather symbol that you have explained, have them make blank charts.
2. For the next two to three days, have the groups take their charts to some location on the school grounds where they can make weather observations. They should use weather symbols to record their observations. *Safety Note:* Be sure that each group is visible to you in a safe location.
3. You can generate additional excitement if you have the children compare the observations from their weather charts with weather maps for the same days.

Key Discussion Questions   1. What kinds of measurements can we make of weather conditions outside? *Temperature, whether it's raining, how hard the wind is blowing, and whether there are clouds in the sky.*
2. How are clouds different from one another? *Some are white and puffy, some are flat and gray, some are high in the sky, and some you can see through.*

Science Content for the Teacher   There are three major types of clouds: *cirrus, cumulus,* and *stratus.* Clouds that are high in the sky and wispy are cirrus clouds. Cumulous clouds are often billowing with white tops. Stratus clouds are sheets of gray clouds that are close to the ground. Depending on your climate, precipitation may take the form of rain or snow. Temperature varies from place to place on a given day as well as from day to day.

Extension   *Science/Art:* Encourage some children to create a cloud display. After consulting reference books for pictures of various types of clouds, they can use cotton balls, cotton batting, and Styrofoam to create their displays.

For Middle-Level Learners [ESS 4]

How Do Layers of Sediment Form?

Objectives
- The children make a model and use it to discover the order in which particles of different sizes settle to the bottom.
- The children make drawings to document the results of their experimentation and discuss their results.

Sciences Processes   Observing   Communicating
Emphasized   Experimenting

Materials for Each   Large glass jar with lid   Pebbles   Soil
Child or Group   Source of water   Gravel   Sand

Motivation   This is a good activity to do before the children begin studying how various types of rocks are formed. Display at the front of the room or at a learning station all of the materials in the materials list. Ask the children to guess what this activity will be about. After some initial discussion, focus their attention on the soil, pebbles, gravel, and sand. Ask them to think about what would happen if a stream carrying these materials slowed down. Once the children have begun to think about the materials settling into layers on the bottom of a stream or river, begin the activity.

Directions
1. Have each group fill one-third of a large glass jar with equal amounts of soil, pebbles, gravel, and sand.
2. Have the groups fill the jars the rest of the way with water and screw on the lids.
3. Have the groups shake the jars so that all the materials are thoroughly stirred in the water.
4. Ask the groups to let the materials settle.
5. Have the groups observe the settling and then make drawings of the layers they observe.
6. Engage the class in a discussion of the results of the activity.

Key Discussion
Questions
1. Which of the materials settled to the bottom of the jar first? *The gravel.*
2. How can you explain the results in this activity? *The large pieces of gravel settled first because they were heavier than the other materials. The heaviest materials are at the bottom, and the lightest materials are at the top.*
3. What type of rock is formed from layers of earth materials that settle out of water? *Sedimentary.*

Science Content
for the Teacher   When water moves across the surface of the earth, it picks up tiny rocks, pebbles, grains of sand, and soil. This flow of water and materials eventually reaches streams, rivers, and the ocean, and the particles within the water become known as *sediment.* Whenever a flow of water is slowed, some of the sediment is deposited on the bottom of the flow. Layers of sediment pile up under the water. After hundreds

of years have passed, the weight of these layers may have become so great that the bottom layers are turned into rock.

Extension   *Science/Social Studies:* Some children may be encouraged to do research on the effect of moving water on farmland. The loss of topsoil due to water erosion is a significant threat to agriculture. Through research, these children will find that there are many government agencies that assist farmers who are trying to protect their soil from erosion.

For Middle-Level Learners [ESS 4]

Quakes and Shakes: An Earthquake Watch

Objectives
- The children will be able to locate those regions of the earth that have more earthquake activity than others.
- The children will study earthquake occurrence data and make hypotheses to explain any patterns they observe.

Sciences Processes Emphasized
Interpreting data
Making hypotheses

Materials for Each Child or Group
Note: This is a long-term activity in which children plot data from current government information on earthquakes. Thus, you will need to order the *Preliminary Determination of Epicenters: Monthly Listing* from the Superintendent of Documents, Government Printing Office, Washington, DC 20402.

Copies of the epicenter charts   Access to an atlas
Paper   Pencil
World map with latitude and longitude marked

Motivation
Ask the children if they have ever been to a part of the country that has a lot of earthquake activity, such as San Francisco. If any of them have, encourage them to discuss anything they may have heard about earthquakes from persons who live there. If no one has, engage the children in a discussion about earthquakes. Stress their cause and possible hazards. Explain that scientists are able to study information about previous earthquakes to predict the general locations of future earthquakes. Tell the children that they will be working with some of the same information that scientists use. Then display the collection of epicenter charts and the world maps.

Directions
1. Give a map and copies of the epicenter charts to each child or group. Explain that the information on the charts shows where scientists believe the source of an earthquake was; then explain the information. Although there is a lot of information on each chart, the children should work with only the date, time of eruption, latitude, longitude, region, depth, and *magnitude.* Explain that magnitude indicates the strength of the earthquake.
2. Have the children refer to an atlas to find the specific location of each earthquake and then mark their copy of the world map with a symbol for the earthquake. They should plot all earthquakes with a source from 0 to 69 kilometers deep with one symbol, 70 to 299 kilometers with another symbol, and more than 299 kilometers with a third symbol.

3. When they have recorded data from the epicenter chart, you may wish to have a discussion of the patterns they observe.
4. Have the children maintain their maps for a few months and repeat the activity each time you receive a monthly epicenter chart.

Key Discussion Questions
1. Do you see any pattern on your map that tells you what parts of the earth seem to have the most earthquakes? Where are those places? *Yes, along the western portion of the Pacific Ocean, from the Mediterranean Sea across Asia, and along the west coast of North and South America.*
2. What problems do you think are caused by earthquakes? *Answers will vary. Some may include comments such as the following: buildings may fall; earthquakes in the ocean may cause great waves.*

Science Content for the Teacher
An *earthquake* is the shaking of the ground caused by the shifting of the plates that make up the earth's surface and the release of pressure through faults in the earth's crust, which results in the movement of blocks of rocks past each other. The vibrations at ground level are sometimes strong enough to do structural damage to buildings and threaten life. The shaking of the ocean floor can produce gigantic waves that roll across the ocean. Scientists record the presence of an earthquake with an instrument known as a *seismograph.* To pinpoint the source of an earthquake's vibrations, scientists gather data from seismographs all over the world. The *epicenter* is thought to be directly above the place where the initial rock fractures occurred. When the locations of epicenters are plotted on a map, they roughly mark the places on the earth where crustal plates grind against each other.

Extension
Science/Social Studies: Some children may wish to research the effects of the San Francisco earthquake of 1906. They will be able to find pictures in encyclopedias showing how the city looked after the earthquake. Ask the children what effects the earthquake likely had on community life immediately after it occurred and its effect after a few years had passed.

For Middle-Level Learners [ESS 4]

How to Find the Dew Point

Objectives
- The children will find the temperature at which water vapor in the air condenses.
- The children will analyze their data and offer an explanation of how changes in treatment of moisture in the air will affect dew point readings.

Sciences Processes Emphasized
Observing   Interpreting
Gathering data

Materials for Each Child or Group
Empty soup can with one end cut out   Supply of ice cubes
Outdoor thermometer that will fit into the soup can   Rag

Motivation
Begin a discussion with the children about the invisible water vapor present in the air. Ask them if they have ever observed any evidence of the presence of water vapor in the air. They will probably share such observations as the steaming up of mirrors in bathrooms and the steam that seems to come out of their mouths when

they breathe on a cold day. Tell the children that water vapor in the air is usually not observed because the air temperature is sufficiently high to keep the water vapor a gas. As a gas, water vapor is invisible. Display the equipment that will be used for this activity and tell the children that they will be using it to find the temperature at which the water vapor presently in the air will condense. Explain that this temperature is known as the *dew point*. The dew point is the point at which water vapor changes from a gas to a liquid.

Directions

1. Distribute the soup cans to the children and have them remove the labels, scrub the outside of the cans with soap and water, and polish the surfaces.
2. Demonstrate the following procedure for the children: Fill the shiny can about two-thirds full of water at room temperature, and place a thermometer in it. Then add small amounts of ice, and stir the mixture until the ice melts. Have the children observe the outside of the can as you add small amounts of ice and stir. Eventually, the outside will begin to lose its shine, and a layer of moisture will be observable.
3. Have the children do this activity on their own. Ask them to keep track of the temperature on the thermometer and to pay close attention to the outside of the can as the temperature drops. Stress the importance of observing the precise temperature at which the film forms.
4. After the children have found the dew point inside the classroom, you may wish to have them find it outside. When the children have completed the activity, begin a class discussion of their results. Be sure the children understand that the drier the air, the lower the temperature must be in order for moisture to condense.

Science Content for the Teacher

The air's capacity to hold moisture is determined by its temperature. The temperature at which air can no longer hold water vapor is known as the *dew point*. *Condensation*, the change from water as a gas to water as a liquid, is usually observable in the atmosphere as dew, fog, or clouds. Condensation occurs when the air is saturated with water vapor. *Saturation* occurs when the temperature of the air reaches its dew point. In this activity, the air near the outside surface of the can is cooled to its dew point. The moisture in that layer of air condenses on the available surface—the outside of the can.

Key Discussion Questions

1. Why do you think we use a shiny can for this activity? *It makes it easy to tell when the moisture condenses. The moisture makes the shiny can look dull.*
2. Why do you think knowing the dew point might be important to weather forecasters? *If they know the dew point, they will know the temperature at which the moisture in the air will condense. Then they can more easily predict when fog, clouds, or rain will happen.*
3. Why do you think dew forms only at night? *During the night, the temperature of the air falls because the earth is not receiving sunlight. Sometimes the temperature falls so low that the dew point is reached. When this happens, the moisture condenses on grass and on the leaves and branches of plants.*

Extension

Science/Math: You may wish to have some children find the dew point with both Celsius and Fahrenheit thermometers. After they have done this, they can use conversion charts to be sure the dew point expressed in the number of degrees Celsius is equivalent to that expressed in the number of degrees Fahrenheit.

DEMONSTRATIONS

Indoor Rainmaking[1]

Objectives	■ The children will observe the production of rain.
	■ The children will explain how the rainmaking model can be used to illustrate the water cycle.

Sciences Processes Emphasized	Observing	Explaining
	Inferring	

Materials	Hot plate or stove	Large pot	Ice cubes
	Teakettle	Water	

Motivation Show the materials to the children, and ask how the materials could be used to make a model that shows how rain forms. After some discussion, they will be ready to observe the demonstration and follow the path of the water. You may wish to have a volunteer assist you.

Directions
1. Place water in the teakettle and begin to heat it. As the water is heating, put the ice cubes in the pot.
2. When the water in the teakettle is boiling, hold the pot with the ice cubes above the steam emerging from the teakettle. Have children observe the formation of water droplets on the bottom of the pot.
3. Have the children note when the water droplets become large enough to fall.
4. Using the questions below, discuss the rainmaking process as a model illustrating the water cycle.

Key Discussion Questions
1. What do you think the teakettle of boiling water stands for in the model? *Oceans and lakes.*
2. How does water from the oceans and lakes get into the atmosphere? *The sun heats the water and it evaporates.*
3. Where are the clouds in our model? *The steam stands for the clouds.*
4. Rainmaking is part of the water cycle. What do you think scientists mean when they talk about the water cycle? *Water is always moving. Water that leaves the lakes and oceans moves into the air. Water that is in the air forms clouds and sometimes falls to the earth. Rain, snow, sleet, and hail fall onto the land and oceans. Water that reaches the land flows back into the oceans and lakes.*

Science Content for the Teacher Water on the earth is continually recycled. The path that water takes in nature is known as the *water cycle.* Water that evaporates from oceans, lakes, and rivers enters the atmosphere. *Precipitation* forms when this water vapor accumulates around dust particles at low temperatures and high altitudes. The water then returns to the earth.

Extension   *Science/Language Arts:* Some children may wish to use this demonstration as a starting point for writing poetry about the principal form of precipitation in their area. They could write their poetry on large sheets of paper suitable for display.

For Young Learners [ESS 3]

Whose Fault Is It?

Objectives
- The children will observe the occurrence of folds and faults in simulated rock layers.
- The children will infer the causes of changes in rock layers.

Sciences Processes
Emphasized
Observing
Inferring

Materials
2 blocks of wood
4 sticks of modeling clay, each a different color

Motivation
Ask the children how you could use clay to make rock layers. Flatten each stick of clay into a strip that is about 1 centimeter (less than 1/2 inch) thick and 8 to 10 centimeters (about 3 to 4 inches) wide.

Directions
1. Place the clay strips on top of one another. Ask the children to guess whether the strips represent sedimentary, igneous, or metamorphic rocks.
2. Gently press the wood blocks against the ends of the clay layers, and have the children observe changes.
3. Eventually, small cracks will appear on the layers, and the layers will be forced into a hump. *Note:* If the clay is too soft or too warm, the fractures will not occur. You may wish to allow the layers to dry or cool for a day before performing this part of the demonstration.

Key Discussion
Questions
1. If the clay layers were layers of rock, which layer would probably be the youngest? Why? *The top one. The material in it was deposited last.*
2. What causes the bends and breaks in real rock layers? *Answers will vary. Some children may be aware that the pushing together of the plates of the earth's crust produces great forces that change and fracture rock layers.*
3. Do you think that breaks in the rock layers might allow molten rock to move toward the earth's surface? Why? *Yes. The molten rock can flow up through the cracks because there is nothing to hold it back.*

Science Content
for the Teacher
Layers of sedimentary rock provide important clues about the relative ages of rocks. Top layers are *usually* younger than lower layers. Sometimes, however, layers of rocks are turned upside down as a result of the collusion of the crustal plates and the movement of molten rock beneath the surface.

Extension
Science/Art: You may wish to have children construct detailed models of various types of faults described in reference books.

For Middle-Level Learners [ESS 4]

You've Heard of Rock Musicians, but Have You Heard of Rock Magicians?

Objectives	■ The children will observe one unusual characteristic in each of five rocks.
	■ The children will describe each characteristic observed.
	■ The children will name each of the rocks used in the demonstration.

Sciences Processes Emphasized

Observing
Communicating

Materials

Bowl of water	Matches
Sheet of paper	White vinegar or any dilute acid

Samples of the following rocks: pumice, anthracite, asbestos,
  calcite, willemite (or any other rock that will fluoresce)
Any ultraviolet-light source (you may be able to borrow one from
  a high school earth science teacher)

Optional: Bow tie, magic wand

Very optional: Top hat and/or cape

Motivation

Because of the nature of this demonstration, it will take little to get the children's attention. You may wish to be the rock magician yourself, or you may happen to have a child who would be perfect for the part! Be sure that all the children have a good view of what is to transpire.

Directions

1. The rock magician should use the materials in the list to demonstrate the following:
    a. The floating rock: Pumice will float in water.
    b. The writing rock: Anthracite will write on paper.
    c. The rock that can resist flame: Asbestos fibers will not burn.
    d. The fizzing rock: A few drops of vinegar will cause calcite to fizz.
    e. The fluorescent rock: With the room darkened, the willemite will fluoresce when placed under ultraviolet light.
2. Before each demonstration, the magician should name the rock, spell it, and write its name on the chalkboard. The children will thereby learn the name of each rock displayed.
3. Have the children write down their observations.

Key Discussion Questions

1. Why do you think geologists are interested in the special characteristics of these rocks? *They can tell a lot about what the rock is made of if it does certain things.*
2. Why do you think the pumice floated? *It has a lot of air trapped in it.*
3. Do you think the material in your pencils might be something like the anthracite? Why? *Yes, both can make marks on paper. Note:* The material in pencils these days is not lead but graphite. Graphite is essentially carbon. Anthracite is also carbon.

Science Content for the Teacher

Pumice is magma (molten rock) that trapped bubbles of steam or gas when it was thrown out of a volcano in liquid form. When magma solidifies, it is honeycombed with gas-bubble holes. This gives it the buoyancy to float on water. *Anthracite* is a type of coal that results from the partial decomposition of plants. The carbon in the plants is the primary constituent of anthracite and other forms of coal. *Asbestos* is the popular name of the mineral chrysotile. The silky fibers of asbestos can be woven into a yarn that is used in brake linings and in heat- and fire-retardant fabrics. *Calcite* is a mineral found in such rocks as limestone and marble. Geologists test for its presence by placing a few drops of a warm acid on the rock under study. If calcite is present, carbon dioxide gas will be released with a fizz by the chemical reaction. *Willemite* is a mineral that fluoresces; that is, it gives off light when exposed to ultraviolet light. Some other minerals, generally available from science supply companies, that can be used to demonstrate fluorescence are calcite, tremolite, fluorite, and scapolite.

Extension   *Science/Social Studies:* You may wish to follow this demonstration with a map or study exercise in which the children find out where the various rocks come from. They will need some earth science reference books and an atlas.

For Middle-Level Learners [ESS 4]

How to Find the Relative Humidity

Objectives
- The children will observe how to construct a wet/dry bulb hygrometer.
- The children will measure the relative humidity.

Sciences Processes Emphasized
Observing
Using numbers

Materials

2 identical Celsius thermometers	Baby food jar full of water at room temperature
Small piece of gauze	Small board or piece of heavy cardboard
Small rubber band	Relative humidity table (see page 62)

Motivation   Ask the children if they have ever heard the term *relative humidity*. After some discussion, indicate that the term represents a comparison of the amount of water in the air to the amount of water the air could hold at the present temperature. Tell the children that they are about to observe how to construct an instrument that will permit them to find the relative humidity.

Directions
1. With the help of a student volunteer, tape both thermometers about 6 centimeters (about 2 inches) apart on a piece of cardboard. The bulb end of one thermometer should extend 6 centimeters beyond the edge of the cardboard.
2. Wrap the extending end in gauze. Fasten the gauze with a rubber band, but leave a tail of gauze that can be inserted into the baby food jar.
3. Place the tail in the baby food jar filled with water, and moisten the gauze around the bulb. The tail will serve as a wick to keep the bulb moist.
4. Fan both thermometers vigorously. In a few minutes, the volunteer will observe that the thermometers display different temperatures. Use the wet/dry bulb table to find the relative humidity.

Relative humidity expressed as a percentage

DRY BULB READING (°C)	DIFFERENCE BETWEEN WET BULB READING AND DRY BULB READING (°C)									
	1	2	3	4	5	6	7	8	9	10
0	81	64	46	29	13					
2	84	68	52	37	22	7				
4	85	71	57	43	29	16				
6	86	73	60	48	35	24	11			
8	87	75	63	51	40	29	19	8		
10	88	77	66	55	44	34	24	15	6	
12	89	78	68	58	48	39	29	21	12	
14	90	79	70	60	51	42	34	26	18	10
16	90	81	71	63	54	46	38	30	23	15
18	91	82	73	65	57	49	41	34	27	20
20	91	83	74	66	59	51	44	38	31	24
22	92	83	76	68	61	54	47	41	34	28
24	92	84	77	69	62	56	49	44	37	31
26	92	85	78	71	64	58	51	47	40	34
28	93	85	78	72	65	59	53	48	42	37
30	93	86	79	73	67	61	55	50	44	39

Key Discussion Questions

1. Why do you think the wet bulb showed a lower reading than the dry bulb? *Water evaporated from the gauze and cooled the thermometer.*
2. Would more or less water evaporate on a drier day? *More, because water enters the air faster if there is little water in the air to begin with.*

Science Content for the Teacher

Hygrometers are used to measure relative humidity. The evaporation of water lowers the wet bulb temperature. The amount of lowering depends on a variety of factors, including the amount of water vapor already in the air.

Extension

Science/Social Studies: Have the children interview adults to find out if they have lived in places where the relative humidity is high or low. The interviewers can find out how this affected the way of life in each place. Children can practice geography skills by locating various high and low humidity regions on a world map.

NOTE

1. The activity on indoor rainmaking is based on an activity of the same name in J. Abruscato and J. Hassard, *The Whole Cosmos Catalog* (Glenview, IL: Scott, Foresman, 1991), 60.

3A

The Cosmos

Content

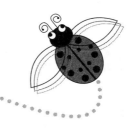

Are We Alone?

Are we all alone in the vastness of space?
Are other planets in orbit around distant stars?

Although we still don't have an answer to the first question, we do have an answer to the second. Humankind has made an extraordinary discovery: There *are* planets around other stars!

Powerful telescopes, the careful study of light spectra from stars, advanced computer software, new techniques for studying the wobbles in the movements of stars (an important clue for the presence of a planet), and diligent work by astronomers have revealed that there are stars in the evening sky that do have planets. The names of three of them are 51 Pegasi in the Pegasus constellation, 70 Virginis in the Virgo constellation, and 47 Ursae Majoris in the Big Dipper. Even more amazing, a family of planets has been discovered orbitting Upsilon Andromedae, a star similar to our sun and 44 light-years away.

So, now we know that planets may be far more common in the universe than we would have ever believed. But where does that leave us? Will we *ever* get the answer to that first question: *Are we alone?* Perhaps, but as we use powerful radiotelescopes to search the sky for signals sent by intelligent life, we can also pursue other questions that are just as interesting. For instance: How did the universe come into existence? When did the universe come into existence? What is the real meaning of *time?* and Did time exist before the universe came into being? There are even more mind-wrenching questions, such as whether universes parallel to ours exist or whether matter that enters a black hole can pop out somewhere else in our universe or another universe—if there are other universes.

All of these questions bring us very close to the edge of what people call *science fiction,* yet each day, real-live and very respectable scientists search for the answers. These esoteric questions, as well as those focused more closely on our planet and solar system, will eventually produce answers. We are moving closer and closer to the time when we'll finally be able to answer the question *Are we alone?*

What Is the Universe and How Was It Formed?

The universe is all of the matter, energy, and space that exists. But how did this matter, energy, and space begin? Scientific debate over how the universe began seems to be endless. One important theory, known as the *Big Bang theory,* suggests that the universe had a definite beginning. According to the theory, approximately 8 to 20 billion years ago, the universe was created as a result of a fiery explosion. Astronomical observations that reveal all galaxies have been moving apart from one another at enormous speeds and other evidence suppports this theory. By reasoning backward from the present outward movement of galaxies, we can assume that all the matter of the universe was once packed together.

The theory of a cosmic explosion is also supported by a discovery made in 1965 by Arno Penzias and Robert Wilson of the Bell Laboratories. Penzias and Wilson discovered and measured the strength of faint radiation that came from every direction in the sky. The entire universe seems to be immersed in this radiation. Measurements of the strengths and forms of radiation coincide with the strengths and forms that would have resulted from an enormous explosion occurring billions of years ago.

Maps of the sky made from data gathered by the Cosmic Background Explorer (COBE) satellite show slight differences in the background radiation discovered by Penzias and Wilson. Advocates of the Big Bang theory claim the data are exactly what a scientist would predict if the universe began with a Big Bang.

Although the Big Bang theory offers many explanations for astronomical phenomena, some recent discoveries have strongly challenged it. Observational studies of galaxies by Dr. Margaret J. Geller and Dr. H. P. Huchra of the Harvard–Smithsonian Center for Astrophysics and others have found some organized patterns of galaxies. However, according to the Big Bang theory, these patterns or structures, including an enormous chain of galaxies about 500 billion light-years across and known as the *Great Wall,* should not exist because galaxies should be homogeneously distributed.

Perhaps future studies will be able to explain the organized pattern of galaxies within the confines of the Big Bang theory. On the other hand, future studies may provide data that suggest alternate theories that better explain the nature of the universe we observe today.

Magnetars

A new type of star has been discovered, and we know of its existence because for one brief moment, it affected our environment. Called a *magnetar,* it is believed to be a neutron star that has a magnetic field billions of times more powerful than the earth's magnetic field. A neutron star is a remnant of a collapsed star and is extremely dense. The forces that form a neutron star are so powerful that the original star's protons and electrons were compressed together to form neutrons.

Some scientists have thought for awhile that this strange type of star existed, but there was no proof until recently, when an intense pulse of x-rays and gamma rays entered our solar system and set off detectors on spacecraft orbiting our earth and surveying other planets. The intensity of the radiation was powerful enough to cause some spacecraft to automatically shut down their instruments to prevent them from being damaged. Fortunately, the radiation didn't penetrate our atmosphere any further than a distance of 48 kilometers (about 30 miles) from our planet's surface. The burst of radiation probably occurred when something caused the magnetic field around the magnetar to become rearranged. No real harm was done, except to disappoint those scientists who were confident that magnetars didn't exist in the first place.

Quasars, Pulsars, and Black Holes

Magnetars aren't the only fascinating objects in the universe. There are faint blue celestial objects that are thought to be the most distant and luminous objects in the universe. There are rotating neutron stars thought to be remnants of *supernovas,* exploding stars that at peak intensity can outshine their galaxies. Astronomers have even found evidence that some stars have collapsed, forming such a powerful gravitational field that no light or any other radiation can escape. These objects, known as *black holes,* along with quasars and pulsars, raise many interesting questions about the universe in which we exist.

Table 3A.1 gives a brief summary of the characteristics of quasars, pulsars, and black holes.

Galaxies

Within the universe are billions of clusters of stars, known as *galaxies.* Each galaxy contains hundreds of millions of stars, clouds of dust, and gas. Galaxies themselves are thought to be parts of clusters of other galaxies and nebulae, which are huge bodies of dust and gas (see Figure 3A.1).

The galaxy of stars that contains our sun is known as the *Milky Way.* The stars in the Milky Way are so far from one another that measurement in kilometers (or miles) would be impossible to imagine. As a result, astronomers use a measuring unit called the *light-year.* A light-year represents the distance that light travels in one year. Light travels 299,792 kilometers (about 186,000 miles) in just one second, so one light-year represents a distance of 9,450,000,000,000 kilometers (about 6,000,000,000,000 miles).

TABLE 3A.1   Characteristics of quasars, pulsars, and black holes

OBJECT	CHARACTERISTICS
Quasar	The name *quasar* comes from the term *quasi-stellar objects.* Quasars are extremely bright objects in the universe that shine with an intensity that's much more powerful than that of hundreds of galaxies. Their energy seems to come from gas and the remnants of stars spiraling into black holes. Quasars are thought to be at the centers of galaxies. Quasars are some of the oldest objects in the universe and are billions of light-years from Earth.
Pulsar	A pulsar is a dense, rapidly spinning remnant of a supernova explosion. (A supernova is the explosive end to the life of a massive star.) The pulsar consists solely of neutrons and produces intense magnetic fields that sweep across space like lighthouse beacons. When the first pulsar was discovered, its extremely regular rate of pulsing was thought to be a signal from another intelligent civilization.
Black hole	Black holes cannot be seen but their presence is detected by studying the behavior of objects near them. Black holes are often thought of as vacuums that take in all that is around them, but that is not completely true. Some black holes emit radiation as matter is drawn in. Observable X-rays and radio waves are then emitted. A black hole is formed by the collapse of an old star into an extremely dense state surrounded by a powerful gravitational field. It is thought that some black holes may contain the masses of millions or billions of stars. These supermassive black holes may begin as ordinary black holes and over a long period of time take in the masses of large numbers of surrounding stars. Another theory is that they were formed during the Big Bang.

FIGURE 3A.1
The Andromeda Spiral Galaxy, which is visible as a faint patch in the constellation Andromeda, is about 2 million light-years from Earth.

Astronomers have estimated that the Milky Way is tens of thousands of light-years in length and one-eighth that distance in width. Their evidence seems to indicate that our galaxy has a spiral shape. The closest star to our sun, Alpha Centauri, is more than four light-years away. The distance from the Milky Way to the nearest galaxy is 1,500,000 light-years.

Constellations

Constellations are groups of stars that seem to form specific patterns when viewed from Earth. Ages ago, people on Earth looked up at the night sky and saw that the stars that make up the Milky Way seemed to be organized into patterns. Each area of the sky containing such a pattern was identified as a constellation, and all the stars within the pattern were considered to be part of it. Many constellations were given names from mythology. Others were named for their apparent resemblance to familiar animals and objects. At present, there are 88 named constellations.

The easiest constellations to recognize are the polar constellations, those groups of stars located around the North Star (Polaris). To locate the North Star, find the constellation known as the Big Dipper. By sighting along an imaginary line between the two stars at the rim of the Big Dipper, you should be able to locate the North Star.

Our Solar System

Our sun, the planets revolving around it, and associated clouds and bodies of matter make up what we call the *solar system,* which scientists believe was formed about 4.6 billions years ago. The sun's gravitational pull is the dominant force in the solar system, and the sun itself is the most massive part of the solar system.

Our Sun, a Star

With all of the new solar data pouring in from spacecraft, the sun is proving to be a more complex star[1] than we ever realized. Of course, the answers to many of our questions may be hidden in the data now on hand. Most scientists seem to agree on how the sun was born and how it will die. They have even calculated how much longer it has to live: 5 billion years as a normal, or main-sequence, star.

Astronomers believe that the sun and planets were formed from an enormous contracting cloud of dust and gas. All parts of this cloud did not move uniformly. Some parts formed local condensations that eventually became our planets, moons, comets, and asteroids. Gradually, the main cloud became spherical. Gravitational contraction increased its temperature. Eventually, the core temperature rose to a point at which the cloud's hydrogen nuclei began to fuse. Nuclear energy then produced enough outward pressure of heated gas to balance the inward force of gravity and maintain the sun as a glowing star. This process is believed to have begun about 5 billion years ago.

About 5 billion years from now, the sun will have depleted the hydrogen fuel in its core. Its thermonuclear reactions will then move outward where unused hydrogen exists. At the same time, the tremendous nuclear heat at the sun's core will also move outward, expanding the sun by as much as 60 times. As the sun cools by expansion, its surface color will become a deep red. It will then be a *red giant*—not a main-sequence star. Looming across much of our sky, it will boil off our water and air and incinerate any remnants of life.

When the sun exhausts its hydrogen fuel, it will no longer be able to withstand gravitational contraction. Eventually, it will shrink to a *white dwarf,* no bigger than the earth but so dense that a piece the size of a sugar cube would weigh thousands of kilograms. Eventually, after billions of years, our sun will cool and dim to a *black cinder.* Only then will eternal night fall upon the solar system.

The Moon

Earth has a single natural satellite: the moon. The first human footsteps on the moon were made by American astronauts, who explored its dusty surface in 1969. Six two-man crews brought back a collection of rocks and soil weighing 382 kilograms (842 pounds) and consisting of more than 2,000 separate samples.

Rocks collected from the lunar highlands date from 4.0 to 4.3 billion years ago. The first few million years of the moon's existence were so violent that little trace of this period remains. As a molten outer layer gradually cooled and solidified into different kinds of rock, the moon was bombarded by huge asteroids and smaller objects. Some of the asteroids were the size of Rhode Island or Delaware, and their collisions with the moon created huge basins hundreds of kilometers across.

The catastrophic bombardment died away about 4 billion years ago, leaving the lunar highlands covered with huge overlapping craters and a deep layer of shattered and broken rock (see Figure 3A.2). Heat produced by the decay of radioactive elements began to melt the inside of the moon at depths of about 200 kilometers (124 miles) below its surface. Then, from 3.1 to 3.8 billion years ago, great floods of lava rose from

FIGURE 3A.2

This lunar landscape photo was transmitted to Earth by a *Surveyor* spacecraft.

inside the moon and poured over its surface, filling the large impact basins to form the dark parts of the moon, called *maria,* or seas. Surprisingly, recent analysis of data from the moon has revealed the presence of water trapped as ice at its polar regions.

The Planets

Nine planets, including Earth, revolve around the sun. Four of these planets—Mercury, Venus, Mars, and Pluto—resemble Earth in size, density, and chemical composition. The other four—Jupiter, Saturn, Uranus, and Neptune—are larger and have thick, gaseous atmospheres (see Figure 3A.3).

It's important to be aware of the key physical characteristics of each planet in our solar system, the nature of any atmosphere that exists, and the kind and number of satellites it has. Table 3A.2 (page 70) provides a considerable amount of detail for each planet, including its distance from the sun, diameter, rotation period, and so on. And the following sections detail some of the key characteristics of each planet.

FIGURE 3A.3

The relative sizes of the planets

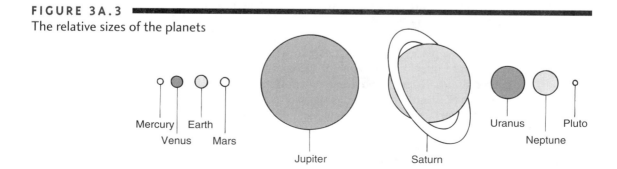

Mercury   Earth

Venus   Mars

Jupiter   Saturn

Uranus   Pluto

Neptune

TABLE 3A.2 Characteristics of the planets

CHARACTERISITC	MERCURY	VENUS	EARTH	MARS	JUPITER	SATURN	URANUS	NEPTUNE	PLUTO
1. Mean distance from Sun (millions of kilometers)	57.9	108.2	149.6	227.9	778.3	1,427	2,871	4,497	5,914
2. Period of revolution	88 days	224.7 days	365.3 days	687 days	11.86 years	29.46 years	84 years	165 years	248 years
3. Equatorial diameter (kilometers)	4,880	12,100	12,756	6,794	143,200	120,000	51,800	49,528	fl2,330
4. Atmosphere (main components)	Virtually none	Carbon Dioxide	Nitrogen Oxygen	Carbon Dioxide	Hydrogen Helium	Hydrogen Helium	Helium Hydrogen Methane	Hydrogen Helium Methane	Methane + ?
5. Moons	0	0	1	2	47	30+	20+	8	1
6. Rings	0	0	0	0	3	1,000 (?)	11	4	0
7. Inclination of orbit to ecliptic	7°	3.4°	0°	1.9°	1.3°	2.5°	0.8°	1.8°	17.1°
8. Eccentricity of orbit	.206	.007	.017	.093	.048	.056	.046	.009	.248
9. Rotation period	59 days	243 days retrograde	23 hours 56 min.	24 hours 37 min.	9 hours 55 min.	10 hours 40 min.	17.2 hours retrograde	16 hours 7 min.	6 days 9 hours 18 min. retrograde
10. Inclination of axis*	Near 0°	177.2°	23° 27′	25° 12′	3° 5′	26° 44′	97° 55′	28° 48′	120°

*Inclinations greater than 90° imply retrograde rotation.

Mercury This is a small, heavily cratered, rocky planet. Dried gullies on and in the surface may indicate the presence of streams and seas millions of years ago. There is possibly water under the surface now. In fact, scientists are reasonably sure they have found water under Mercury's north and south poles. Mercury has a very thin atmosphere that's composed of carbon dioxide and small amounts of nitrogen. No natural satellites orbit this planet.

Venus The planet's surface is covered with lava flows from ancient volcanoes, quake faults, and impact craters. One of the lava-filled basins is larger than the continental United States. There is even one volcano that is taller than Mt. Everest. The atmosphere is a poisonous mixture of carbon dioxide and sulfuric acid. Thick clouds hide the Venusian surface. No natural satellites orbit Venus.

Earth Earth is known as the "blue planet," since most of its surface is covered with water. The land masses on Earth, or continents, have mountains, deserts, forests, and plains. The crust of Earth is active with earthquakes and volcanoes, which are found at various locations. Ancient craters on Earth's surface—for instance, in places such as Arizona and in the Gulf of Mexico—indicate that it has been struck by asteroids over its history.

Earth's atmosphere contains oxygen, nitrogen, carbon dioxide, and other gases. There is also an ozone layer, which protects living things from solar ultraviolet radiation, and clouds, which are part of Earth's water cycle. Earth has one natural satellite: the moon.

Mars   A tiny, toy-like robotic vehicle called *Sojourner* was sent to Mars in 1977 (see Figure 3A.4). It successfully traveled over a small portion of the Martian surface and sent back pictures to Earth. Although *Sojourner* showed us some Martian rocks, our telescopes and other instruments have provided a larger view of the Martian landscape. The surface has dried gulleys, which may indicate that Mars had running water and streams at one time. Additionally, geological features resembling shorelines, gorges, riverbeds, and islands have also been observed. Finally, Mars has polar ice caps, which likely consist of water.

The Martian atmosphere, like that of Venus, is composed primarily of carbon dioxide with small amounts of nitrogen, oxygen, and argon. The small amount of water vapor in the air condenses to form clouds along the slopes of volcanoes. Some fog even forms in Martian valleys. Mars has two moons—Phobos and Deimos—and each has a heavily cratered surface.

Jupiter   This planet, the largest in our solar system, has an atmosphere that is mostly hydrogen and helium whirling above a ball of liquid hydrogen. Jupiter's extraordinarily large atmosphere includes the Great Red Spot: a giant storm that is at least three times the size of Earth.

FIGURE 3A.4
Sojourner on the surface of Mars

A number of natural satellites travel around Jupiter. The four largest are Ganymede, Callisto, Io, and Europa, and two of next largest are Amalthea and Himalia. The moon Europa has a deep ocean of liquid water under an icy crust.

Saturn   This planet seems to have no solid surface and is composed of hydrogen gas. The sixth planet from the sun, Saturn is known for its intricate ring system. The rings are made of ice and rock particles, which vary in size from being as small as dust to as large as boulders. The rings appear to be held in their respective orbits by the gravitational attraction of the planet and its satellites (see Figure 3A.5).

Saturn has at least 30 moons. Titan is the largest, and the next six in size are Rhea, Iapetus, Dione, Tethys, Enceladus, and Mimas. The moon Titan has an atmosphere rich in nitrogen, as did Earth's atmosphere in its early days. Consequently, this moon holds great interest to scientists searching for extraterrestrial life.

Uranus   This, the third-largest planet in our solar system, rotates on its side! It has no solid surface, although it may have a small, silicate-rich core. The atmosphere of Uranus contains hydrogen, helium, water, ammonia, and methane. The blue-green color of the planet is due to the presence of methane gas above the cloud layers. Astronomers have detected a system of faint rings around the planet. Uranus has over 20 moons. Five of the largest are Miranda, Titania, Oberon, Umbriel, and Ariel.

Neptune   This gaseous planet is composed of hydrogen, helium, and methane, and these gases are thought to surround an Earth-sized liquid core. Like Uranus, there is sufficient methane on Neptune to give it a slightly bluish color. Winds in the atmosphere of Neptune are the fastest anywhere. They are three times stronger than any winds on Earth and nine times more powerful than the winds of Jupiter.

Neptune has several faint rings. The farthest ring has been named Adams, and within it are arcs named Liberty, Equality, and Fraternity. The moons of Neptune include Naiad, Thalassa, Despina, Galatea, Larissa, Proteus, Triton, and Nereid. The

FIGURE 3A.5 ━━━━━━━━━━━━━━━━━━━━━━━━━━━━━━━━

This photomontage of Saturn and its rings
and moons was created by an artist who
juxtaposed a series of photographs
transmitted by the *Voyager* spacecraft.

largest of these moons, Triton, travels in an orbit opposite to the planet's rotation direction. This means that Triton is continually getting closer to the planet and will crash into it in about 10 to 100 million years!

Pluto   This is the smallest and farthest planet from the sun, and very little is known about its characteristics. It is thought that the surface of Pluto is covered with a layer of frozen methane, nitrogen, and carbon monoxide. And while its travels take it farther from the sun than the other planets, its orbit periodically moves inside Neptune's orbit. It takes 248 Earth years for Pluto to make one complete orbit of the sun. Its orbit is also highly inclined, meaning that it is above and below the orbital planes of the other planets.

Even less is known about this planet's atmosphere, due to its great distance from observers on Earth. Moreover, spacecraft have not been able to get very close to it. Some useful data have been gathered using the infrared astronomical satellite (IRAS) and the Hubble Space Telescope. However many important questions about Pluto and its moon, Charon, will not be answered until robotic spaceflight missions approach the planet.

Meteors

Meteors are masses of stone and iron from space that sometimes strike Earth. Some meteors have a mass of less than one gram; others have masses of thousands of kilograms. Although many meteors enter Earth's atmosphere, few reach the planet's surface. Most are simply burned up by the friction they produce as they move through the atmosphere. Some meteors are so large that parts of them remain after their journey through the atmosphere. If they reach Earth's surface, they are known as *meteorites*. Scientists have various theories about the origin of meteorites. Most think they originated in our solar system, perhaps from the band of planetlike objects between the orbits of Mars and Jupiter.

Comets

Comets are heavenly bodies surrounding the solar system. They move in large orbits; occasionally, a comet may be pulled from its normal orbit and move toward the sun. Comets are thought to be composed of solidified ammonia, carbon dioxide, and ice. The solid portion of a comet is known as its *head.* The comet's *tail* is formed by the evaporation of solidified matter by energy from the sun. The tail of a comet always points away from the sun. Although comets do not produce light themselves, energy from the sun causes the material in their heads and tails to give off light.

Asteroids

Between the orbits of Mars and Jupiter lies a belt of objects that are smaller than any of the planets. These objects are called *asteroids.* Scientists are not sure how the asteroids were formed. Some believe they are the remnants of a planet that once existed between Mars and Jupiter. Others think they are leftovers from the materials that combined to form Mars and Jupiter.

Some asteroids leave their orbits and cross the paths of planets or moons. Craters observed on the moon and on Mars are probably the result of collisions with asteroids. Some craters on Earth can be explained most easily as the results of collisions with asteroids millions of years ago.

Exploring Space: The First Steps

The development of powerful rockets has made possible the exploration of outer space. (An explanation of the scientific principles involved in rocket propulsion may be found in Chapter 8A.) The first step toward space exploration began in earnest in 1957 with the Soviet Union's launch of the first artificial space satellite: *Sputnik I.*

On August 17, 1958, the United States attempted its first launch of a rocket to the moon. Intended to place an artificial satellite in orbit around the moon, this mission was a failure. On July 2, 1959, the Soviet Union fired a rocket that went into orbit around the sun. A later rocket in the launch series was sent past the moon and transmitted pictures from its far side, but humans did not visit the moon until July 20, 1969, when Neil Armstrong stepped upon its surface. This was one of the many outcomes of the *Apollo* space exploration program, which witnessed visits on the moon's surface by 12 astronauts in all from 1969 to 1972. To date, however, the moon is the only place in space that humans have visited.

Four years earlier, in 1965, both American and Soviet unmanned spacecraft had flown by Mars and taken pictures of its surface. In 1971, *Mariner 9* was placed in orbit about that planet. The pictures it transmitted to Earth showed a surface that looked as if it had been sculptured by intensive flooding millions of years ago. Curiosity about another planet—Mercury—led to the launch of *Mariner 10*, which flew within 720 kilometers (about 450 miles) of the planet in 1974. Television cameras and scientific instruments sent back information concerning temperature, solar wind, and the planet's surface.

Since that time, various spacecraft have been used to explore Venus and other planets. American *Mariner* and Soviet *Venera* rockets both have reached the Venusian atmosphere and transmitted information. *Venera IX* and *X* landed on the surface of Venus in 1975. A year later, in 1976, more detailed information about the surface of Mars was gathered by the spacecraft *Viking 1* and *2*, which dropped small instrument packages to the surface.

The first American spacecraft to orbit Venus was *Pioneer Venus I,* which reached the Venusian atmosphere on December 5, 1978. A few days later, *Pioneer Venus 2* discharged five probes toward the planet's surface. Each transmitted important information about the Venusian atmosphere before being destroyed by the planet's heat. Soviet *Venera* spacecraft parachuted instrument packages to the surface of Venus in 1978. These landers sent information to orbiting spacecraft, which reflected it to Earth.

Space Probes

Voyager 1 and *2* are rocket probes launched in 1977 to observe phenomena on Jupiter, Saturn, Uranus, and Neptune. It is hoped that one or both of these probes will be able to reach the edges of our solar system and beyond. At present, the probes are sending back an enormous amount of data about the outer planets. Data gathered by *Voyager 2*'s flyby of Uranus in 1986 provided extremely sharp pictures of its major satellite.

If they are not destroyed, the *Voyager* spacecraft will escape the solar system at a speed of 62,000 kilometers (about 38,700 miles) per hour. On board each spacecraft are a phonograph record, sound-reproduction equipment, and playing instructions. The records include music, spoken languages, and common sounds from nature. Also included is a plaque that shows pictures of humans and describes, in scientific symbols, Earth, its location, and its people. The *Voyager* spacecraft will reach the first star in their interstellar voyage in about 40,000 years. Perhaps someone or something will interrupt them before then and learn about our planet and its people from the information, equipment, and pictures on board.

The *Magellan* spacecraft was deployed by the space shuttle *Atlantis*. Its interplanetary journey includes a careful study of Venus. *Magellan's* onboard instruments, which include radar imaging systems, have transmitted rather spectacular images of the Venusian surface. Early radar images include that shown in Figure 3A.6, which shows 75 kilometer (46 mile) long valleys that have been nicknamed "Gumby" by photoanalysts.

The National Aeronautics and Space Administration (NASA) has an aggressive schedule for sending spacecraft to explore Mars. Additional orbiter/landers—using more advanced technology than the *Pathfinder* mission that placed *Sojourner* on the surface—will be launched. In the first decade of the twenty-first century, we should expect some landers to reach Mars, retrieve soil and rock samples, and carry them back to Earth. The success of these missions will lay the foundation for astronauts to visit Mars some time in the not too distant future.

The Hubble Space Telescope

The Hubble Space Telescope (HST) was deployed from a space shuttle launched on April 24, 1990, and just one month later, on May 20, humans saw the first pictures transmitted from the telescope. The HST was designed to gather the sharpest pictures ever of astronomical objects (see Figure 3A.7, page 76). Unfortunately, defects in one of the Hubble's mirrors limited its effectiveness. To correct this problem as well as upgrade related equipment, astronauts from the space shuttle *Endeavor* carried out the

FIGURE 3A.6
This *Magellan* radar image of Venus shows a set of valleys nicknamed "Gumby."

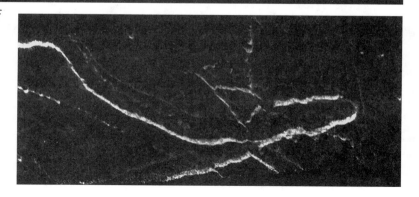

FIGURE 3A.7   Compare these photographs of the nearest starburst spiral galaxy, NGC-35. The image on the left was taken with a land-based telescope. The detailed area shown on the right is an image by the Hubble Space Telescope (HST). The HST's high resolution allowed astronomers to quantify complex structures in the starburst core of the galaxy for the first time.

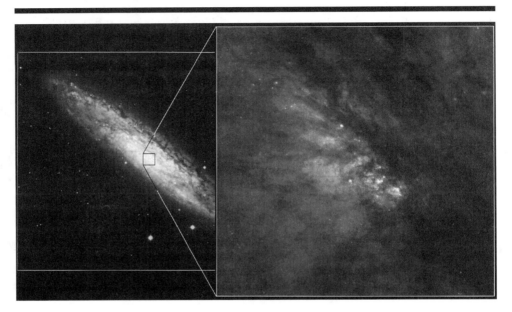

most complicated space repairs ever attempted. They secured the HST in the shuttle cargo bay, replaced its solar panels, installed a device to correct the mirror defects, re-placed gyroscopes (instruments that sense the telescope's orientation in space), re-placed one of its cameras, and released the upgraded HST into orbit. The Hubble Space Telescope is continually repaired and upgraded and is now able to detect stars that are 13 billion or more light-years away.

The Space Shuttle

The American space shuttle[2] continues to offer great potential in the exploration of outer space because of its ability to carry scientists and its great maneuverability. It can orbit Earth like a spacecraft and land like an airplane. The shuttle is designed to carry heavy loads into orbit around Earth. Other launch vehicles have done this, but unlike these vehicles, which can be used only once, each space shuttle orbiter can be reused more than 100 times (see Figure 3A.8).

The shuttle permits the checkout and repair of satellites in orbit and the return of satellites to Earth for repairs that cannot be done in space. Thus, the shuttle makes pos-sible considerable savings in spacecraft costs. The types of satellites that the shuttle can orbit and maintain include those involved in environmental protection, navigation, energy, weather forecasting, fishing, farming, mapping, and oceanography.

Principal Components

The space shuttle has three main units: the *orbiter*, the *external tank*, and two solid rocket *boosters.* The orbiter is the crew- and payload-carrying unit of the shuttle system. It is 37 meters (122 feet) long, has a wingspan of 24 meters (78 feet), and without fuel weighs about 68,000 kilograms (150,000 pounds). It is about the size and weight of a DC-9 commercial airplane.

The orbiter can transport a payload of 29,500 kilograms (65,000 pounds). It carries its cargo in a cavernous payload bay 18.3 meters (60 feet) long and 4.6 meters (15 feet) in diameter. The bay is flexible enough to provide accommodations for unmanned spacecraft in a variety of shapes and for fully equipped scientific laboratories.

The orbiter's three main liquid rocket engines are fed propellants from the external tank, which is 47 meters (154 feet) long and 8.7 meters (28.6 feet) in diameter. At liftoff, the tank holds 703,000 kilograms (1,550,000 pounds) of propellants, consisting of liquid hydrogen (fuel) and liquid oxygen (oxidizer). The hydrogen and oxygen are in separate pressurized compartments of the tank. The external tank is the only part of the shuttle system that is not reusable.

A Typical Shuttle Mission

In a typical shuttle mission, lasting from 7 to 30 days, the orbiter's main engines and the booster ignite simultaneously to rocket the shuttle from the launch pad. Launches are made from the John F. Kennedy Space Center in Florida for east-west orbits and from Vandenberg Air Force Base in California for north-south orbits.

FIGURE 3A.8
A successful shuttle launch

At a predetermined point, the two solid rocket boosters separate from the orbiter and parachute to the sea, where they are recovered for reuse. The orbiter continues into space, jettisoning its external propellant tank just before orbiting. The external tank enters the atmosphere and breaks up over a remote ocean area.

The orbiter then proceeds on its mission in space. When its work is completed, the crew directs the orbiter on a flight path that will take it back to the Earth's atmosphere. Various rocket systems are used to slow its speed and adjust its direction. Previous spacecraft followed a direct path from space to the predetermined landing area. The orbiter is quite different. It can maneuver from the right to the left of its entry path a distance of about 2,035 kilometers (about 1,270 miles). The orbiter has the capability of landing like an airplane at Kennedy Space Center or Vandenberg Air Force Base. Its landing speed is about 335 kilometers (about 210 miles) per hour.

Successes and Tragedies

The NASA space shuttle program has enjoyed many successes during its 20-plus years. Its first success was in April 1981, when the orbiter *Columbia* carried out a two-day mission that proved the shuttle could put a spacecraft in orbit and return safely. Missions that followed included the deployment of satellites, scientific explorations, the deployment of the Hubble Space Telescope, and flights to assist in the building and servicing of the International Space Station.

These successes have not been without human costs, however. On January 28, 1986, the orbiter *Challenger* exploded just 73 seconds after liftoff. This accident took the lives of all seven crew members, including the first teacher-astronaut, Christa McAuliffe. On February 1, 2003, the space shuttle *Columbia* suffered a catastrophe on re-entry into the earth's atmosphere. Again, all seven crew members were killed. Each of these tragedies was followed by an intense investigation in order to determine the cause and to hopefully prevent a similar event from happening in the future. To be sure, the exploration of space will continue and the mysteries of the universe will continue to be revealed.

Exploring Space: The Next Steps

The X-37: A Starting Place

> *"May we have your attention please? Those preparing to board the X-37 for an orbital Earth flight should kindly unfasten their seat belts and proceed to hatch #9. The X-37 is in the cargo bay and now prepared for boarding. Please check under your seat and in the luggage compartment above your head for any personal items you may have brought onboard the shuttle. Have your boarding pass available for the flight attendant at hatch #9. Enjoy your '21-Day Eye-on-the-Earth Excursion.' We'll see you on the ground."*

At some point in your life, or in the lives of the children you teach, ordinary people will view wondrous Earth from space with their own eyes. It's difficult to predict when and how it will happen, but research to develop cost-effective ways to achieve orbital flight is well underway. Through contracts with private companies, NASA is now ex-

FIGURE 3A.9

The X-37 advanced technology flight demonstrator will operate in both the orbital and re-entry phases of flight.

ploring the design of spacecraft that will reduce the cost of putting 1 pound (about 2.2 kilograms) of payload into space from $10,000 to $1,000. That means that space travel may be in your future!

The space vehicle in your future will have some of the same characteristics as the *X-37,* an experimental test vehicle (see Figure 3A.9). Known as a "spaceplane," the X-37 is intended to be ferried to Earth's orbit by a shuttle, to remain in Earth's orbit, and then to land on its own on a conventional airport runway. In the years ahead, new versions of the X-37 will be developed and tested. Perhaps some will even have solar panels that can be used to power the craft in orbit. For now, building a reusable passenger-carrying spaceplane poses an enormous challenge. But one thing is certain: Testing will continue and sometime, somewhere, in some yet undesigned spaceplane, a tourist will be awakened by "May we have your attention please . . . "

The International Space Station: A Rest Stop on the Road to Mars?

High above our heads, men and women are at work in and on the *International Space Station.* This space laboratory is permanently orbiting Earth at a distance of 200 miles (323 kilometers). As you read these words, scientists in the space station are conducting an intensive study of how the human body and other biological systems respond to prolonged time in space. They are also at work constructing additional internal and external parts for the space station using twenty-first-century materials and techniques adapted for use in space.

The International Space Station is a cooperative venture of a number of countries. Each is making its own unique contribution to this, the largest cooperative scientific and engineering effort in human history. When it is complete, the space station will contain facilities for biotechnology, fluids and combustion, a space station furnace, gravitational biology, centrifuge, and human research.

Crews are continually onboard the space station and busily at work. The United States and Russia have delivered people, equipment, and supplies to the station, including materials created by other nations. Additionally, unmanned rockets have been used as "freighters" to carry equipment and supplies to the International Space Station. So, the science fiction of our childhood has become today's reality: We have space "ferries"!

Given this, we can only wonder what humankind will accomplish next, as today's science fiction frontier becomes tomorrow's rest stop on our journey to Mars and beyond!

Summary Outline

I. The universe is all the matter, energy, and space that exist.
    A. Recent discoveries of patterns of galaxies pose a challenge to the Big Bang theory.
    B. In recent years, scientists have discovered and begun studies of extraordinary astronomical phenomena, such as magnetars, quasars, pulsars, and black holes.

II. The solar system consists of the sun, its nine planets, and associated clouds of matter, including meteors, comets, and asteroids.
    A. The sun is a star that will use up its supply of hydrogen and come to the end of its existence in about 5 billion years.
    B. The moon, which is a satellite of Earth, is airless and lifeless.
    C. The nine planets that circle the sun are Mercury, Venus, Earth, Mars, Jupiter, Saturn, Uranus, Neptune, and Pluto.

III. Powerful rockets have enabled humans to explore outer space in a variety of ways.
    A. Manned and unmanned space probes have explored space since 1957.
    B. The space shuttle is a space vehicle that can return to Earth and be reused in subsequent space journeys.
    C. The *X-37* will serve as the prototype for a spaceplane.
    D. The *International Space Station* will be a permanently orbiting scientific laboratory. It may also serve as a launching pad for the human exploration of Mars.

N O T E S

1. The discussion of the sun was excerpted with modifications from *Our Prodigal Sun*, a pamphlet prepared by the National Aeronautics and Space Administration. This pamphlet (stock number 3300-00569) can be purchased from the Superintendent of Documents, Government Printing Office, Washington, DC 20402.

2. The discussion of the space shuttle was excerpted with minor modifications from *NASA Facts: The Space Shuttle*, prepared by the National Aeronautics and Space Administration. This publication (stock number 003-000-00679-9) is available for purchase from the Superintendent of Documents, Government Printing Office, Washington, DC 20402.

3B The Cosmos

Attention Getters, Discovery Activities, and Demonstrations

ATTENTION GETTERS

For Young Learners [ESS 2]

Can You Move Like the Planets?

Materials   9 sheets of 8½ × 11 in. pastel paper for each group
1 larger sheet of orange paper
Crayons or water-based markers for each group

Motivating Questions
- What are some of the things you see in the sky on a bright day?
- Display a globe and ask: Do you think our earth moves or stays still?

Directions
1. Write the planet names on the chalkboard, distribute the paper, and assign a planet name to each group.
2. Write the word *sun* on the orange sheet, and have each group write the name of its planet on the paper it received.
3. Have volunteers from each group join you at a central place in the room. Arrange the volunteers in proper sequence from the sun (the orange sheet that you are holding), and have the children circle around you.
4. Finally, indicate that the planets spin (rotate) as they move (revolve), and have the children do the same, slowly.

Science Content for the Teacher
Nine major planets travel around the sun in orbits. These planets do not emit light. They reflect the sun's light. The sun is a star whose apparent motion is due to the earth's rotation. Seasonal changes are due to the change in the relative position of the earth as it orbits around the sun.

For Young Learners [ESS 3]

Can You Move Like the Moon?

Materials   1 orange sheet of paper   1 blue sheet of paper
1 white sheet of paper   Crayons or water-based markers

Motivating Questions
- Do you think the earth moves around the sun, or do you think the sun moves around the earth?
- Do you think the moon moves around the earth, or do you think the earth moves around the moon?

Directions
1. Write the word *sun* on the orange sheet of paper, the word *earth* on the blue sheet, and the word *moon* on the white sheet. (You may wish to have children copy the words from the board.)
2. Select one student to stand and hold the orange sheet to represent the sun.

3. Select another student to hold the blue sheet and move in orbit around the sun.
4. Finally, select a student to hold the white sheet and orbit the earth as it travels around the sun.

Science Content for the Teacher   The moon is a satellite of the earth. This means that the moon revolves around the earth as the earth rotates and revolves around the sun. The moon also rotates as it orbits the earth.

For Young Learners [ESS 1]

Why Is Earth Called the "Blue Planet"?

Materials   1 model car, plane, and doll   1 globe

Motivating Questions
- Is this a real car, plane, or person?
- How are these the same or different from real cars, planes, and people?

Directions
1. Write the words *sun* and *earth* on the chalkboard.
2. Pronounce each word, and then display the toys. Discuss how models are different from real things.
3. Display the globe, and ask what it is a model of. Have children point out the locations of lands and oceans on the globe, and discuss the relative amounts of each.
4. Move the globe as far from the children as possible, and ask how astronauts in space might describe the earth.

Science Content for the Teacher   Scientists often use models. Just as toys stand for real things, a globe stands for, or is a model of, the earth. A globe is roughly the same shape as our planet and shows the predominant colors as seen from space.

For Middle-Level Learners [ESS 6]

Is Day Always as Long as Night?

Materials   1 tennis ball   Chalk
1 steel knitting needle   1 m of string
1 small lamp without lampshade   1 marking pen

Motivating Questions
- If you didn't have to go to school, would you have more time to play outside in the summer months or in the winter months?
- Are the lengths of the days and nights the same all through the year?

Directions
1. Before class, carefully push the knitting needle through the tennis ball from top to bottom. Use a marking pen to make a dot that stands for your city or town on the tennis ball.

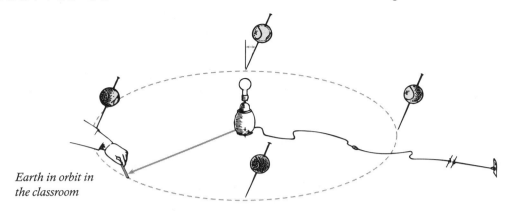

*Earth in orbit in
the classroom*

2. Use the string to make a circle on the classroom floor. Put the lamp at the center of the circle. Use the chalk to label the furthest-left part of the circle *June 21*. Label the furthest-right part of the circle *December 21*, the topmost point *March 21*, and the lowest point *September 21*.

3. At the start of class, have the children gather around the model. Explain that the circle *almost* represents the path of the earth.

4. Tell the children that the path is really a flattened-out circle called an *ellipse*. Convert the circle to an ellipse by using the original circle as a guideline and drawing an ellipse with chalk.

5. Incline the tennis ball approximately 23° from the vertical, and have a child hold it at the spot marked March 21 and slowly rotate it. The children will note that their town gets light for half the rotation (12 hours). When this procedure is repeated at June 21, the children will note that the town is lit for approximately two-thirds of a rotation (16 hours). At the December 21 spot, the children will note their town gets few hours of sunlight (8–10 hours). To make this more obvious, have a child sit at sun's location and tell whether she or he sees the town for a long or short period of time on June 21 and December 21.

Science Content for the Teacher   Spring and fall are times when the earth's axis is not tilted toward or away from the sun. At these times, day and night are of equal length. During summer in the Northern Hemisphere, the earth's axis is tilted in the direction of the sun, so any location in the Northern Hemisphere has longer days.

For Middle-Level Learners [ESS 6]

Can You Draw an Orbit?

Materials   1 m of string
1 large sheet of paper
1 pencil
2 pushpins or thumbtacks
1 sheet of cardboard about the same size as the paper

Motivating Questions	■ What shape is the earth's path around the sun? ■ Do you think the shape is a circle?

Directions

1. Place the paper on the cardboard. Stick the pushpins through the paper and cardboard toward the center of the paper but about 20 centimeters apart.
2. Tie a knot in the string to make a closed loop, and put the loop around the pushpins.
3. Holding the pencil vertically inside the loop and pushed against the string, move it in a complete path around the pins. Be sure to keep the tension of the pencil against the loop constant.

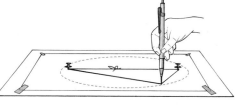

How to make an ellipse

4. Explain to the children that the figure you have drawn is an *ellipse* and that the planets travel in ellipses around the sun. If you wish, remove one of the pushpins after you have drawn the ellipse and explain that the remaining pushpin represents the sun.

Science Content for the Teacher

Although people often describe the orbits of the planets as circles, they are in fact ellipses. An ellipse has two foci. The sun is at the location of one of the foci for the earth's orbit.

For Middle-Level Learners **[ESS 6]**

Where Does the Sun Rise and Set?

Materials

2 sheets of drawing paper for each child
Pencils, crayons, or markers

Motivating Questions

■ Can you remember where the sun sets?
■ Can you remember where the sun rises?

Directions

1. Have each child place the drawing paper so the long side runs from left to right in front of him or her.
2. On one sheet of paper, have each child draw some of the objects he or she would see while looking toward the east of where he or she lives: buildings, trees, fields, forests, parks, or whatever is toward the east of his or her home. On the other sheet, have each child do the same for the west.
3. Next, have each child draw a rising sun on the sheet at the place that represents where the sun rises and a setting sun at the place that they think represents where the sun sets.
4. Have the children take both papers home for a few days to correct, if they need to, the locations of their suns. *Safety Note:* Remind the children never to look directly at the sun.

Science Content   It seems to us that the sun is moving across our sky every day, rising in the east and
for the Teacher   setting in the west. However, the sunrise and sunset that we see are due to the
                   earth's rotation. In this activity, the children simply compare their memories of
                   where the sun rises and sets to the actualities.

For Middle-Level Learners [HNS 2 and 3]

Earth Centered versus Sun Centered:
The Great Debate

                   Note: To be successful, this Attention Getter will require a little acting on your part!

Materials   Access to the Internet
                   Science resource books and encyclopedias
                   Assorted art materials
                   Assorted fabric pieces

Motivating   ▪ Let's do some voting! How many of you agree with each of the following
Questions   hypotheses, and how many disagree?
                   "The sun moves around the earth."
                   "The earth moves around the sun."
              ▪ If you agree with the first hypothesis, what evidence do you have to support
                it?
              ▪ If you agree with the second hypothesis, what evidence do you have to
                support it?

Directions   1. Have two volunteers stand at the front of the room. Ask the other students to
                 shut their eyes for a moment. Say, "When I ask you to open your eyes, I will be
                 two different scientists!"
              2. Have the students open their eyes. Using your best acting voice, slowly walk
                 around one student and say, "I am Ptolemy. *I* believe the sun moves around the
                 earth." Then walk around the other student and say, "I am Copernicus. *I* believe
                 the earth moves around the sun." Return to your normal voice and continue.
              3. Have half of the cooperative groups focus on Ptolemy and half on Copernicus.
                 Ask each group to research the life and beliefs of their scientist and to select one
                 member to play the scientist. He or she must state his or her hypothesis and
                 supporting evidence. The group must prepare any notes, drawings, props, and
                 costuming.
              4. After research time, have each "scientist" speak to the class. Then lead a discus-
                 sion about what we know today about our solar system.

Explanation/   Ptolemy proposed that the earth was at the center of the universe and that the sun
Science Content   moved around it. Everyday observations supported his hypothesis. Some 1,500
for the Teacher   years later, Copernicus proposed that the earth moved around the sun and sup-
                   ported his hypothesis with careful observations of the planets' orbits.

D I S C O V E R Y   A C T I V I T I E S

Planets on Parade

Objective	■ The children will place the planets in sequential order from the sun.
Science Processes Emphasized	Using numbers Using space/time relationships
Materials for Each Child or Group	1 deck of 9 index cards, each labeled with a different planet name
Motivation	Tell the children that they are going to play a game that will help them learn about the planets. Display the nine index cards you will be distributing.
Directions	1. Before beginning this activity, create a set of clues for each planet, such as "I am Venus; I am closer to the sun than the Earth"; "I am Neptune; I am further from the Sun than Mars." 2. Distribute a randomly sequenced deck of index cards to each group. Explain that each card represents a planet that is traveling around the sun but that the cards are not in the proper order. Challenge the groups to rearrange the cards based on the clues you give. 3. Read each clue, and encourage the children to rearrange the cards on the basis of the clues.
Key Discussion Questions	1. Which planet is closest to the sun? *Mercury* 2. Which planet is furthest from the sun? *Pluto* 3. Which planet is just before Earth, and which planet is right after Earth? *Venus, Mars*
Science Content for the Teacher	The nine known planets of our solar system in order from the sun are Mercury, Venus, Earth, Mars, Jupiter, Saturn, Uranus, Neptune, and Pluto.
Extension	*Science/Math:* After the children have put their decks in order, have them turn the decks over and number each card sequentially from 1 to 9. Have pairs of children play a game in which one child removes one of the numbered cards and the other child has to guess the planet name that is on the reverse side.

Making a Simple Sundial

Objectives	■ The children will use numbers to write time measurements. ■ The children will predict the actual time from the position of the shadow on a sundial.

Science Processes Emphasized	Using numbers Predicting
Materials for Each Child or Group	Sheet of light cardboard 25 cm (10 in.) square Masking tape Straw
Motivation	Display the materials and tell the children that they are going to be making their own clocks. Indicate that they will be strange clocks because they will only work when the sun is shining.
Directions	1. Prior to class, make a 20 centimeter (about 9 inch) circle on each sheet of cardboard and punch a small hole at the center of each circle. Be sure to have a compass available for step 3. 2. Distribute a straw and a few strips of masking tape to each group. Have the groups insert one end of the straw into the hole and tape the straw so that it can stand upright. Tell them to write the letter *N* at any point along the edge of the circle. 3. On a sunny day, take the groups and their sundials outside. Using the compass, point north and have the children orient their sundials so that the *N's* are pointed north. Have them mark the location of the straw's shadow, and then tell the children the actual time. Have them write the time on the cardboard at the end of the shadow. 4. After repeating this procedure at various times on consecutive days, have the children predict where the straw's shadow will be at a given time and take them outside at that time to check. As a final step, take the children outside and have them use their sundials to tell you the time.
Key Discussion Questions	1. There is one time in the day when the shadow is shortest or does not exist at all. What time is that? *When the sun is directly overhead.* 2. What are some of the problems with using sundials to tell time? *You can't tell the time on a cloudy day or at night.*
Science Content for the Teacher	Since Earth is constantly changing its position in relation to the sun, the sundials made in this activity will be fairly accurate for only a few days. Sundials in gardens or parks are constructed to compensate for Earth's changing position. They usually do not use a vertical object for the shadow but rather a rod that is inclined at the angle of the location's latitude and pointed toward the North Star.
Extension	*Science/Social Studies:* Do library research to locate pictures or drawings of various time-keeping devices used through the ages. Show the pictures to the children and ask them to suggest any problems, such as the size of the devices, that people might have had using these devices.

Sunlight in Winter versus Summer

Objective	■ The children will observe that light striking an inclined surface does not appear as bright as light striking a surface directly.
Science Process Emphasized	Measuring

Materials for Each Child or Group

Black construction paper	Book	Flashlight
Chalk	Tape	

Motivation Ask the children if they have ever wondered why it is colder in winter than in summer. Tell them that they will discover one of the reasons in this activity.

Directions
1. Be sure to have a globe available before beginning this activity. Darken the classroom and distribute a book, tape, chalk, paper, and flashlight to each child or group.
2. Have each child or group tape the paper to the book and hold the book vertically on a flat surface. Ask them to shine the flashlight on the paper and use the chalk to draw a circle outlining the lit area.
3. Next, tell the children to keep the flashlight at the same distance from the book but to move it so the light strikes a different part of the paper. Have them tilt the book away from the flashlight and outline the lit area.
4. Turn the lights on and display the globe. Use a flashlight to represent the sun, and tilt the globe to show that the earth's tilt causes the Northern Hemisphere to be angled away from the sun during the winter months. Relate this to the light striking the paper that was tilted away from the light source.

Key Discussion Questions
1. How are the drawings you made different from one another? *The first was smaller.*
2. Was the patch of light brighter the first or second time you had the light strike the paper? *The first.*

Science Content for the Teacher Although many people believe that winter occurs because the earth is farther from the sun at that time of the year than it is in summer, the principal cause for winter is the earth's tilt, not its orbit. This tilt serves to spread out the sun's energy more in the Northern Hemisphere during the winter months. Sunlight strikes the Northern Hemisphere more directly in June than in December.

Extension *Science/Social Studies:* Have the children look at the globe and consider how their lives would be different if they lived in an equatorial region, which receives a great deal of direct sunlight all through the year, or in a polar region, which receives much less sunlight.

For Young Learners [ESS 2]

Make a Solar System Mobile

Objective
- The children will construct mobiles showing the nine planets of the solar system.

Science Processes
Emphasized
Measuring
Using space/time relationships

Materials
1 wire coat hanger   3 or 4 straws
String   Scissors
Crayons   Tape
9 circles of oak tag 8 cm (about 3 in.) across

Motivation
Tell the children they are going to create an art project that illustrates some science knowledge they have. You may wish to display a sample planet mobile at this point.

Directions
1. Prior to class, create a mobile using a coat hanger as a base and an arrangement of strings and horizontal straws. Attach the nine oak tag circles to the strings that dangle from the straw ends.
2. Display the mobile, and explain that each circle represents one of the planets in the solar system. Write the names of the planets on the chalkboard, and distribute the materials. Tell the children to write the name of a planet on each circle.
3. Once the circles are labeled, have the children construct the mobiles. Be ready to assist those children who need help tying knots to attach string to straws or to oak tag circles. Some children may find it easier to tape the parts of their mobile together. You may wish to suggest that the children construct some of the subparts of the mobile first—for example, a straw with two or three planets hanging from it. If you are fortunate enough to have parent volunteers or assistants in the classroom, urge them to help those children who have limited psychomotor abilities.
4. When the children are done, have them hang their mobiles in the classroom.

Key Discussion
Questions
Since this activity is focused on the construction of a mobile, the questions you raise should facilitate the children's use of psychomotor skills.
1. If you wanted to hang two planets from a straw, where would you tie them? *One at each end.*
2. If you hung one planet from each end of a straw, where would you tie the string that attaches the straw to the hanger? *At the center.*

Science Content
for the Teacher
Be sure to remind the children that although their planets are all the same size, the real planets are of different sizes.

Extension
Science: Children with advanced reading and writing skills may be asked to use resource books to locate key descriptive words and write them on the planet circles. Challenge these children to find words that tell about the colors or temperatures of the planets.

How to Build an Altitude Finder (Astrolabe)

Objectives
- The children will construct a simple device for measuring the heights of planets and stars above the horizon.
- The children will measure how many degrees an object is above the horizon.

Science Processes Emphasized
Observing
Using numbers
Measuring

Materials for Each Child or Group
Piece of cardboard 25 × 25 cm (about 10 × 10 in.)
25 cm (10 in.) length of string
Small weight, such as a washer or nut
Protractor
Tape

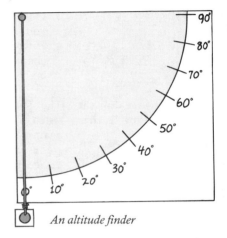

An altitude finder

Motivation
Tell the children that they will be building an instrument that the Greeks invented long ago to discover how far above the horizon the planets and stars are. Explain to the children that scientists call this instrument an *astrolabe* but that they can call it an *altitude finder* because it finds altitudes.

Directions

1. Distribute a protractor to each child or group. Show the children that the protractor scale can be used to measure angles from 0° to 180°.
2. Distribute a cardboard square to each group, and have the children place a 0° mark at the lower-left-hand corner of the cardboard. Have them place a 90° mark at the upper-right-hand corner.
3. Have the children attach one end of the string to the upper-left-hand corner of the cardboard with the tape and tie a pencil to the free end of the string. Now they can use the string and pencil as a compass to draw an arc from the lower-left-hand corner to the upper-right-hand corner.
4. Have the children divide the arc they have drawn into 10° intervals from 0° to 90°—that is, 0°, 10°, 20°, . . . , 90°. The protractor can be used to help mark these divisions.
5. The children should now untie the pencil and tie the nut or washer to the string. The string should cross the 0° mark when the upper edge of the cardboard is held horizontally. Tell the children that they will be sighting objects along the top of the cardboard with the string on the edge of the cardboard that is farthest away from them.
6. When the children have constructed their altitude finders, you may wish to take them outside to find how many degrees such things as chimneys, treetops, or lampposts are above the horizon. Be sure they do not try to sight the sun with their altitude finders.
7. Encourage the children to take their altitude finders home and measure the number of degrees the visible heavenly bodies are above the horizon.

Key Discussion Questions

1. Why do you think we attached a weight to the string? *To pull the string straight down.*
2. Sometimes people use the term *angle of elevation* when they use an astrolabe. What do you think the term means? *How many degrees the object is above the horizon.*
3. Does the altitude finder tell you anything about the direction the object is from you? *No.*
4. How could you find the direction? *Use a compass. Note:* The next activity in this chapter involves creating an instrument that measures the angle of a heavenly body from true north.

Science Content for the Teacher

The astrolabe was invented by the Greeks for observing heavenly bodies. It consisted of a movable rod that was pointed at a star or planet. The position of the rod against a circle indicated the altitude of the sun, moon, and stars. The astrolabe was eventually refined for use as a navigational tool. The sextant, a more accurate device that fulfills the same purpose, came into use in the eighteenth century. It uses a small telescope and a system of mirrors to compare the position of a heavenly body with the horizon.

Extension

Science/Social Studies: You may wish to have a group of children do some library research to find out more about the extent to which the ancient Greeks were involved in astronomy. This group can also research the importance of the astrolabe and sextant in the exploration of the world by seafaring countries.

For Middle-Level Learners [S&T 4]

How to Build an Azimuth Finder

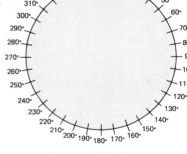

An azimuth finder

Objective

■ The children will construct a simple device that will tell them how many degrees from north, measured in a clockwise direction, a heavenly body is.

Science Processes Emphasized

Observing   Measuring
Using numbers

Materials for Each Child or Group

Magnetic compass
50 cm (20 in.) square of cardboard
25 cm (10 in.) length of string
Pencil
Protractor

Motivation

Tell the children that astronomers usually keep track of both the positions of heavenly bodies above the horizon and their direction in relation to north. Write the word *azimuth* on the chalkboard, and explain that this term refers to how far an object is from north. Distribute the materials, and begin a discussion of how they can be used to make an azimuth finder.

Directions

1. Have the children use the protractor and pencil to draw a circle on the cardboard square.

2. Show the children that they can divide the circle into 10° units by placing the protractor so that its center measuring point is at the center of the circle. Have the children label any point on the circle 0° (north). Then have them mark off 10° positions from 0° to 360°, going in a clockwise direction. Once they have marked off the 10° units, they can use the bottom of the protractor as a straight-edge. *Note:* Since the protractor goes from 0° to 180°, the children should simply turn it upside down in order to continue around the circle in 10° intervals from 180° to 360° (0°).

3. When the azimuth finders are complete, take the children outside to use them to find the azimuths of chimneys, treetops, and other tall objects. In order to do this, they must first rotate the case of the compass so the needle is pointing north. (You may wish to introduce the difference between true north and magnetic north at this point. Refer to Science Content for the Teacher for information on this subject.) Have each child align the azimuth finder so that the 0° mark is oriented to the north.

4. The children can find various azimuths by noting the number of degrees clockwise the object is from the 0° reading.

5. Encourage the children to take their azimuth finders home to make evening measurements of the positions of heavenly bodies. They will need flashlights to read the finders.

Key Discussion Questions

1. What would be the azimuth of a planet that was due east of you? *90°.*
2. What would be the azimuth of a planet that was due south of you? *180°.*
3. What would be the azimuth of a planet that was due west of you? *270°.*

Science Content for the Teacher

You can readily find the azimuth of a heavenly body by using true north as a reference point. Navigators generally label true north as 0° and describe the azimuth of an object in terms of the number of degrees, measured in a clockwise direction, by which its direction differs from true north. (Astronomers tend to use true south as 0°. However, for school use, the 0° north reading used by navigators is a perfectly acceptable method of measurement.)

One problem in the use of an azimuth finder is that the magnetic north measured by a compass is displaced from geographic north, except for a small portion of North America. The amounts of deviation for some representative cities are as follow:

Portland, Oregon	21°E
San Francisco	17°E
Denver	13°E
St. Paul	5°E
Atlanta	0°
Cleveland	5°W
Philadelphia	9°W
Portland, Maine	17°W

Extension

Science/Social Studies: You may wish to have some children do library research on the history of astronomy. The children can find information on Egyptian, Babylonian, Chinese, and Mayan astronomy in most reference books. They may also be interested in gathering pictures of Stonehenge to share with the rest of the class.

For Middle-Level Learners [S&T 4]

Using Altitude and Azimuth Finders to Follow the Motion of a Planet

Objective
- The children will use simple altitude- and azimuth-measuring instruments to observe the motion of a planet.

Science Processes Emphasized
Observing   Communicating
Measuring

Materials for Each Child or Group
Altitude-measuring instrument (see first Discovery Activity for Middle-Level Learners, pages 91–92)
Azimuth-measuring instrument (see previous activity)
Chart with the following headings: *Observation, Date, Time, Altitude, Azimuth*
Paper and pencil

Motivation
Ask the children if they have ever seen planets in the evening sky. They may have observed that planets do not twinkle and that some appear other than white in color. Discuss with the children the importance of making observations of planets over an extended time in order to see patterns of motion. Indicate that this activity is going to extend over a period of months and will require them to do their observations at home.

Directions
1. Review the use of the altitude and azimuth measurers described in the two previous activities. If the children have not constructed these instruments, they will need to do so before beginning this extended activity.
2. Have each child prepare an observation chart.
3. Explain to the children that they should attempt to locate one planet in the evening sky and record observations at the same time each day. To help them locate a planet, find one for yourself and determine its altitude and azimuth. (You can get help from any almanac that describes the locations of visible planets for your area at various times of the year.) Share the location of this planet with the class. The children can then try to find it on their own with their measuring devices.
4. Every few months, hold a class discussion of the observations that have been made as of that time.

Key Discussion Questions
1. What planet did you observe? How did you know what planet it was? *Answers will vary.*
2. What problems did you have during the activity? *Answers will vary but may include such problems as cloud cover obscuring the planets, precipitation making outdoor work difficult, misplacing instruments, and forgetting to make observations at the same time every day.*

Science Content for the Teacher
See the content presented in the previous two activities.

Extensions   *Science:* You may wish to encourage a group of children to carry out some long-term library research to coincide with this extended activity. Children can focus on such topics as the astronomers Tycho Brahe and Copernicus, the invention of the telescope, and the use of modern astronomical instruments, such as the radio telescope.

Science/Social Studies: You may wish to have some children explore the resistance of society to Copernicus's and Galileo's conclusion that the sun is the physical center of the solar system.

DEMONSTRATIONS

For Young Learners [ESS 2]

Moon Watcher

Objectives
- Using a model, the children will observe the phases of the moon.
- The children will explain why the moon seems to change in shape.

Science Processes Emphasized
Observing
Communicating

Materials
Small lamp with ordinary light bulb and removable shade
Orange
Paper and pencil
Signs with the labels *Earth, Moon,* and *Sun*

Motivation
Ask the children to describe and draw the various shapes that the moon seems to take. Have them show their drawings to the class. Ask if they think the moon really changes shape. After some discussion, display the materials for the demonstration, and tell the children that they will be observing a model of the moon in orbit around Earth that will help them understand the changes in its shape.

What phase of the moon is this?

Directions

1. Remove the lampshade, and place the sun label on the lamp. Place the sun at the center of the front of the room. Select one child, and affix the *Earth* label to him or her.
2. Darken the room by drawing the shades and shutting off the classroom lights.
3. Now have the child hold the orange (the moon) so that his or her hand is fully outstretched. Have the child first stand so that he or she is facing the sun and holding the moon directly in line with it. The child should be about 1 meter (a little more than 3 feet) from the sun.
4. The lamp should be turned on at this point. Have the child holding the orange describe how much of the orange's lit surface is seen. None of the lit surface should be seen; the moon is not visible in the sky.
5. Have the child turn sideways, and ask him or her how much of the lit surface of the orange he or she can see. Half the lit surface should be visible; the child sees a half-moon.
6. Have the child stand so that his or her back is to the lamp and the orange is about 30 centimeters (1 foot) away from his or her eyes and slightly to the left of the head. Ask how much of the lit surface of the moon can be seen. All of it should be visible; the child sees a full moon.
7. Repeat the demonstration so that the crescent moon and three-quarter moon can be seen.

Key Discussion Questions

1. Does the moon produce light? *No, it just reflects light from the sun.*
2. What name do we give to the shapes that the moon seems to take? *Phases.*
3. Does the moon really change in shape? Why? *No. The only thing that changes is the pattern of the light we can see bouncing off the moon.*

Science Content for the Teacher

The sun shines on only half the surface of the moon. This entire lit surface is not always visible from the earth. The apparent shape of the moon at any given time is really the portion of the lit surface that is visible. The different portions of the surface that are lit at different times are the phases of the moon. The *full moon* is that phase in which we see the entire lit surface. When full, the moon appears as a round disk in the sky. We refer to the phase in which we see half the lit surface as the *half-moon*. The *crescent moon* is a phase in which we see only a sliver of the lit surface. The *new moon* is the phase in which none of the lit surface can be seen.

Extensions

Science: You may wish to encourage a group of children to use the lamp, orange, and other round objects to demonstrate other astronomical phenomena, such as lunar and solar eclipses.

Science/Arts: A group of children may wish to draw a sequence of pictures to represent an imaginary incident that occurs as astronauts explore a mysterious crater on the moon.

The Shoebox Planetarium

Objective
- The children will observe the Big Dipper constellation projected in the classroom and will be able to locate it in the night sky.

Science Processe Emphasized

Observing

Materials

Shoebox with lid   Electrical tape
Index card   Scissors
Flashlight

Motivation

Tell the children that they will observe something they can then ask a parent or other adult to help them find in the night sky.

Directions

1. Tape the lid to the shoebox. At one end, cut out a hole sufficiently large for you to insert the lamp end of a flashlight. Cut a rectangular window the size of a small index card in the other end.
2. Using the electrical tape, seal one end of the box around the flashlight so that the switch is not in the box.
3. Poke small holes in an index card in the shape of the Big Dipper. Attach the index card to the window in the shoe box. *Note:* For somewhat older children, you may wish to prepare additional index cards to use to project images of other constellations.
4. Darken the room, turn on the flashlight, and project the Big Dipper on a screen or wall. Have the children note the shape of the handle and the cup. Encourage the children to ask an adult to help them find it in the night sky.

Key Discussion Questions

1. Look at the sides of the Big Dipper. What do you notice about them? *Answers will vary. If no one mentions that sides of the dipper slope inward, do so.*
2. Look at the handle of the Big Dipper. What do you notice about it? *Answers will vary. If no one mentions that the handle is curved, do so.*

Science Content for the Teacher

We are able to observe thousands of stars with the naked eye. Groupings of stars that seem to move together in an apparent path around the North Star are known as *constellations.* The following is a sample of the many constellations visible from the northern latitudes at various times in the year: *spring,* Leo, the Lion; *summer,* Cygnus, the Swan; *fall,* Andromeda, the Maiden; *winter,* the Hunter. This demonstration focuses on the constellation known as the Big Dipper, which is visible throughout the year. The Big Dipper is part of another constellation known as Ursa Major, the Bear, with the tail of the bear made from the handle of the Big Dipper.

Extension

Science/Math: Have the children create their own connect-the-dots puzzles that include numbers representing the seven stars of the Big Dipper. Have the children exchange papers so each can complete a puzzle made by someone else.

For Middle-Level Learners [ESS 6]

Space Journey

Note: Due to the unique nature of this demonstration, Motivation, Directions, Key Discussion Questions, and Extensions have been integrated under one heading.

Objectives
- Each child will take the role of a member of a space exploration team and describe his or her imaginary adventure.
- The children will explain the similarities and differences between their imaginary journeys and a possible real journey into outer space.

Materials   A classroom that can be darkened by shutting off the light and adjusting the blinds

Motivation, Directions, Key Discussion Questions, and Extensions

Through this simulation of a journey into outer space, children have an opportunity to use their knowledge of the solar system to form mental images of the planet their spaceship lands on. The experience encourages children to use their imagination, to communicate orally with the remainder of the class, and at a later time, to use their creative writing and artistic abilities.

Prior to the simulated space journey, divide the class into teams of space explorers. Each team will have four members: a pilot, a navigator, a scientist, and a medical officer. Allow group members to select their roles, and change the classroom seating arrangement so that team members can sit side by side. Have various team members explain what their jobs will be at the time of launch and during planetary exploration. You may, with the assistance of the class, redecorate the classroom so it looks like the interior of a spacecraft. To add realism to the experience, play a sound effects record of a rocket launch during blastoff.

Have each team prepare for the launch by sitting quietly in their seats for a few seconds. Indicate that you will soon begin the countdown for blastoff. Tell them that they should shut their eyes and listen to your words.

Begin the countdown. Tell the children that the rocket engines are beginning to work. When you reach 0, tell them that the rocket is lifting off the launchpad.

Use phrases such as the following to guide their thinking during the flight:

You are being pressed backward. . . . You are in the most dangerous part of the flight, a time when a group of astronauts once lost their lives. . . . Your journey will be a safe one. Imagine that you are looking back at the earth. . . . You are flying higher and higher. . . . The earth is getting smaller and smaller. . . . It is a tiny blue dot. Ahead of you is the blackness of space. . . . The stars are bright. Brighter than you have ever seen them before. . . . Way ahead you see a tiny reddish-colored dot. . . . The pilot puts the spacecraft on automatic pilot and all the members of the crew go to special sleeping compartments, where they will sleep for months as the spacecraft approaches its target. . . . You are sleeping.

Many weeks later, a buzzer rings to awaken you. You return to your seats and see that the planet is now a large reddish ball directly ahead.

As the spacecraft gets closer, the pilot prepares for a landing. The spacecraft gently lands. You look out the windows and see the surface of the planet. . . . Think about the way it looks. Is it flat or bumpy? Does it have mountains? Don't answer. Just think about how it seems to you.

The science officer checks some instruments that tell about the planet's surface and atmosphere. The science officer says that it is safe to explore the planet if you wear spacesuits.

Imagine that you put the bulky spacesuits on. You check each other's suits to be sure they are working properly. Imagine that the pilot opens the door and you go down a ladder to the surface of the planet.

You look around and then look back at one another. You check to be sure that your radios are working. Now each of you starts out in a different direction. After you've walked for a few minutes, you stop and look around to see if you can still see the other crew members. You can see each of them. Keep walking and making observations. . . . You notice something very interesting at your feet. You bend down, pick it up, and gently place it in your collection bag. You reach a large boulder and walk behind it. There on the ground, you see something in the shadows. You are amazed at what you see. You try to move it but you can't. You pull and pull and finally get it free. Just as you are getting ready to call the other crew members to tell them what you have found, you hear the pilot's voice: "Emergency, get back to the ship immediately." You take what you discovered and race back to the ship. You and the other crew members are safely on board. Relax . . . the pilot makes a safe liftoff. You begin the long journey back to Earth. . . . A few months later, you see a tiny blue speck straight ahead. It gets larger and larger. . . . It is Earth, your home. The pilot makes a safe landing. . . . You may open your eyes. Welcome home!

When all the spacecraft have made safe landings, engage the participants in discussions of what they observed and how their observations compare with what they have learned about the solar system and planets. You may wish to have the children prepare illustrated written reports about their adventures.

Science Content for the Teacher   Prior to this demonstration, study the physical characteristics of the various planets in our solar system as well as the stars. This knowledge will enable you to assist the children when they discuss their experiences.

For Middle-Level Learners [ESS 6]

What Is a Light-Year?

Objectives
- The children will interpret data given to them and calculate the distance light travels in one year.
- The children will interpret data given them and develop a strategy for finding the time it takes for light to reach the earth from the sun.

Science Processes Emphasized   Interpreting data
Using space/time relationships

Materials   Transparency and transparency pen   Clock with second hand
Flashlight   Globe

Motivation   Clap your hands, and ask the children how long they thought it took the sound waves to reach them. Write down their estimates. Then position yourself so that they can watch you clap and also see the clock. Tell them that you want them to try to time the travel of sound waves. Clap once again. The children will note that it was either impossible to time the sound waves or that it took less than a second. Explain that they have been trying to time the rate at which sound travels and that the speed of sound, although high (340 meters/second, 1,090 feet/second at 0° Celsius), is much less than the speed of light. Tell the children that they are going to discuss the speed of light.

Directions

1. Write *300,000 km/sec* on the transparency. Aim the flashlight toward the children, and turn it on briefly. Explain that light from the flashlight traveled to their eyes at the rate shown on the transparency. Tell them that at this speed, if light could travel around the earth, it would circle the earth seven times in 1 second. Hold up the globe and illustrate the seven trips by moving your finger around the equator as the children snap their fingers to represent 1 second. As you obviously cannot get your finger around a tiny globe seven times in 1 second, the children should appreciate the magnitude of the speed of light.

2. Challenge the children to calculate the actual number of kilometers a beam of light can travel in a year. Begin by having them determine the number of seconds in a year (60 seconds/minute /60 minutes/hour/24 hours/day/365 days/year = 31,536,000 seconds/year).

3. Again direct the flashlight toward the students, and flick it on and off. Tell them to imagine that the flashlight is the sun. Ask them how long it takes light to travel from the sun to the earth. Write *149,600,000 km* on the transparency. Indicate that this is the average distance that the earth is from the sun as it travels in orbit. Have the children invent a strategy for finding out how many seconds it takes for light to get to the earth. *Hint:* Round off the kilometer distance to 150,000,000 and divide it by 300,000 kilometers per second, which will equal 500 seconds. Remind the children that they did some rounding, so the actual number of seconds is somewhat less.

Key Discussion Questions

1. How far away from the flashlight would you have to be in order for the light to reach you in exactly 1 second? *300,000 kilometers.*

2. If the sun were to stop shining right now, how long would it be before we would notice it? *Between 7 and 8 minutes.*

Science Content for the Teacher

Light waves travel at a speed of 300,000 kilometers per second (about 186,000 miles per second). Light does not require a medium and can travel through empty space. The speed of light is constant in the universe. Scientists use the distance that light can travel in one year, a *light-year,* as a standard measurement of distance.

Extension

Science/Math: Ask the children to determine how long it takes light to travel from the sun to Pluto (about 5 hours) and from the sun to Proxima Centauri, the closest star to the sun (about 4 years). This extension requires library research, the ability to round numbers, and the use of a calculator.

PART TWO

The Life Sciences and Technology

History and Nature of the Life Sciences

Life always has been and always will be a wondrous mystery. The tiniest ocean creature sneaking up on an even tinier prey, a grizzly bear growling as she dips a giant paw into a river full of salmon, and even a man waiting in line to get fast food and answer the "Do you want fries with that?" question are all trying to get energy as efficiently as possible. If they are successful, they will be able to move through their individual life cycle and possibly bring forth more life.

Biologists, zoologists, botanists, medical researchers, and others strive to understand how and why energy is captured, cells grow, and species reproduce. What they learn provides the foundation for the everyday work of people in a wide range of careers in the life sciences. The results of that work touch all our lives.

Careers in the Life Sciences

Many career paths are available for women and men who have the required knowledge, skills, and motivation to explore the nature of life and how life, in all its forms, can be protected and enriched. Here are a few of the many possibilities:

- *Physician.* Physicians undergo training that will bring them knowledge and skills in a variety of the life sciences. And that training will ultimately support their practice in any of a wide variety of specialties: internal medicine, emergency room care, orthopedics, reconstructive and cosmetic surgery, ophthalmology, nervous system disorders, obstetrics and gynecology, oncology, and cardiology.

■ *Medical Technologist.* Medical technologists are assistants to physicians, pharmacists, laboratory scientists, and others who perform medical research. Technologists are usually employed in physicians' offices, hospitals, blood banks, pharmacies, and laboratories—all places where blood and cell specimens are analyzed for the presence of bacteria, parasites, fungi, cancer, and so on.

■ *Horticulturalist.* If you've ever wondered why the flowers in a flower shop or the fruits and vegetables in a supermarket are so abundant and appear to be so perfect, then you've seen the results of work done by horticulturalists. They are trained in certain aspects of the life sciences and use their knowledge and skills to improve the quality and production of plant life.

Key Events in the Development of the Life Sciences

350–341 B.C.E. Aristotle classifies the animals on Earth into eight distinct groups.

350 B.C.E. Diocles writes a book on anatomy and a book on herbal remedies.

190–209 Galen, a Greek physician, organizes all the medical knowledge of that time into a coherent work that will be used by physicians until the Middle Ages.

1665 Robert Hooke publishes *Micrographia*, which displays drawings of natural objects he has studied with a microscope.

1673 The Royal Society of London receives correspondence from Dutch naturalist Antoni van Leeuwenhoek, describing his discoveries using a tool called a *microscopia*.

1735 Carl von Linné (whom we refer to as *Linnaeus*) publishes *Systema Naturae*, which proposes the system of binomial nomenclature (i.e., the use of a genus and species name for each organism) that is still used today.

1837 Charles Darwin begins work that will, after many years, lead to the development of the theory that changes in species over time are the result of *natural selection*, which is the fundamental idea of evolution. His thoughts were based on both his personal study of plants and animals gathered along the coast of South America and his study of the work of Thomas Malthus. Unfortunately, Darwin feared that others would react negatively to his ideas and delayed publishing his conclusions.

1858 Alfred Russell Wallace concludes, as Darwin did, that natural selection propels the evolution of species. Wallace's and Darwin's papers are both presented at a meeting of the Linnaean Society.

1859 Charles Darwin, provoked by Wallace's work, finally publishes a complete book that puts forth his theories. *On the Origin of Species* will become one of the most important books in the history of science.

1860s   Louis Pasteur disproves the idea that flies and other small living things can spontaneously arise from living matter. He shows that new living things can only be created through the reproduction of existing living things.

1866   Gregor Mendel, an Austrian monk, proposes the basic laws of heredity.

1871   Charles Darwin publishes *The Descent of Man.*

1902   Walter Sutton discovers that chromosomes separate for reproduction, an idea that will become the foundation for other scientists' work as they attempt to fully understand inheritance.

1925   Tennessee schoolteacher John Thomas Scopes is brought to trial for teaching evolution. William Jennings Bryan is the lead prosecutor, and Clarence Darrow defends Scopes.

1938   Fishermen find a *coelacanth,* a fish that was thought to be extinct, off the coast of South Africa.

1953   James D. Watson and Francis H. C. Crick publish their paper on the molecular structure of deoxyribonucleic acid (DNA) in *Nature* magazine.

1959   In Africa, Mary Leakey, a paleontologist, finds a hominid skull belonging to *Australopithecus boisei.*

1971   Stephen Jay Gould and Niles Eldredge propose their theory of punctuated equilibrium, which states, essentially, that evolution often occurs in short bursts followed by longer periods in which no or only very modest changes occur in a species.

1974   Donald Johanson and others discover the fossils of a female fossil hominid, *Australopithecus afarensis.* The team names her *Lucy* and proposes that hominids walked upright before they developed large brains.

1974   Bob Bakker proclaims that birds are the descendants of dinosaurs.

1978   Mary Leakey discovers fossil footprints at Laetoli in Africa, which demonstrates that hominids walked upright 3.6 million years ago.

1990   Headed by James D. Watson, the 15-year Human Genome Project formally begins, representing an effort to "find all the genes on every chromosome in the body and to determine their biochemical nature."

1992   A yeast chromosome (*S. cerevisiae*) gene sequence is published.

1993   Biologist E. O. Wilson concludes that there may be as many as 30 million species of insects on Earth.

1995   The *haemophilus* influenza genetic sequence is published by Venter, Smith, Fraser, and others.

1996   The yeast genome sequence is investigated and published by an international consortium.

1997   The Roslin Institute, in Edinburgh, Scotland, successfully clones a sheep, producing Dolly the Lamb. She is the first mammal to be cloned from an adult.

1999   Gunter Blobel, a cell and molecular biologist at Rockefeller University, receives a Nobel Prize for identifying how and where proteins move in the cell. He shows that new proteins move to their correct locations by using a molecular "bar code" that the cell can read.

1999   The DNA of the first human chromosome, chromosome 22, is sequenced.

2000   A "draft" of the human genome is completed. Researchers essentially receive a road map that will result in the identification of the entire human genome DNA sequence.

2003   Sequencing of the human genome is finished, and researchers celebrate the completion of the Human Genome Project, begun in 1990.

Women and Men Who Have Shaped the Development of the Life Sciences

ANDREAS VERSALIUS (1514–1564) secured corpses for the earliest scientific dissections. As a professor at the University of Padua in Italy, he conducted many of these dissections for the benefit of future medical students. He summarized and categorized his lifetime of work in *De humani corporis fabrica libri septem,* which, when translated from Latin, means "The Structure of the Human Body in Seven Volumes."

CARL VON LINNE (CAROLUS LINNAEUS) (1707–1778) was known for his careful study and classification of plants, animals, and minerals. Although he was a physician, he is most famous for his book *Systema Naturae,* which still provides the foundation for the methods used to observe and classify natural objects.

JEANNE VILLEPREUX-POWER (1794–1871), a French-born woman, was a self-taught naturalist who studied in Sicily. She was one of the first scientists to use aquariums for experimentation with living organisms. In honor of this and other scientific achievements, a crater on the planet Venus was named for her.

ELIZABETH BLACKWELL (1821–1910) received the first medical degree granted to a woman in the United States. She specialized in the treatment of women and children and established what came to be the New York Infirmary for Women and Children.

ALEXANDER FLEMING (1881–1955) spent much of his life searching for an effective antiseptic and ultimately discovered that a sample of mold from the *penicillium* family was extraordinarily effective in killing microbes.

GEORGE WASHINGTON CARVER (1896–1943) experimented widely in the field of plant genetics. He crossed plants of various types to produce new flowers, fruits, and vegetables and was known as an expert in the study of molds and fungi. His work did much to speed the progress of agriculture in the United States.

PERCY LAVON JULIAN (1899–1975) received his bachelor's degree from DePauw University, his master's in chemistry from Harvard University, and his Ph.D. in chemistry from the University of Vienna. Although trained as a chemist, he devoted most of his life's work to the development and refinement of chemicals that could be used as medicines.

BARBARA MCCLINTOCK (1902–1992) was a biologist who specialized in the study of genetics. She received the Nobel Prize for medicine in 1983 for the analysis of mechanisms that affect genes and, in fact, evolution itself.

RITA LEVI-MONTALCINI (1909–), an Italian-born biologist, came to St. Louis, Missouri, where she studied cellular reproduction and growth in the human body at Washington University. Her research led to her sharing of the Nobel Prize for physiology and medicine in 1986.

FRANCIS HARRY COMPTON CRICK (1917–) was trained as a physicist but is known for his work with James D. Watson, in which they proposed that DNA has a double-helix structure and then explained how it is replicated. With Watson and Maurice Wilkins, Crick received the Nobel Prize for medicine and physiology in 1962.

JONAS SALK (1914–1995), as head of the Virus Research Laboratory at the University of Pittsburgh, worked to improve a previously developed influenza vaccine; his synthesis of data from other scientists led to strategies that would create a vaccine to stop the polio virus. His work led to the large-scale vaccination of schoolchildren and the reduction of polio as a threat to public health worldwide.

GERTRUDE BELLE ELION (1918–1999) focused her scientific research on the creation of drugs to treat cancer, malaria, leukemia, and other diseases. She shared the 1988 Nobel Prize for physiology.

JAMES DEWEY WATSON (1928–), who had earned a Ph.D. in genetics, joined Francis H. C. Crick, Maurice Wilkins, and Rosalind Franklin in the study of the structure of DNA. Watson, Crick, and Wilkins shared the Nobel Prize for medicine and physiology in 1962. The year 2003 marked the fiftieth anniversary of the Watson/Crick discovery and the successful completion of the Human Genome Project, of which Watson was the head.

Personal and Social Implications of the Life Sciences

No area of scientific exploration has clearer implications for our health and well-being than the life sciences. But along with progress comes certain risks and benefits. Let's consider a few areas of our personal and societal lives that are affected by developments in the life sciences.

Personal and Community Health

Many life scientists spend their careers in search of the causes and cures of illnesses and injuries. Some of that work has looked at the roles of proper nutrition and sanitation. And other research has led to the discovery that some illnesses and predispositions for particular illnesses may come from a person's genetic makeup. The discovery has led to enormous strides in biomedical research.

The study of the sources and effects of pollution is another area of study that has implications for personal and community health. The effects of water pollution, acid rain, and the depletion of ozone in the atmosphere are a few examples of topics that have drawn the attention of life scientists.

Hazards, Risks, and Benefits

The life sciences have brought us new knowledge about natural hazards in the environment, including the risks for becoming infected with sexually transmitted diseases (STDs), the effects of eating food containing parasitic organisms, and even ways for coexisting with large predators. How well we cope with these natural hazards is, to some extent, grounded in how well we understand the life sciences in all of its forms. Each of us must make careful decisions, assessing the risks and benefits associated with the choices we have about the kinds of food we eat, whether to smoke, and whether to use alcohol or potentially dangerous drugs.

We have enjoyed great benefits as the result of pharmaceutical technologies, surgical procedures, and even organ transplantation. But these benefits have sometimes been achieved through medical research that has used human subjects. Individuals who volunteer for treatment with new drugs and procedures must be made aware of the possible risks and benefits of doing so.

Life Science Technology: Its Nature and Impact

You might not think of the life sciences as having a significant technological component, but they do! Moreover, that technology touches you in some very specific ways.

Modern health care—from making eyeglasses to performing cardiovascular surgery—overflows with instrumentation that has been brought to your health care provider (and ultimately, to you) by engineers who have applied their expertise to the life sciences. Even something as banal as a visit to the dentist will give you a visual display of electromechanical devices to probe, unearth, and repair cavities; carry out root canal procedures; and even administer anesthetics.

Of course, biomedical research is only one aspect of the life sciences that receives the attention of engineers. Other engineering challenges include improving crop production, removing contaminants from water supplies, and designing facilities to help preserve endangered species.

The Design of Life Science Technology

Whether they work in environmental protection, criminal investigation, horticulture, or health care, life scientists require devices whose design meets the following criteria:

1. It does no harm or as little harm as possible to living things and the environment.
2. It addresses a problem that has been clearly identified and for which data can reasonably be expected to be obtained.
3. It presents data in a manner that is readily interpretable by life science researchers or health care providers, as appropriate.
4. If it is a tool, it can be easily used and safely operated.
5. It provide the users of life science technology with constant feedback about the accuracy of the data being represented and/or the health and welfare of the living things being treated.

Examples of Life Science Technology

A variety of instruments are used to gather information about living things and to improve their health and welfare:

Binoculars
Optical microscope
Electron microscope
Autoclave (microorganism culturing device)
Heart/lung machine
Blood pressure monitoring devices
Conventional pharmaceuticals

Genetically engineered pharmaceuticals
Prosthetic devices
Cardiac pacemaker
CAT (computerized axial tomography) scan devices
MRI (magnetic resonance imaging) devices
Safe capture traps (to study living things)

Long-Term Implications of Life Science Technology

The technology that has come from the wellspring of life science research has done much to improve the quality of our lives and our environment. We now have the tools to analyze and solve almost any problem imaginable.

But along with this capability comes concern about how to reduce the biological dangers new technology sometimes creates. This is truly a double-edged sword, as these examples point out:

- Oral contraceptives are widely available, but their use may have as an unintended consequence an increase in sexually transmitted diseases (STDs).
- X-ray technology permits exploration of the human body and the treatment of some cancers, but it may lead to increased health risks—including a risk for cancer.

- False-positive results on medical tests can lead to unnecessary treatment regimens.
- The biological control of some insects can result in the increased population of other more harmful insects, who have lost their natural predators.
- The use of antibiotics that do not have bacteria as a root cause may inadvertently result in increasing the number of species of bacteria that are resistant to antibiotics.

Finally, the increased use of technology in all fields of the life sciences traditionally brings increases in the costs of goods and services. The implications of these increases for the consumer—whether a farmer calculating the cost of the foods he or she produces or a patient dealing with increases in the costs of his or her health care—must be considered as new technologies are invented and applied.

4

The Life Sciences and Technology

Unit, Lesson, and Enrichment Starter Ideas

The Tapper

The sound of John Williams's footsteps bounced off the walls lining the dimly lit hallway and echoed after him as he counted down the classroom numbers. Room 12, 11, 10, 9, 8. And there it was—Room 7. With excitement and more than a little apprehension, he opened the door. His first quick look around the room brought a sinking feeling. Drab, drab, drab—25 desks with firmly attached chairs, an old wooden teacher's desk, green chalkboards, bookshelf after bookshelf filled with school books, and some bulletin boards swiss-cheesed with tack holes. No real tables or even counter space for science work or hands-on projects of any kind.

John walked to the front of the room and sat down behind the old wooden desk. The eerie silence and warmth of the last days of summer soothed him only slightly. What would it be like teaching in this school? Would the other teachers accept him? Where was he going to get the materials he was going to need? What would the children be like? That was his primary question: What would the children be like?

He didn't notice the tapping sound for a while. Finally, a particularly loud tap broke him from his reverie. He turned to his right and saw the concerned face of a child outside, tapping on the window pane with one hand to get his attention. He left his chair, walked to the window, and opened it wide.

"Hi, I'm Mr. Williams. I'm going to be the teacher in this room."

"I found this nest in the bushes. It was on the ground."

John asked, "What grade are you going to be in?"

"It's got some pieces of eggshell in it," the Tapper answered.

John tried again, "What's your name? Do you live near here?"

"The birds. What happened to the little birds?"

Children are concerned about life. They want to know what happens to baby birds, and they want to know the names for the colorful, creepy-crawly caterpillars they find on the way to school. In this chapter, you will find ideas and resources to assist you as you plan discovery-oriented life science experiences for children that will develop and extend their curiosity, knowledge, and concern for life in its multitude of forms.

Assessing Prior Knowledge and Conceptions

"But we learned all that in Mr. Greeley's class last year."

Have you ever been in a classroom and observed a teacher getting "ambushed"? That's what happens when teachers assume that children know little or nothing about a topic, only to discover too late that they know a lot. The results are also disastrous when teachers assume that children know a lot about a topic and, in fact, know very little. (Plus, valuable lesson-planning time will have been wasted.) Even assumptions about children's beliefs about phenomena in the natural world can stop teachers in their tracks. Children may have very strongly held beliefs that are totally incorrect, and that may not be discovered until the class is deep in a lesson or unit.

So, as a teacher in the real world of schools and classrooms, how can you quickly get a sense of what the children know, what skills they possess, and what they believe? Part of the answer is to use *probes:* basic questions and simple activities that get children thinking and talking about particular topics. The answers children give will provide very direct guidance about what you should include in science units and lessons.

The probes and sample responses that follow come from informal interviews that I or my students have done with children. I think you'll be amazed at some of the responses and motivated to develop probes that you can use *before* planning units and lessons.

Probe	*Responses That Reveal Prior Knowledge and Conceptions*
■ *Is the wind a living thing?*	"Yes. It moves things." "No. It just blows stuff around." "No. It's just cold." "No. You can't see it."
■ *Is fire a living thing?*	"No. It burns things." "Yes. It makes smoke." "Yes. It's hot and red and moves." "No. I don't know why."
■ *Is the sun a living thing?*	"Yes. If it wasn't, it couldn't make things hot." "No. It's like a star."
■ After pointing out some clouds overhead: *Are those clouds living things?*	"Yes. They work by bringing the rain down." "No. They are just a bunch of rain." "No. They are just puffy and float." "No. They don't breathe or have babies."
■ *What is a seed?*	"Something you stick in the ground." "A thing that makes flowers grow." "A plant grows out of them." "Little thing you put in the ground." "They get bigger to make a plant."
■ After having the child observe a variety of seeds: *Where do seeds come from?*	"Plants. Some have things that make the air put it somewhere else. They have fuzz on them." "Other plants." "Flowers." "Pumpkins. Sometimes if you eat one, it will stay there and grow."

(continued)

Probe	Responses That Reveal Prior Knowledge and Conceptions
(*Where do seeds come from?*)	"When someone plants two seeds and if one of them doesn't grow, then someone digs the other seed up." "Sometimes ants make them and lay them like eggs." "They come from big, big bags."
■ *Do you eat any plants or parts of plants?*	"Yes. Raspberries." "Yes. I eat carrots." "We can eat berries and beans." "Corn. I eat the whole thing." "No. Brian eats clovers. He's bad." "No way. They are bad for you."
■ After showing a collection of forest pictures: *What animals and plants live in a forest?*	"All of them except dogs and cats." "Spiders. Lots of spiders." "Trees and wolves." "Lions and bears." "People could, but they don't. I don't think anybody lives there now."
■ After showing a child pictures of the desert: *What animals and plants do you think live in a desert like this one?*	"No dogs and cats." "Snakes." "Tigers." "Dinosaurs used to live there." "Some cows do." "Wolves . . . No, maybe no wolves."
■ *What is pollution?*	"Dirty air." "Cars give pollution." "Big cities have pollution." "Garbage on the ground." "It comes from cars on the street." "Where the air gets dirty and mixes up with the bad stuff then we can't breathe." "When people litter with cars." "Air . . . disgusting air." "Stuff that flies around the world."

Unit Plan Starter Ideas

That great idea for a science-teaching unit may come from deep within your brain, your school curriculum guide, a state science curriculum framework, a science resource book, a course, a workshop, a discussion you have with children, or some other source. Unfortunately, a great idea (like a friend, an umbrella, and a good restaurant with cheap food) is sometimes hard to find when you really need one.

To make it easier for you to come up with great ideas for science units, I have prepared two different sources of unit starter ideas:

1. The first is based on the National Science Education (NSE) Standards for science content. I created these starter ideas for standards related to grades K–4 and 5–8.

2. The second source of starter ideas is based on my study of life science topics that commonly appear in school curriculum guides. These are shown by grade level.

I am certain that the unique compilation of starter ideas that follows will help you plan and create wonderful discovery-based teaching units.

Ideas Based on the NSE K–8 Content Standards

CONTENT STANDARD K–4: Life Sciences [LS]

As a result of activities in grades K–4, all students should develop an understanding of:

> The characteristics of organisms
>
> Life cycles of organisms
>
> Organisms and environments[1]

■ Starter Ideas for the Characteristics of Organisms

UNIT TITLE: *Taking Care of Plants*

UNIT GOAL: Children care for classroom plants for a two-week period and then prepare charts and drawings to show how they helped the plants meet their requirements for life (e.g., air, water, nutrients, and light).

UNIT TITLE: *Taking Care of Animals*

UNIT GOAL: Children care for classroom chameleons, gerbils, and guinea pigs and identify through diagrams and written explanations how they have helped the animals meet their requirements for life (e.g., air, water, and food).

■ Starter Ideas for Life Cycles of Organisms

UNIT TITLE: *Cycles in a Garden*

UNIT GOAL: Children maintain an outdoor garden, observe plants growing into adulthood from seeds, and maintain logs that show the changes that occur as the plants go through their life cycles.

UNIT TITLE: *Seed Cycles/Frog Cycles*

UNIT GOAL: After raising plants from seeds and frogs from eggs, children compare plant and animal life cycles, including attention to birth, adulthood, reproduction, and death.

■ Starter Ideas for Organisms and Environments

UNIT TITLE: *Find the Chains*

UNIT GOAL: Through library research, Internet research, and direct observations at a local nature area, children prepare diagrams to show five sample food chains that could be found in each of the following environments: forest, desert, tundra, meadow, and ocean.

UNIT TITLE: *The Grasshopper's Lawn*

UNIT GOAL: Children make careful observations of the school lawn and identify the living things, food, and water present in the grasshopper's environment.

CONTENT STANDARD 5–8: Life Sciences [LS]

As a result of the activities in grades 5–8, all students should develop an understanding of:

Structure and function in living systems

Reproduction and heredity

Regulation and behavior

Populations and ecosystems

Diversity and adaptation of organisms

■ Starter Ideas for Structure and Function in Living Systems

UNIT TITLE: *Cells—What Are They? What Do They Do?*

UNIT GOAL: Children prepare written reports on cell structure and function based on their study of cells using a microscope and library research.

UNIT TITLE: *Body Systems*

UNIT GOAL: Children describe the characteristics of body systems that provide for digestion, respiration, reproduction, circulation, excretion, movement, control and coordination, and protection from disease.

■ Starter Ideas for Reproduction and Heredity

UNIT TITLE: *You and Heredity*

UNIT GOAL: Children describe how each new human being receives a "set of instructions" that specifies his or her inherited traits.

UNIT TITLE: *My Traits and My Environment*

UNIT GOAL: Children identify five of their inherited traits and five traits that may have been acquired from their environment.

■ Starter Ideas for Regulation and Behavior

UNIT TITLE: *Changes on My Inside*

UNIT GOAL: Children describe and prepare labeled diagrams to show how the human nervous system senses internal environmental changes and the body adapts to changes in internal stimuli.

UNIT TITLE: *Changes on My Outside*

UNIT GOAL: Children describe and prepare labeled diagrams to show how the human nervous system senses external environmental changes and the body adapts to changes in internal stimuli.

■ Starter Ideas for Populations and Ecosystems

UNIT TITLE: *Producers*

UNIT GOAL: Children identify those organisms that capture the sun's energy in a desert, a woodland, a meadow, and an ocean ecosystem.

UNIT TITLE: *Consumers*

UNIT GOAL: Children identify those organisms that use energy captured by others in a desert, a woodland, a meadow, and an ocean ecosystem.

■ Starter Ideas for Diversity and Adaptation of Organisms

UNIT TITLE: *Special Species*

UNIT GOAL: Children identify the external adaptations and the related advantages possessed by five birds of prey, five land predators, and five ocean predators.

UNIT TITLE: *Dinosaurs' Disappearance*

UNIT GOAL: As a result of library research and classroom discussion, children identify and prepare support for three hypotheses that explain why dinosaurs became extinct.

CONTENT STANDARDS RELATED TO:
Science and Technology [S&T]
Science in Personal and Social Perspectives [SPSP]
History and Nature of Science [HNS][2]

UNIT TITLE: *Acid Rain*

UNIT GOAL: Children write and perform a classroom skit that identifies the natural and human causes of acid rain and its environmental impact.

UNIT TITLE: *They Study Life*

UNIT GOAL: Children conduct library and Internet research to gather information about the lives and work of three scientists in the field of ecology and present their information through oral reports.

Ideas Based on Typical Grade-Level Content

■ Starter Ideas for Kindergarten

UNIT TITLE: *The Senses*

UNIT GOAL: Children learn that the senses of touch, sight, hearing, taste, and smell are their tools for exploring the world around them.

UNIT TITLE: *Plant or Animal?*

UNIT GOAL: Children learn the characteristics they can use to classify things as plants or animals.

■ Starter Ideas for First Grade

UNIT TITLE: *What Do Green Plants Need?*

UNIT GOAL: Children learn that green plants need sunlight, air, and water to live.

UNIT TITLE: *What Do Animals Need?*

UNIT GOAL: Children learn that animals need food, air, water, and shelter to live.

■ Starter Ideas for Second Grade

UNIT TITLE: *Plants Have Parts*

UNIT GOAL: Children learn the basic structures and functions of such plant parts as roots, stems, leaves, flowers, and seeds.

UNIT TITLE: *Animals Have Parts*

UNIT GOAL: Children learn the basic structures and functions of the principal organs outside and inside animals.

■ Starter Ideas for Third Grade

UNIT TITLE: *Looking for Plants*

UNIT GOAL: Children learn that plants display characteristics that reflect adaptations to the environments in which they live.

UNIT TITLE: *Looking for Animals*

UNIT GOAL: Children learn that animals display characteristics that reflect adaptations to the environments in which they live.

■ Starter Ideas for Fourth Grade

UNIT TITLE: *Life Is a Cycle*

UNIT GOAL: Children learn the life cycles of various plants and animals.

UNIT TITLE: *What Is a Population?*

UNIT GOAL: Children learn that a *population* is all the individuals of a particular species in an environment and that populations are affected by changes in the environment.

Children's curiosity about plants makes this topic an excellent source of starter ideas.

■ Starter Ideas for Fifth Grade

UNIT TITLE: *Cells Tell*

UNIT GOAL: Children learn to use a microscope and reference material to identify basic structures in animal and plant cells.

UNIT TITLE: *Cells, Tissues, Organs, Systems*

UNIT GOAL: Children learn that their bodies and other living things are composed of a variety of systems and subsystems.

■ Starter Ideas for Sixth Grade

UNIT TITLE: *Taking Care of Your Business*

UNIT GOAL: Children learn about the basics of personal health care, the existence of sexually transmitted diseases (STDs), and the general modalities for the prevention of STDs, including abstinence.

UNIT TITLE: *The Dinosaurs*

UNIT GOAL: Children learn the characteristics of various species of dinosaurs and their places in the food chains that existed when they did; then they make hypotheses about whether particular species could survive in the climatic conditions that now exist in the students' region.

■ Starter Ideas for Seventh Grade

UNIT TITLE: *Animals without Backbones*

UNIT GOAL: Students learn the basic characteristics and biological adaptations of sponges, coelenterates, worms, mollusks, echinoderms, and arthropods.

UNIT TITLE: *Animals with Backbones*

UNIT GOAL: Students learn the basic characteristics and biological adaptations of fish, amphibians, reptiles, and birds.

■ **Starter Ideas for Eighth Grade**

UNIT TITLE: *Plants with Flowers, Plants Without*

UNIT GOAL: Students learn how flowering (angiosperms) and nonflowering (gymnosperms) plants reproduce.

UNIT TITLE: *Our Earth, Our Ecosystem*

UNIT GOAL: Students learn that the earth can be studied as one large ecosystem, which is affected by our technologies.

Lesson Plan Starter Ideas for Common Curriculum Topics

Sometimes, you will be responsible for teaching lessons that are part of units prepared by committees of teachers in your school district or units that are commercially available. You may wonder how to break these units into lessons. To help you come up with lesson ideas for the life sciences, I have analyzed a variety of teaching units and prepared a list of lesson plan starter ideas based on topics usually covered in these units. The lesson descriptions are very specific, so each description may also be viewed as the lesson's principal objective.

■ **Starter Ideas for Characteristics of Living Things**

- Observe and measure the growth and movement of living things that are kept in the classroom.
- Count the number of living things in the classroom, and prepare a bar graph that shows the number of each type of living thing.
- Orally describe the similarities and differences between plant and animal parts.
- Analyze the conditions under which animals at a local zoo are kept, and list the observed conditions on a chart.

■ **Starter Ideas for Plant and Animal Life Processes**

- Analyze food samples provided by the teacher to determine whether they are sweet, sour, bitter, or salty.
- Identify from a list of foods those that are the best sources of protein, fiber, carbohydrates, and fat, and locate each food in the nutrition food pyramid.
- Explain orally how humans can prevent the spread of diseases, including sexually transmitted diseases (STDs).
- Explain orally the effects of tobacco, alcohol, and drug use on the human body.
- Evaluate the effectiveness of posters created by classmates to encourage people not to smoke, use alcohol, or take drugs.
- Recognize and identify different patterns of animal growth (continuous, molting, metamorphosis).
- Identify the functions of the principal organs of the human reproductive system for both males and females.

■ Starter Ideas for Populations

- Identify factors that might cause a population of animals or plants to become extinct.
- Explain the factors that trigger the migration of a population from one place to another.
- After doing library and Internet research to evaluate explanations for successful migration to distant locations, select the two most likely explanations.
- Explain the similarities and differences in the survival needs of the following populations: bees, ants, deer, humans.
- Make a labeled diagram that shows the role decomposers play in returning water, minerals, and other nutrients to a population.

■ Starter Ideas for the Environment

- Describe the adaptations that an organism has that help it fit into its environment.
- Predict the impact of humankind on plants and animals.
- Infer the requirements for keeping an ecosystem self-sustaining.
- Create a timeline for the last 100 years that shows the changes described by senior citizens in the local environment.
- Identify the human use of natural resources found in the environment.

■ Starter Ideas for How Life Adapts and Changes

- Evaluate how an animal's characteristics increase its chances for survival in its environment.
- Given illustrations of the ancient and modern forms of horses and dogs, infer any advantages the modern form would have over the ancient form in today's world.
- Create a timeline that shows when life began on Earth, the origin and extinction of dinosaurs, and the origin of humans.
- Identify the major changes that have occurred in the bodies and behaviors of humans over the past 3 million years.
- Predict changes that will occur in human bodies as the species adapts to increased water and air pollution.

■ Starter Ideas for Ecosystems

- Explain how all animals depend on the food-making ability of green plants.
- Classify the members of a community as producers, consumers, and decomposers.
- Count the number of organisms found in a sample of water from a pond ecosystem.
- Explain that an ecosystem consists of the physical environment and a group of interacting living things that also interact with the environment.
- Infer how changes in the characteristics of an ecosystem can affect the balance among producers, consumers, and decomposers.
- Given specific information about the components of an ecosystem, infer how the introduction of a population of new producers changes the rest of the ecosystem.
- Describe an experiment that could test the effects of drastic changes in each of the following on an ecosystem: water, food, temperature, and availability of light.

MAKE THE CASE   *An Individual or Group Challenge*

■ **The Problem**

Children need science experiences that range across the earth/space, life, and physical sciences. Teachers may tend to emphasize those topics they feel most comfortable with and thus inadvertently limit the scope of children's learning.

■ **Assess Your Prior Knowledge and Beliefs**

1. When you compare your knowledge of the life sciences to your knowledge of the earth/space sciences and physical sciences, do you believe you have acquired more, less, or the same amount of basic science content in each?

	More	*Less*	*Same*
Earth/space sciences	_____	_____	_____
Physical sciences	_____	_____	_____

2. When you were a student in grades K–8, were you exposed to more, less, or the same amount of life science content as you were to earth/space science content and physical science content?

	More	*Less*	*Same*
Earth/space sciences	_____	_____	_____
Physical sciences	_____	_____	_____

3. Whether life as we know it exists on other planets is an ever-popular life science topic for children. Identify five discrete items of knowledge that you have about the topic.

_____

_____

_____

_____

_____

4. Now identify five things about the requirements for life that you think you should know but do not.

_____

_____

_____

_____

_____

■ **The Challenge**

You are part of a team of teachers planning a unit on the requirements for life. Give examples of life science activities you might include.

WebQuest Starter Ideas

Imagine the WebQuest possibilities for your students when you teach the life sciences! They'll be able to use the vast resources of the Internet to discover fascinating information about animals, plants, their own bodies, and the incredible web of life of which they are a part.

The starter ideas in this section will help you plan your own life science Web-Quests. As you study the ideas, please keep the following in mind:

1. The WebQuests are correlated with the NSE Standards for grades K–8 (which are printed inside the front cover).

2. In the WebQuest context, the term *reports* has a very broad meaning and includes poster preparation, skits, dance, video presentations, labeled diagrams, and, of course, traditional written reports, if and when appropriate.

■ Starter Ideas for WebQuests

WEBQUEST TITLE: *Help the Polar Bears*

SUGGESTED GRADE LEVELS: K–1 (to be done with an adult)

NSE CONTENT STANDARDS: LS 1 and 3; SPSP 4

CHALLENGE—MOTIVATION: Have you ever seen a polar bear? Sometimes, young polar bears become orphans. What would a zoo need to raise polar bear orphans?

CHALLENGE—REPORTS: Pretend you are going to start a zoo for polar bear orphans. List what you will need to keep them healthy. Draw and label the parts of their new zoo home.

KEY TERMS FOR SEARCH ENGINES: Polar Bear, Arctic Animals, Alaskan Bears

WEBQUEST TITLE: *Save the Tigers*

SUGGESTED GRADE LEVELS: 2, 3

NSE CONTENT STANDARDS: LS 1, 2, and 3; SPSP 4

CHALLENGE—MOTIVATION: The sign outside a zoo says "Donate Money So We Can Raise Endangered Bengal Tigers." You ask the zoo manager what a Bengal tiger is and why they are in danger. She goes into her office and takes out a poster about the Bengal tiger to help answer your questions about . . .

CHALLENGE—REPORTS: What might be on the zoo manager's poster? Make a poster that you could use to tell others about Bengal tigers. Be sure to include . . .

KEY TERMS FOR SEARCH ENGINES: Bengal Tiger, Royal Bengal Tiger, Asian Tiger

WEBQUEST TITLE: *Rain Forest Animals*

SUGGESTED GRADE LEVELS: 4, 5

NSE CONTENT STANDARDS: LS 7 and 8; SPSP 10

CHALLENGE—MOTIVATION: You are getting ready to lead a team of scientists in exploring a South American rain forest. They will be all coming to your laboratory next week to learn about . . .

CHALLENGE—REPORTS: Prepare an outline for the speech you will give to your team. Tell them where they'll be going, what they should wear, which species they should look for, and . . .

KEY TERMS FOR SEARCH ENGINES: Rain Forest Animals, Costa Rica Rain Forests, Rain Forest Habitat, Amazon Rain Forest

WEBQUEST TITLE: *Your Healthy Heart and Lungs*

SUGGESTED GRADE LEVELS: 5, 6

NSE CONTENT STANDARDS: LS 4; SPSP 6

CHALLENGE—MOTIVATION: You've seen many signs and posters that tell people not to smoke. Have you ever wondered what health problems are caused by smoking?

CHALLENGE—REPORTS: Make two posters for your class that will help keep your friends from becoming smokers. Make one poster that shows how smoking affects the heart and another that shows . . .

KEY TERMS FOR SEARCH ENGINES: Secondhand Smoke, American Heart Association, American Lung Association

WEBQUEST TITLE: *Watch the Whales*

SUGGESTED GRADE LEVELS: 5, 6, 7

NSE CONTENT STANDARDS: LS 4, 6, 7, and 8; SPSP 10

CHALLENGE—MOTIVATION: Imagine that you are going on a whale-watching trip. You pack art supplies and very powerful binoculars for the adventure.

CHALLENGE—REPORTS: Select either the Pacific or Atlantic Ocean for your trip. Then make five labeled drawings that show the kinds of whales you expect to see. Be sure to show . . .

KEY TERMS FOR SEARCH ENGINES: Marine Mammals, Humpback Whales, Sea World Shamu

WEBQUEST TITLE: *What's Your Biome?*

SUGGESTED GRADE LEVELS: 5, 6, 7

NSE CONTENT STANDARDS: LS 7 and 8; SPSP 7

CHALLENGE—MOTIVATION: You have just been given a scientific award from the Metropolis Museum that includes enough money to travel to and live in any biome you want to for one year. But there is a catch: . . .

CHALLENGE—REPORTS: To get the money, you must write a letter to the museum that tells what biome you have chosen, why you chose it, what animals and plants you expect to study, and . . .

KEY TERMS FOR SEARCH ENGINES: Biome, Plant Adaptation, Animal Adaptation

WEBQUEST TITLE: *Sense or Nonsense?*

SUGGESTED GRADE LEVELS: 5, 6, 7

NSE CONTENT STANDARDS: LS 6; SPSP 6

CHALLENGE—MOTIVATION: You have just been made president of the Ajax Advanced Robot Company. The owners have told you that they want you to produce a robot that has at least three human senses.

CHALLENGE—REPORTS: Select three senses, identify the organs that gather information for each sense, and explain how information travels to the brain. Draw a robot that has each of the three senses. Label all the parts that allow the robot to have the three senses. Be sure to . . .

KEY TERMS FOR SEARCH ENGINES: Five Senses, Nervous System, Sense Organs, Spinal Cord, Ganglia

WEBQUEST TITLE: *What Is a Human Population?*

SUGGESTED GRADE LEVELS: 6, 7, 8

NSE CONTENT STANDARDS: LS 7; SPSP 7 and 10

CHALLENGE—MOTIVATION: You have just been assigned the job of reporting to your country's leaders the size of the population and where the population is the most dense. This is important for future planning because . . .

CHALLENGE—REPORTS: The report must include a map showing where population is most and least dense, a chart showing resources that will be needed if the most dense areas keep growing, and . . .

KEY TERMS FOR SEARCH ENGINES: Population Map, Population Density, Overpopulation, World POPClock

Classroom Enrichment Starter Ideas

In-Class Learning Centers

A well-prepared in-class learning center offers children many opportunities to make their own discoveries. In order to be well prepared, such a center must provide a wide range of materials that encourage hands-on, discovery-based learning, ranging from print and audiovisual resources to art supplies and games. In addition, the learning center must be located where children have ready access to it yet can also be somewhat removed from the larger classroom setting while doing independent activities.

The following starter ideas for in-class learning centers should get you thinking about how to create centers in your own classroom. Note that the relevant NSE Standard is identified for each starter idea and that asterisks indicate those that are particularly suited for young children.

■ Starter Idea for a Learning Center

CENTER TITLE: *The Wonder Machine*

NSE CONTENT STANDARD: LS 4

IDEA: A corner of your classroom would be a good location for this learning center. Allow enough floor space for children to make outlines of themselves by rolling out shelfpaper and tracing around their bodies. You may want to cover part of the floor with newspapers, on which the children can work with clay and paste. If you have computer software or videos related to the human body, make them available in this center, too.

So that students will know what to do in the center, prepare activity cards or guide sheets that give directions for activities based on the following ideas:

- *Find Your Pulse* Children use a stopwatch or the second hand of a clock to count heartbeats, do mild exercise, and count heartbeats again. The children should graph their results.

- *Take a Breather** Children breathe on a mirror and record what they observe.

- *Bright Eyes* Children observe changes in their partners' eyes when they briefly shine a flashlight at them.

- *Different Bodies** Children trace each other while lying on shelfpaper and then refer to materials on the principal organs of the body and their locations and draw the organs on the shelfpaper. Some children may use a tape measure to gather data for a chart on foot sizes.

- *What's Inside?* Children use clay, construction paper, and other art materials to construct models of organ systems.

This in-class learning center—the Wonder Machine—holds a host of activities to interest children.

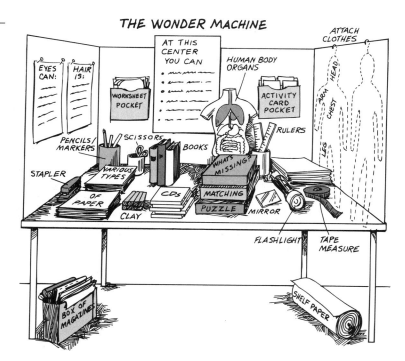

THE WONDER MACHINE

■ Additional Starter Ideas for Learning Centers

CENTER TITLE: *Rain Forest Adventure**

NSE CONTENT STANDARDS: LS 1 and 3

IDEA: Use art materials to draw pictures of and make models of living things unique to the rain forest; tell in which layer of the rain forest each is found.

CENTER TITLE: *Save a Species**

NSE CONTENT STANDARDS: LS 1 and 3

IDEA: Carry out research in books and the Internet to identify five endangered plants and animals, and locate on a world map where each species is found.

CENTER TITLE: *Worm Wonders*

NSE CONTENT STANDARD: LS 4

IDEA: Identify the body parts of an earthworm, describe the function(s) of each, and carry out resource book and Internet research to discover the nature of the earthworm's life cycle.

CENTER TITLE: *Something Fishy*

NSE CONTENT STANDARDS: LS 4 and 8

IDEA: Using a whole, dead (but refrigerated) fish, identify its body parts and adaptations that enable this species to swim efficiently, respire, capture prey, reproduce, and carry out its life cycle.

Bulletin Boards

Good bulletin boards have the potential to be something that children can both look at and learn from. There are many ways to use classroom bulletin boards to enhance life science units and extend your teaching to nonscience areas. The following list offers a few starter ideas for you. Again, asterisks indicate activities that may be particularly appropriate for young children.

■ Starter Ideas for Bulletin Boards

BULLETIN BOARD TITLE: *Flower Power**

IDEA: Create vocabulary word cards for the words *stem, leaf, roots, petals, soil, air, sun,* and *water.* Make construction paper cutouts of a plant stem, leaves, petals, roots, the sun, clouds, soil, and raindrops, and display them on the bulletin board with the word cards. After the children have become familiar with the vocabulary on the word cards, have them attach the cards to the appropriate parts with push-pins. Provide a self-correcting key.

BULLETIN BOARD TITLE: *I'm Lost**

IDEA: Divide a bulletin board into six areas, all of which can be reached by a young child. Each area should have one of the following labels and magazine pictures illustrating the label: *Insects, Fish, Amphibians, Reptiles, Birds, Mammals.* Place at the bottom of the bulletin board a folder or envelope containing a random assortment of pictures or drawings for each of the six categories. Provide some age-appropriate method for attaching the pictures to the areas, and encourage the children to spend free time at the bulletin board, placing each picture from the folder in the appropriate category.

BULLETIN BOARD TITLE: *Desert Animal Homes**

IDEA: Cover the bulletin board with easel paper, and use colored paper, crayons, pastels, paint, and other art supplies to create, with the children's assistance, a desert scene without animals. Include cactus, sand, rocks, blue sky, a shining sun, and so forth. Draw or cut out 10 magazine pictures of desert animals (e.g., a hawk, rattlesnake, scorpion, and lizard), and place these in a folder or envelope at the bottom of the bulletin board. Provide an age-appropriate method for children to attach the pictures to the bulletin board. Encourage children to use their free time to work on putting the animals in their proper places.

BULLETIN BOARD TITLE: *Plant Munchers**

IDEA: Create a large, generic plant that includes a flower, seed, fruits, leaves, stems, and roots. Add unlabeled arrows that point to each part. Put pictures of commonly eaten fruits and vegetables in a large envelope attached to the bulletin board. In their free time, have children attach the pictures to the appropriate arrows.

BULLETIN BOARD TITLE: *Producers, Consumers, and Decomposers*

IDEA: Cover the bulletin board with easel paper. Divide it into three equal-sized parts, and label each with one of these headings: *Producer, Consumer*, or *Decomposer.* As the children have free time, ask them individually or in groups to draw and label an example of each organism following this rule: "The three organisms must interact with one another."

BULLETIN BOARD TITLE: *Body Systems*

IDEA: Place a large drawing of the human body at one side of the bulletin board. Each week, place a large index card with the name of a body system (e.g., digestion, circulation, respiration) at the top of the other side of the bulletin board. Challenge children to attach smaller cards with labels to show the sequence of steps that occur in the identified system. For example, if the system was digestion, the children might attach cards under it that said "Food eaten," "Food enters stomach," and so on.

Field Trips

Field trips provide amazing opportunities for discovery learning, as they take children out of the classroom and immerse them in the real world. Whether you teach in a city, suburban, or small-town school, you can find ideas for field trips all around you. To understand just how true that is, think about how you could tailor each of these topics to the resources of the community in which you teach:

Seasonal changes
Local foods
Area plants
Area animals

A field trip to an aquarium gives children the chance to see animals up close that they would otherwise only see in books or on television.

The field trip may be to the regional aquarium or the pond down the street, but either way, children will be eager to see what the day will hold. After all, children *love* field trips!

Here are starter ideas for field trips for all schools. Note that asterisks indicate activities that may be particularly appropriate for young children.

■ Starter Ideas for Field Trips

FIELD TRIP TITLE: *Animal Study**

IDEA: Visiting a zoological park, aquarium, or farm gives children the opportunity to observe some of the animals they have seen only in pictures, movies, and tele-vision shows. Consider having individual children or cooperative learning groups become "experts" on one animal they will see during the trip, and have them compare their research with what they actually observe during the trip. Any nearby stream, field, or park also can offer the children a chance to obtain firsthand knowledge about animal life. Because such trips can also provide opportunities for students to draw and write about interesting animals, art materials and notebooks should be available. If the location is easily accessible, visit it at different times in the year so variations in animal life can be observed.

FIELD TRIP TITLE: *Is It Alive?**

IDEA: A field trip on school grounds or to a nearby park or nature area will provide many opportunities for young children to differentiate between living and nonliving things. Prior to the trip, have children discuss the characteristics of living and nonliving things. You may wish to create a checklist that children can take along on the trip. They may discover that some objects do not easily fit into the two categories. Such an observation could prompt a good discussion of the problems that arise when objects are classified.

FIELD TRIP TITLE: *Searching for Changes*

IDEA: A walk through the school neighborhood can provide opportunities to observe how the environment has been modified to meet the needs of people. If farmland has been converted to a residential area, you may see some signs of previous farm use. Have the children look for evidence of resources being brought into the environment, such as electric poles, water pipes, and so forth. Also look for evidence of materials being taken out of the area, such as sewage pipes and trash bins. Emphasize that an environment may look stable, but if we observe it for any length of time, we can see many changes occurring.

FIELD TRIP TITLE: *Plants on Parade*

IDEA: A nature walk focused on plants may reveal a great deal to children about the types and quantities of plants that live on or near the school grounds. Prior to the trip, have children predict the number of different plants they will see. During the trip, have them keep track of the kinds of plants they observe.

Many of the factors that make the city an interesting and exciting place to live also make it a place that overflows with field trip possibilities. Here are additional starter ideas that should stimulate your thinking about field trips for children in city schools:

▪ Starter Ideas for Field Trips

FIELD TRIP TITLE: *Mud Puddle Life*

IDEA: Children observe living things in and at the margins of a mud puddle after a rainstorm.

FIELD TRIP TITLE: *Dandelion Detectives*

IDEA: Children count dandelions, note where they are found, and observe their structures.

FIELD TRIP TITLE: *Squirrel Detectives*

IDEA: Children count the squirrels they see on a nature walk and note their behavior.

FIELD TRIP TITLE: *Bushes Change*

IDEA: Children study hedges and other plants growing on the school grounds to observe seasonal changes.

FIELD TRIP TITLE: *City Birds*

IDEA: Children study pigeons, sparrows, starlings, and other birds that live in the city.

FIELD TRIP TITLE: *Bug Business*

IDEA: Children go on a nature walk to locate (without touching) as many insects as they can and note what the insects are doing.

FIELD TRIP TITLE: *Is There Life in That Lot?*

IDEA: Under close supervision and at a vacant lot that is safe in every respect, children note the presence of such living things as ragweed and milkweed plants, fungi, moths, butterflies, and so forth.

FIELD TRIP TITLE: *Pyramid Power*

IDEA: Children visit restaurants and neighborhood grocery stores to learn what foods people from various cultures enjoy and then use the nutrition food pyramid to classify the foods.

Additional Field Trip Destinations

Aquarium	Food-processing facility
Botany or zoology department at local college	Forest preserve
	Natural history museum
Bird/wildlife sanctuary	Orchard
Commercial greenhouse	Pet store
Fish hatchery	Ranch, dairy, chicken, or vegetable farm
Flower or garden show	

Cooperative Learning Projects

As you consider the following starter ideas for cooperative learning projects, keep in mind the importance of stressing the three key aspects of cooperative learning:

1. Positive interdependence
2. Individual accountability
3. Development of group process skills

■ Starter Ideas for Cooperative Learning Projects

PROJECT TITLE: *"Life's My Game, Amy's the Name"*

IDEA: Have each group research career options available to people interested in the life sciences. After the groups have finished their research, have each group select one career and train one person in the group to present the career to the remainder of the class. Emphasize that the group is responsible for getting the information needed, rehearsing the person, and providing constructive feedback. On the presentation day, the person trained should come to class dressed as a person in the career is dressed and prepared to describe what he or she does, the working conditions, the rewards, and the educational background required.

PROJECT TITLE: *We Are the . . .*

IDEA: Give each group a choice of an animal or plant phylum (you may wish to include protists), and have the groups prepare presentations that creatively teach the characteristics of the phyla. Groups should be encouraged to use music, dance, art, puppets, poetry, and other media for their presentations. Each group should build into the presentation a way of assessing whether the audience has learned the characteristics.

PROJECT TITLE: *Big as a Whale*

IDEA: Have each group prepare life-sized outlines of three animals on the school lawn using lengths of clothesline pulled around popsicle sticks that have been placed at points marking the ends of the animal's tail, head, feet, and other body parts. In preparation for this project, each group should choose the three animals they will create and carry out library research to acquire the needed information. All the groups should create their animals on the lawn at the same time. This will permit the children to compare their own size to the sizes of various animals.

■ Additional Starter Ideas for Learning Groups

- Have each group select a human body system, research the system, and then present the system to the remainder of the class in a creative way.
- Challenge groups to raise popcorn plants to see which group can produce the healthiest and largest plants in the shortest period of time.
- Have groups prepare arguments for or against the operation of zoos. This can serve as the basis for a debate or discussion among groups.
- Have groups research and design a truly healthy breakfast that reflects knowledge of the nutrition food pyramid. Groups can be challenged to prepare portions of their proposed breakfasts that can be sampled by the rest of the class.

RESOURCES FOR DISCOVERY LEARNING

Internet Resources
Websites for Life Science Units, Lessons, Activities, and Demonstrations

The Electronic Zoo

netvet.wustl.edu/pix.htm

If your students are engaged in discovery units, lessons, or Internet research about animals, this page will prove to be extremely valuable. In addition to subsections on all major areas of the animal kingdom, you will find excellent photographs, graphics, and even animal sounds! Be advised that some of the links on the pages will take young people to rather advanced science content. You may wish to spend some time at this site yourself so you can tailor your students' web research to content that is at an appropriate difficulty level for them. Older students will also find career-awareness information, if they have an interest in veterinary medicine.

ERIC Life Science Lesson Plans

ericir.syr.edu/Virtual/Lessons/Science/

This is one of the best-organized compilations of science lesson plans on the Internet. When you reach the site, first select "Science" and then select "Biological and Life Sciences," which will take you to an alphabetized list of lessons at all grade levels. Be advised that although the lessons have been placed in a consistent format, they come from a variety of sources. (Or to put it more directly, they vary in quality.)

The Natural History Museum (London) "Quest"

www.nhm.ac.uk/education/quest/index.html

This is the "Quest" portion of a rather amazing site. The Natural History Museum provides virtual tools that your students can use to explore at least 12 different objects related to the natural sciences. Each Quest excursion can easily be adapted to a discovery-based lesson for your classroom. Imagine the possibilities as your students explore science materials in London using the Internet.

The Natural History Museum (London) "The Life Galleries"

www.nhm.ac.uk/museum

At this site, students can view a variety of the life science exhibits available at the Natural History Museum. To begin, they should select "Life Galleries." Each location—whether on birds, mammals, ecology, or any of the other important topics presented—contains extremely well done visual presentations and an abundance of information about the topic. Creative teachers will find this a useful site to direct students to.

The Wild Ones

www.thewildones.org

This site, sponsored by the Wildlife Preservation Trust International, seeks to provide "students ages 7 to 14 with an international perspective, opportunities for cooperative science activities, and a positive outlook on their capacity as individuals to improve the prospects for endangered species." At this Interent location of The Wild Ones, you will find a variety of resources, including classroom, school yard, and field trip activities related to the organization's mission. An interesting feature of this site is that a portion of the resources are presented in *Spanish*.

Sea World: Science Information Content

www.seaworld.org/infobook.html

This beautifully presented and quite helpful site represents Sea World's presence on the Internet. This specific portion of the site includes science content and illustrations on a variety of topics related to ocean and shore life and other environmental topics: beluga whales, coral reefs, endangered species, and many other topics commonly taught in the schools. The information about particular species of animals is quite extensive, and the photographs and related graphics are of the highest quality.

Sea World: Science Information Resources

www.seaworld.org/teacherguides/index.html

This portion of the Sea World site focuses directly on teaching resources (in contrast to the previous site, which presents science content). This is one of the very few places on the Internet that provides complete science units referred to as "Teacher's Guides," including "All About Seals, Sea Lions, and Walruses," "Ocean Olympians," and "Animals Abound." Again, some of the units are in *Spanish*.

The Tree of Life

tolweb.org/tree/phylogeny.html

Don't be misled by the use of the word *tree* in the name for this site. It's about *all* life on our planet. Be advised that this site presents science content in a somewhat sophisticated manner, which should be understandable to you and perhaps a few of your most advanced students. Even so, this is one of the most carefully organized and well-presented compilations of science content on the Internet and must be visited by any teacher who wants to be sure that he or she presents accurate scientific content to children when life on Earth is being studied. Use the "Search" choice on the opening page, and key in the name of a living thing your class is studying. You will be amazed at the information and associated graphics available.

Print Resources

Articles from Science and Children and *Science Scope*

Aram, Robert J. "Habitat Sweet Habitat." *Science and Children* 38, no. 4 (January 2001): 23–27.

Bradway, Heather. "You Make the Diagnosis." *Science Scope* 24, no. 8 (May 2001): 23–25.

Coverdale, Gregory. "Science Is for the Birds: Promoting Standards-Based Learning through Backyard Birdwatching." *Science Scope* 26, no. 4 (January 2003): 32–37.

Galus, Pamela. "Snail Trails." *Science Scope* 25, no. 8 (May 2002): 14–18.

Gates, Donna M. "Pond Life Magnified." *Science Scope* 25, no. 8 (May 2002): 10–13.

Giacalone, Valerie. "How to Plan, Survive, and Even Enjoy an Overnight Field Trip with 200 Students." *Science Scope* 26, no. 4 (January 2003): 22–26.

Hammrich, Penny L., and Kathleen Fadigan. "Investigations in the Science of Sports." *Science Scope* 26, no. 5 (February 2003): 30–35.

Houtz, Lynne E., and Thomas H. Quinn. "Give Me Some Skin: A Hands-On Science Activity Integrating Racial Sensitivity." *Science Scope* 26, no. 5 (February 2003): 18–22.

Keena, Kelly, and Carole G. Basile. "An Environmental Journey." *Science and Children* 39, no. 8 (May 2002): 30–33.

Keteyian, Linda. "A Garden Story." *Science and Children* 39, no. 3 (November/December 2001): 22–25.

Koschmann, Mark, and Dan Shepardson. "A Pond Investigation." *Science and Children* 39, no. 8 (May 2002): 20–23.

Lawry, Patricia K., and Judy Hale McCrary. "Someone's in the Kitchen with Science." *Science and Children* 39, no. 2 (October 2001): 22–27.

Lebofsky, Nancy R., and Larry A. Lebofsky. "Modeling Olympus Mons from the Earth." *Science Scope* 25, no. 7 (April 2002): 36–39.

Mannesto, Jean. "The Truth about Wolves." *Science and Children* 39, no. 8 (May 2002): 24–29.

McGinnis, Patricia. "Dissect Your Squid and Eat It Too." *Science Scope* 24, no. 7 (April 2001): 12–17.

McWilliams, Susan. "Journey into the Five Senses." *Science and Children* 40, no. 5 (February 2003): 38–43.

Mitchell, Melissa, and James K. Mitchell. "A Microbial Murder Mystery." *Science Scope* 25, no. 5 (February 2002): 24–30.

Morrison, Geraldine, and JoAnn Uslick. "Summer Science Camp, Anyone? *Science and Children* 39, no. 7 (April 2002): 34–37.

Norrell, Mark A. "Science 101: What Is a Fossil?" *Science and Children* 40, no. 5 (February 2003): 20.

Rule, Audrey, and Cynthia Rust. "A Bat Is Like a . . ." *Science and Children* 39, no. 3 (November/December 2001): 26–31.

Science Scope 26, no. 4 (January 2003) (Entire issue emphasizes addressing science misconceptions)

Sitzman, Daniel. "Bread Making: Classic Biotechnology and Experimental Design." *Science Scope* 26, no. 4 (January 2003): 27–31.

NOTES

1. This standard, as well as the others identified in later sections, are excerpted with permission from the National Research Council, *National Science Education Standards* (Washington, DC: National Academy Press, 1996), pp. 104–171. Note that the bracketed symbol to the right of each standard was prepared by this author. See also the list of all the K–8 content standards inside the front cover of this book.

2. Note that I have related this sampling of NSE Standards E, F, and G to the life sciences.

5A Living Things

Content

Living or Nonliving? That's the Question

Dust from the surface of an African plain, dotted with grass and small plants, is kicked into clouds by the plodding feet of a rhinoceros. As the huge, lumbering beast moves along munching plants, it frightens insects into confused flight. Some of these insects land on the rhino's body and are carried to greener pastures as the rhino moves across the plain. Some of these insects become food for the tick birds that also ride on the rhino's back (see Figure 5A.1). As the rhino feeds on grasses and weeds, the tick birds flutter about, feasting upon the newly arrived insects. The rhino, the insects, the tick birds, and the grass are all living things, but the dust, of course, is not.

What makes the dust fundamentally different from the rhino, insects, tick birds, and grass? When scientists make observations to determine whether something is living or nonliving, they search for these eight characteristics, or *functions,* of life:

1. The ability to respire, or to release the chemical energy locked in nutrients (respiration)
2. The ability to produce or acquire and use food
3. The ability to get rid of waste products (secretion and excretion)
4. The ability to move a variety of materials within it (transport)
5. The ability to move
6. The ability to respond to changes (irritability)
7. The ability to grow
8. The ability to produce more of its own kind (reproduction)

Scientists who study the characteristics of living things are known as *biologists.* Life on Earth is so complex that biologists can specialize in one or more parts of biology:

Zoology, the study of animals

Botany, the study of plants

Anatomy, the study of the structure of living things

Ecology, the study of the relationships among living things and their surroundings

Similarities in Living Things

Believe it or not, you have a lot in common with a cactus plant! This hopefully doesn't apply to your outward appearance, but it most definitely applies to your inside appearance. You, the cactus plant, and every other living thing is made up of one or more *cells.* Within every cell is a gelatinlike, colorless, semitransparent substance called *protoplasm,* which is made up of a variety of elements: carbon, hydrogen, oxygen, potassium, phosphorous, iodine, sulfur, nitrogen, calcium, iron, magnesium, sodium, chlorine, and traces of other elements.

In living things that contain more than one cell, any group of cells that performs a similar function is called a *tissue.* A group of tissues that function together is called an *organ.* And a group of organs that work together to perform a major function is known

FIGURE 5A.1

The tick birds and the rhinoceros both benefit from their relationship.

as a *system*. For instance, in plants, the various cells and tissues that enable the food made in the leaves to be transported to the stems and roots make up the vascular system. Plants contains many different systems that all perform different functions. So does the human body. Those systems include the skeletal system, muscular system, respiratory system, nervous system, excretory system, and reproductive system.

Differences in Living Things

You and that cactus plant are also different in many ways. The protoplasm in the cells of a particular type of living thing is unique to that thing. The ptotoplasm of a cactus enables cactus cells to carry on the unique functions that permit the cactus to function as a cactus. So it is with the protoplasm of the human body and every other living thing.

The cells that make up living things also differ. Most have clearly defined nuclei, but some one-celled organisms do not. And while plants and animals have clearly defined nuclei in their cells, the cell walls of plants contain cellulose while the cells of animals are bound by membranes that do not contain cellulose. Plants and animals, of course, possess other characteristics that allow us to distinguish between them:

Plants	Animals
Organs are external to the plant's body—for example, leaves and flowers.	Most organs are internal to the animal's body—for instance, the heart and the stomach.
They produce their own food.	They cannot produce food internally.
They show little movement.	Most can move freely.
No organs have a specific excretory function.	They possess excretory organs.
They respond slowly to changes in the environment.	They can respond quickly to changes in the environment.

Even within any given multicellular living thing, the cells are not all similar to one another. For example, your skin cells, although they contain protoplasm and a nucleus, differ in many ways from the cells that make up the muscles of your heart. Similarly, every plant and every animal contains a variety of very specialized cells that make up its tissues and organs.

Classifying Living Things

Long ago, biologists classified all living things into just the two categories we've already discussed: plants and animals. With further study and more sophisticated equipment, biologists were surprised to discover living things that really didn't fit into either group.

The Five Kingdoms

Modern biologists use a classification system that includes five distinct kingdoms (see Figure 5A.2):

1. *Monera*—This kingdom includes one-celled living things that don't have a membrane around the cell's genetic material. In other words, none of these things has a nucleus. Monerans include bacteria, which don't produce their own food, and blue-green algae, which can produce food through photosynthesis. Most of the earth's oxygen is produced by blue-green algae. A few species of bacteria live deep underwater near thermal vents and are able to manufacture food using chemical energy.

2. *Protista*—This group includes single-celled organisms that do have a membrane surrounding the cell's genetic material—for example, diatoms, protozoa, and euglena. Common amebas and paramecia are also protozoans. All protists are found in moist or aquatic habitats and get their nutrition in a variety of ways. Protists are believed to be early examples of the types of life forms that eventually became the fungi, plants, and animals that live on the earth today.

3. *Fungi*—This group of living things may be one celled or multicelled. They gain their nutrition by absorbing nutrients from their surroundings, and they store energy in the chemical compound glycogen, which makes them different from plants that store food as starch. Fungi can reproduce sexually or asexually. Asexual reproduction is carried out through the production and release of tiny spores that can be carried long distances through the air. Sexual reproduction occurs from the fusion of cell material from two types of fungi competing on the same food source.

4. *Plantae*—This kingdom includes living things that are multicellular and have true cell nuclei and cell walls. Most use photosynthesis to produce food. The green plants in this kingdom—mosses, ferns, grasses, trees, and so on—reproduce sexually or asexually.

5. *Animalia*—This group is made up of multicelled living things that are able to ingest food directly from their environments. Animal cells contain nuclei. Members of this kingdom reproduce sexually, with a few exceptions. Sponges, for example, reproduce asexually by forming buds that can break free of the parent sponge and be carried to a place they can develop into a complete sponge. Although some animals, such as sponges, are sessile (i.e., they remain in one specific place during their life cycle), most are able to move freely from place to place.

FIGURE 5A.2   A five-kingdom classification system

Kingdom	Characteristics	Examples			
Monera	One celled, lack nuclear membranes and other cell structures with membranes, sometimes form groups or filaments, nutrition usually by absorption, reproduction usually by fission or budding	Bacteria Blue-green algae			
Protista	Includes one-celled and multicelled living things, have an organized nucleus and organelles with membranes, reproduction usually by fission	Ameba Paramecium			
Fungi	Some one celled, some multicelled, nutrition by absorption, cell walls made of chitin, sexual or asexual reproduction	Bread molds Mildews Yeasts Mushrooms			
Plantae	Multicellular, produce own food through photosynthesis, cells surrounded by cell wall, sexual and asexual reproduction	Mosses Ferns Trees Grasses Palms Roses			
Animalia	Multicellular, nutrition by ingestion, cells surrounded by cell membrane, have complex organ systems, mainly sexual reproduction	Sponges Flatworms Starfish Insects Amphibians Reptiles Mammals			

How to Classify a Particular Living Thing

When biologists classify an organism, they must first decide which of the five kingdoms provides the best fit. Then, because kingdoms are divided into various categories and subcategories, biologists must identify the appropriate subcategory. They do so by looking at how other living things with the identical characteristics as the mystery organism have already been classified.

Every living thing is classified according to the following system, in order from the largest (most general) to the smallest (most specific) group:

Kingdom
Phylum
Class
Order
Family
Genus
Species

This means, of course, that every living thing actually has seven names that ultimately specify its exact place among all living things. Let's see how this would work for a relatively easy-to-find organism—the common grasshopper:

Kingdom   Animalia
Phylum   Arthropoda
Class   Insecta
Order   Orthoptera
Family   Acridiidae
Genus   *Schistocerca*
Species   *americana*

The grasshopper is an animal, so its kingdom is Animalia. And since the animal kingdom has so many members, it is further classified as a member of the Arthropoda phylum. There are thousands of other arthropods, so the grasshopper is placed in the class Insecta. The process continues until the grasshopper is identified by the series of seven names. Notice how the classification of a grasshopper and a human differ:

	Grasshopper	**Human**
Kingdom	Animalia	Animalia
Phylum	Arthropoda	Chordata
Class	Insecta	Mammalia
Order	Orthoptera	Primates
Family	Acridiidae	Hominidae
Genus	*Schistocerca*	*Homo*
Species	*americana*	*sapiens*

The use of a classification system helps biologists avoid confusion when they talk and write about living things.

The Plant Kingdom:
A Closer Look

Recent classification systems have grouped the organisms of the plant kingdom into two major phyla: the Bryophytes (Bryophyta) and the Tracheophytes (Tracheophyta). *Bryophytes* are small plants that lack conducting vessels for transporting water and nutrients. This phylum includes mosses, liverworts, and hornworts. The phylum *Tracheophyta* includes all vascular plants—that is, plants that have vessels for transporting water and nutrients.

Ferns, conifers, and flowering plants are all tracheophytes. Ferns do not produce true seeds. Both conifers and flowering plants are seed-producing tracheophytes. These seed-producing plants are grouped into two classes: the Gymnosperms and the Angiosperms. Most Gymnosperms do not produce flowers—they produce cones. Evergreen trees such as pines, redwoods, and spruces are all Gymnosperms. Angiosperms produce flowers. Fruit trees, rose plants, and daisies are all examples of Angiosperms.

The Structure of Flowering Plants

Incredibly, there are over 250,000 species of flowering plants, or *Angiosperms*. As the most advanced form of plant life on Earth, this class can survive and even thrive in a variety of climates and soil types. The structure of these plants is what enables them to survive (see Table 5A.1, page 140).

Sexual and Asexual Reproduction in Flowering Plants

Most flowering plants have both male and female organs, Thus, in Angiosperms, reproduction is generally accomplished by the union of sperm and egg cells to form seeds. This is called *sexual reproduction*. However, fruit and vegetable growers are able to produce new plants without using seeds. *Asexual reproduction* can happen in the natural world when separated plant parts reach soil and moisture. They will grow into a new plant that has the exact genetic makeup of the original plant. Table 5A.2 (page 141) presents key points about sexual and asexual reproduction in flowering plants.

The Animal Kingdom:
A Closer Look

Animals are multicellular organisms that obtain food from their environments. Most have systems that allow them to move, and most reproduce sexually. Almost 1 million different kinds of animals inhabit the earth. In order to keep track of them, biologists have found it useful to classify them into two major groups: animals without backbones and animals with backbones. Animals without backbones are called *invertebrates*. They

TABLE 5A.1   The structure of flowering plants

ELEMENT	CHARACTERISTICS	FUNCTION(S)
Roots	Roots grow downward and outward into the soil. Tiny root hairs behind the root tip absorb water and minerals.	Anchors the plant. Absorbs water and minerals. May store food.
Stems	*Monocot* stems emerge from seeds with one cotyledon or seed leaf (such as corn, grasses). *Dicotyledonous* stems emerge from seeds with two cotyledons (such as tomatoes, roses). *Herbaceous* (soft and green) stems are found in short-lived plants (such as dandelions, tomatoes, grasses). *Woody* stems are found in longer-lived plants (such as forsythia, lilac, trees).	Serve as a pipeline, carrying produced foods downward and water with dissolved minerals upward. Displays the leaves to sunlight.
Leaves	Leaves come in many shapes and sizes. *Monocot* leaves are narrow and have smooth edges and parallel veins. *Dicot* leaves are broad and have veins that spread out. Water vapor leaves the plant through leaf openings called *stomata*.	Carry out photosynthesis (food making) because they contain chlorophyll. Assist the plant in losing excess water through transpiration.
Reproductive organs	A typical flower has sepals, petals, stamens, and a pistil. *Sepals* form the leaf-like outer covering of the developing flower bud, which is usually green. *Petals* are usually bright colored, have an odor that's attractive to insects, and produce a sugary nectar (a food source for insects and birds). *Stamens* are male reproductive organs that produce pollen containing a sperm nucleus. At the top of each stamen is an *anther*, or pollen box, that releases pollen. The *pistil* is the female reproductive organ. At the top of the pistil is the *stigma*, to which pollen can stick.	Produces fruits containing seeds, which produce new plants.

TABLE 5A.2   Sexual and asexual reproduction in flowering plants

TYPE OF REPRODUCTION	CHARACTERISTICS
Sexual	The sperm and egg nucleus unite in the process known as *pollination*. Pollen grains are carried to the *stigma* and produce a tube that grows downward to the *ovary*, or enlarged bottom part of the pistil. The sperm nucleus travels down the tube and unites with egg cells in the ovary to eventually produce seeds.
Asexual	Parts of plants—such as leaves, stems, and roots—are used to produce new plants. Examples include "cuttings" (containing a stem with leaves) from begonias, bulbs (which have large, food-storing, underground stems) from lilies and tulips, and potato pieces that contain buds, or "eyes."

include sponges, jellyfishes, starfishes, worms, mollusks, lobsters, spiders, and insects. The second major group, those with backbones, are called *vertebrates*. This group includes fishes, frogs, snakes, birds, and mammals. Vertebrates and invertebrates are divided into various phyla.

Vertebrates: Mammals

Mammals are vertebrates who nourish their young with milk produced by mammary glands. Their bodies are usually covered with hair or fur, although in some mammals, the hair takes the form of a few whiskers around the mouth. While many mammals have four legs, some mammals—for example, whales, dolphins, and manatees—do not. In other mammals, the forelegs and rear legs are modified to perform particular functions. For instance, the forelimbs of kangaroos enable them to grasp food, whereas their strong, enlarged back legs enable them to hop.

The eggs of mammals are usually fertilized internally, and most mammals produce young by giving birth to them (although the duck-billed platypus, which is a monotreme mammal, does lay eggs). Female mammals suckle their young and care for them as they mature. The amount of time for a young mammal to mature into an adult varies greatly. Mammals seem able to teach their young to perform functions that will ensure their survival. Some mammals care for their young until they are fully grown and able to survive on their own.

Female opossums and kangaroos are marsupial mammals. They have pouches in which they place their young as soon as they are born. Although bats appear to be birds, they have hair rather than feathers. Bats can fly through the use of a leathery membrane stretching between their forelimbs and hind legs.

Although whales look like fish, they are really sea-living mammals. The hair on their bodies takes the form of whiskers around the mouth. The blue whale can reach almost 30 meters (about 100 feet) in length and weigh more than 140,000 kilograms (about 150 tons).

The primates, which include monkeys and apes, are the most intelligent of the mammals. They have the best-developed brains of all animals, fingers that are able to grasp objects, opposable thumbs, and nails instead of claws. (An opposable thumb can be positioned opposite of the other fingers, making it possible to manipulate objects with one hand.) The largest of all apes is the gorilla, which can weigh as much as 180 kilograms (about 400 pounds). The gorilla is able to walk upright and to support itself by placing its hands on the ground. The most intelligent of all animals is probably the chimpanzee, though some people feel that a sea mammal, the dolphin, may be more intelligent than the chimpanzee and perhaps as intelligent as humans.

Biologists usually group the human species with the primates. The characteristics that have traditionally differentiated humans from other primates include the ability to reason, the use of complex communication systems, and the use of tools. In recent years, the observation of chimpanzees and gorillas in the wild, as well as laboratory research, has revealed that primates may have capabilities that challenge traditional views.

Sexual Reproduction in Vertebrates

Vertebrates reproduce in a variety of ways. Some lay eggs; others give birth to living young. Fertilization may occur externally or internally. The young may be born fully developed, or they may be born in a very immature condition. Table 5A.3 provides an overview of vertebrate reproduction using three types of animals: frogs, birds, and mammals. (Human reproduction is discussed in Chapter 6A.)

Bioterrorism: What Today's Teachers Must Know

The events of "9/11," along with prior and subsequent terrorist acts, have affected us all in countless ways. Perhaps the most insidious effect has been the *fear* that's been generated. Much of that is fear of the unknown—What else is going to happen? And one of the most frightening possibilities is *bioterrorism,* in which individuals and groups use biological agents to achieve terrorist goals.

By becoming a teacher, you have become part of your community's defense against present and future attacks. Your contact with children will enable you to teach them—in a prudent and age-appropriate manner—about diseases that may affect their present and future health and well-being.

Previous generations of teachers have assumed this responsibility in the context of *natural* disease threats. Now, with a new sense of urgency, you must teach children about diseases that may be *purposefully* introduced into a specific human population. Thus, the scientific knowledge that children learn in your classroom will lay the foundation for lives in which these individuals learn to take sensible precautions to preserve

TABLE 5A.3   Sexual reproduction in vertebrates

TYPE OF VERTEBRATE	METHOD OF REPRODUCTION
Frog	Although the frog is an amphibian, its reproductive cycle occurs in the water. The male fog releases sperm cells over egg cells expelled into the water by the female. The many-celled embryo becomes a tadpole that's capable of absorbing oxygen through its gills. The tadpole changes with time: Its gills shrink, its lungs form, and it becomes reliant on air for oxygen. With these changes, it has become a young frog.
Bird	Birds reproduce as a result of internal fertilization. An ovary within the female bird produces eggs, which may be fertilized if sperm is deposited by a male. The fertilized egg becomes covered with a shell that protects it when it passes from the female's body and reaches the outside world. Nearly all birds sit on their eggs in a nest to provide the best temperature for the embryos within them to mature. The eggs are turned and moved by the incubating parent so that they are evenly warmed. Once hatched, most baby birds are completely dependent on their parents for food, nearly naked except for down feathers, and generally helpless. Baby birds mature quickly, however. They develop other kinds of feathers, learn to fly, and eventually leave the nest.
Mammal	Sperm cells enter the female reproductive system and internally fertilize an egg cell. The fertilized egg travels to the female's uterus, where it grows and develops. The time in the uterus is known as the *gestation period;* for a human, it is about 9 months. A few mammals, such as the spiny anteater and the duck-billed platypus, lay eggs in a manner similar to birds and reptiles. Marsupials, such as kangaroos and opossums, carry their young, who are very undeveloped at birth, in a pouch. Newborn mammals cannot survive on their own. They rely on their parents to provide food, warmth, and a secure place to sleep.

their health. Additionally, with this knowledge, perhaps a few of your students will become motivated to enter health care fields, in which they will make personal contributions to keeping us all safe from bioterrorism.

Although there are a variety of disease processes that you must consider as part of your science content, two are particularly important in light of recent events: anthrax and smallpox.

Anthrax

Imagine an assassin that can lie in wait for its victims for decades and is too tiny to see with the naked eye. Although it usually causes disease in grazing animals, we have sadly learned that the spore-forming bacterium *Bacillus anthracis* can be successfully targeted at humans, as well.

The disease, called *anthrax,* is purposefully spread by putting spores into the air, which are then inhaled by victims or come into contact with the skin. Although a person can be accidentally infected by eating the undercooked meat of an infected animal or by working with the hide or fur of such an animal, these infections are rare. Using the spores of the bacteria in an act of bioterrorism is a much more serious threat to us all.

Process and Symptoms

Whether an anthrax infection originates on the skin or through the respiratory system, the effect has been known to turn the body's natural immune system against the rest of the body. The toxins in the bacteria cause *macrophages*—natural disease-hunting and -killing cells—to overreact, summoning so many chemical agents that the blood vessels begin to leak and the organs begin to fail. If the person or animal dies, the bacteria consume the remaining nutrients. And when the bacteria run out of nutrients, they turn back into the spore state, in which they are dormant until they infect another animal or person.

The immediate symptoms of anthrax vary, depending on whether the person has inhaled spores or bacteria, ingested them, or had them enter the body through a cut or open area of the skin. Inhaled anthrax begins with symptoms that resemble those of the common cold or flu; these symptoms can lead to breathing problems. Ingested anthrax produces symptoms that include loss of appetite, vomiting, and fever. Eventually, the victim has abdominal pain, vomiting of blood, and severe diarrhea. When spores or bacteria enter the skin, they produce a sore that becomes a blister and then develops a black scab at its center.

All three types of anthrax can result in death.

Transmission and Treatment

There is some good news about anthrax: It can be successfully treated if detected at an early stage of infection. Antibiotics such as penicillin, doxycycline, and fluoroquinolones can all be effective. There is also a vaccine that can work against anthrax, but it isn't widely available.

Fortunately, anthrax is not a contagious disease—in other words, incidental contact between an infected and an uninfected person will not transmit the disease. To become infected, you must have direct contact with the bacterium or spores.

Smallpox

The virus has the scientific name *Orthopoxvirus,* and the most serious disease it causes in humans is *variola major.* In common language, it is *smallpox,* an extremely contagious disease and probably the largest bioterrorist hazard faced by the world today.

The virus itself is one of the smallest living organisms presently known. Given this small size, it can become an aerosol very easily, and once airborne, it can infect virtually everyone in a crowded area. The sneeze or cough of a person infected with smallpox will release millions of virus particles into the air, which will, in turn, infect anyone who inhales them.

Since smallpox is a virus, not a bacterium, antibiotics will not kill it. A vaccine against the virus does exist, but its use was discontinued in the 1970s. Large-scale vaccinations were discontinued because the risk of getting seriously ill from the vaccine had become much higher than actually getting the disease, which had pretty much been wiped out. This means that today, there are enormous numbers of children and adults who have not been inoculated against smallpox. Thus, an outbreak of smallpox—resulting from either bioterrorism or natural causes—would devastate any population.

Process and Symptoms

The symptoms of smallpox include fever, headache, and a rash that starts on the face, arms, and mucous membranes of the mouth and throat and eventually spreads to the trunk of the body and the legs. The rash eventually becomes raised, infected bumps on the skin. The patient will likely die as a result of respiratory problems. The mortality rate may be as high as 30%. If the patient survives, he or she will be left with considerable scarring.

Transmission and Treatment

Smallpox is transmitted from person to person in a number of ways. As noted earlier, simply inhaling the air exhaled by an infected person is the most common means of transmission. Contact with secretions from the bumps of a smallpox rash can also result in transfer of the virus from one person to another and eventual inhalation of the virus. Even contact with the bedding or other materials that have been touched by the infected person can cause infection in others.

Because smallpox is so highly contagious, patients must be quarantined (or separated from others) for at least three weeks. The same is true for any unprotected person who has come in contact with a patient. In addition, bedding and other materials must be destroyed or sterilized.

Clearly, the best course of action is prior vaccination. Health care workers, first-responders to smallpox outbreaks, police, teachers, and others in direct contact with children will all be vaccinated over time. Additionally, the smallpox vaccine may once again become widely used for infants and children.

In short, the only effective long-term choice in addressing the threat of smallpox is to vaccinate entire populations. Early efforts to do so have been met with some resistance, however, as legitimate concerns have been raised over the possible side-effects that may occur during such a massive vaccination program. These concerns will have to be weighed against the threat of bioterrorism before a vaccination program will be started again.

Summary Outline

I. Living things can be distinguished from nonliving things on the basis of characteristics known as functions of life.
   A. The life functions are respiration; food production, acquisition, and use; secretion and excretion; transport; ability to move; irritability; growth; and reproduction.
   B. *Biology* is the study of living things.
   C. All living things are made up of one or more cells. Plants have cellulose in their cell walls; animals do not.

II. Living things can be classified into groups based on their common characteristics.
   A. The major groupings are the five kingdoms: Monera, Protista, Fungi, Plantae, and Animalia.
   B. Living things can be further classified into the following categories: phylum, class, order, family, genus, and species.

III. The plant kingdom can be divided into several phyla and subdivided into several classes.
   A. Flowering plants, or Angiosperms, are the most advanced form of plant life on the earth.
   B. Plants can reproduce through sexual or asexual reproduction

IV. The animal kingdom includes the invertebrates and vertebrates.
   A. Invertebrates are animals with backbones, including hydra, jellyfishes, corals, worms, mollusks, and jointed-leg animals.
   B. Vertebrates are animals with backbones, including fish, frogs, birds, and mammals.

V. Bioterrorism is the use of biological agents to achieve a terroristic cause.
   A. Anthrax is an infectious disease that humans get most commonly through inhalation or direct skin contact with the spore-forming bacterium *Bacillus anthracis.*
   B. Smallpox is a highly contagious disease resulting from contact with the virus *Orthropoxvirus,* one of the smallest living organisms presently known.

5B Living Things

Attention Getters, Discovery Activities, and Demonstrations

ATTENTION GETTERS

Is It a Plant or an Animal?

Materials for Each   Scissors   3 mailing envelopes
Child or Group   10 colorful magazine pages that show plants and animals

Motivating   ▪ Do you see any living things in the pictures?
Questions   ▪ What is the same (different) about all the plants (animals)?

Directions   1. Distribute the materials, and ask the children to cut out all of the pictures they
                 find of living things.
             2. Write the words *animals* and *plants* on the board, pronounce them, and have the
                children write each word on one of the envelopes. Tell the children that there
                is another type of living thing called a *protist*. Make a protist envelope, and then
                explain that most protists are too small to see.
             3. Have the children sort their pictures into the plant and animal envelopes.

Science Content   There are many different ways to group living things. A common classification
for the Teacher   system uses three categories: plants, animals, and protists. Plants have cell walls
                 that have cellulose and make food through photosynthesis. Animal cells do not have
                 cell walls. Their cells are bounded by cell membranes. Animals take food into their
                 bodies. Bacteria, viruses, protozoa, and slime molds are classified as protists.

How Does Color Help Animals?

Materials for Each   Sheet of green construction paper   Scissors
Child or Group   Sheet of brown construction paper   Paper leaf pattern

Motivating   ▪ What kinds of animals eat insects?
Questions   ▪ What are some ways that insects can escape from other animals?

Directions   1. Distribute the materials, and have the children use the leaf pattern to draw and
                 then cut out one brown leaf and one green leaf. Have them cut out a few small
                 green and brown squares that are about 2.5 centimeters (1 inch) on edge.
             2. Tell the children that they should pretend the squares are insects. Have them
                place the green insects on the brown leaf and the brown insects on the green leaf.
             3. Ask them how hard they think it would be to find the insects if they were birds.
             4. Have the children put the green insects on the green leaf, and ask the question again.

Science Content   Many animals have protective coloration that increases their chances of escaping pred-
for the Teacher   ators. Insects that have the same color as their background stay still when predators
                 are near and blend into their background, which increases their chances of survival.

Are You a Good Animal Detective?

Materials	Sheet of easel paper

Marking pen

Motivating Questions
- What animals do you think we will see outside?
- How many animals do you think we will see?

Directions
1. Take the children on a 10-minute nature walk around the school grounds to identify the animals that live around the school.
2. On your return to the classroom, prepare a three-column chart and list the children's recollections of the types and quantities of animals seen. Also note where the animals were seen—for example, under a rock.

Science Content for the Teacher Life is both diverse and widespread. Any lawn, playground, or natural area on or near the school will have an abundance of animals. Depending on your locale and the season, expect to see squirrels, birds, cats, and dogs. Search for insects and other small creatures under rocks and near moist areas such as the ground near a water fountain or a mud puddle as well as on the bark of trees.

How Are Seeds the Same and Different?

Materials for Each Child or Group One common fruit per group. (*Note:* Try to have a variety of fruits available, including oranges, apples, pears, grapefruit, peaches, and plums.)
Lightweight plastic serrated knives (if you are working with older children)
Paper towels
Drawing paper
Hand lens

Motivating Questions
- Do you think your fruit has a seed?
- Do you think your fruit has more than one seed?
- What do you think the seed or seeds in your fruit will look like?
- Do you think different fruits will have seeds that are the same or different?

Directions
1. Distribute the materials, and give each group one or more fruits. Before they cut open their fruits, have the groups predict the number, shape, size, and color of the seed or seeds and then draw what they think their seed or seeds will look like.
2. Have the groups cut open the fruits and examine the seeds. *Safety Note:* Cut open the fruit for younger children after the groups have completed their drawings.
3. Have the groups compare the seeds, and then discuss the variety in the number and types of seeds in fruits.

Science Content for the Teacher Although there is great variety in the seeds of common fruits, fruits of the same type have the same type of seeds. An interesting addition to your discussion would be a consideration of the great size and variation in seeds, with the coconut as one of the largest seeds in the natural world. You may wish to point out to the children that many types of seeds are important to humans. Examples include corn, oats, and wheat.

Can You Grow a Sweet Potato Plant Indoors?

Materials	1 small sweet potato 6 toothpicks
	1 glass that is wider than the potato's diameter Water

Motivating Questions
- Do you think the sweet potato is a root or a stem?
- Where does a new potato plant get food?

Directions
1. Distribute the materials and have the children wash the sweet potatoes to remove any excess dirt.
2. Have each group of children stick the toothpicks into the potato so it can be suspended in the glass with the narrow end submerged in the water. (About one-fourth should be in the water.)
3. After each group has prepared its potato, put the potatoes in a warm, well-lit area of the room. Children will need to add water periodically to replace that used by the growing potato plant and lost through evaporation.

Science Content for the Teacher Unlike the white potato, which is a tuber, or underground stem, the sweet potato is a root. The rapid root and leaf growth that will occur is partially due to the availability of starch in the fleshy material within the potato root.

Do Insects Have the Same Kinds of Body Parts?

Materials 1 collection of common insects with different insects in different jars with net tops (grasshoppers, crickets, butterflies, flies, ants)
Hand lens
Drawing paper

Motivating Questions
- Are all these animals insects?
- How are these animals alike? How are they different?

Directions
1. Have the groups observe the insect or insects in each jar. Provide a hand lens for those who want to make closer observations. Encourage the children to make a drawing of each insect.
2. After each group has made observations and drawings, begin a discussion of how the insects are the same and different.

| Science Content for the Teacher | Although insects vary greatly in size, color, and the detailed shapes of their body parts, all insects have three main body parts: head, thorax, and abdomen. Unlike spiders and other arachnids that have eight legs, insects are six-legged creatures. Insects have two antennae and wings. They are invertebrates with exoskeletons, relatively hard exterior body coverings that protect the softer interior parts. |

For Middle-Level Learners [HNS 2 and 3]

The Mystery of the 17-Year Locust

| Materials | Access to the Internet
Science resource books and encyclopedias
Posterpaper and markers
Drawing or picture of an adult cicada (misnamed the *17-year locust*) |

| Motivating Questions | ■ What does this picture remind you of?
■ How old do you think this creature is?
■ What hypotheses can you make about its life cycle? |

| Directions | 1. Have the groups do research to learn about the life cycle of the cicada, also known as the *17-year locust*. They should find out where and when it lays its eggs, where the nymph stage of the insect lives, when the nymph becomes an adult, and the effects the adult insect has on its surroundings when it lays its eggs.
2. Have the children make drawings of the cicada at the various stages of its life cycle.
3. Bring the groups back together to discuss what they have learned. In particular, why is the cicada sometimes called the *17-year locust?* |

| Science Content for the Teacher | The species of cicada that has a 17-year life cycle is commonly known as the *17-year locust*. It is a member of the grasshopper family and is not a locust. Its life cycle includes three stages: The adult female lays eggs in slits cut in young twigs, and then larvae develop. The larvae drop from the trees, burrow into the ground, and suck on juices from roots. After 13 or 17 years, depending on the species, nymphs emerge from the ground and become winged adults, which live for about a week. |

DISCOVERY ACTIVITIES

For Young Learners [S&T 3]

How Is a Kitten Different from a Stone?

| Objective | ■ Children will describe three ways in which a kitten (or other small animal) is different from a stone. |

| Science Processes Emphasized | Observing
Classifying | Communicating
Inferring |

Materials for Each Child or Group	Small animal (or a picture of a small animal)
	Stone
	One picture of a living thing and one picture of a nonliving thing

Motivation   Keep both the kitten and the stone out of sight at the beginning of the activity. Secretly pick up the stone and tell the class that you would like them to guess what is in your hand. After a few guesses, show the stone and tell them that today's activity will teach them how a stone is different from a living thing. Show them the kitten (or picture of a kitten), and begin the lesson.

Directions   1. Ask the children to make observations of both the kitten and the stone.
2. Make a list of their observations on the chalkboard.
3. Begin a discussion of their observations of the stone and the kitten, focusing on the differences between living and nonliving things.
4. Distribute one picture of a living thing and one picture of a nonliving thing to each child or group. Have them study the pictures and think about the differences between the living and nonliving things depicted in them.
5. Have the children summarize what they have learned about the differences between living and nonliving things.

Key Discussion Questions   1. What are some nonliving things you have noticed on your way to school? *Water. Sun. Wind.*
2. What are some living things you have noticed on your way to school? *Children. Plants. Animals.*
3. What are some of the living things in this classroom? *Children. Teachers. Plants.*
4. What are some of the nonliving things in this classroom? *Books. Desks. Pencils.*

Science Content for the Teacher   Living things differ in many ways from nonliving things. The characteristics of living things—the functions of life—include reproduction; food production, acquisition, and/or use; growth from within; internal transport of materials; responsiveness to stimuli; secretion and excretion of waste products; and respiration.

Extensions   *Science:* A field trip in conjunction with this activity will enable children to observe living and nonliving things in the environment and begin to differentiate one type of living thing, plants, from another type of living thing, animals. This would be an excellent time for children to begin thinking about the fact that a specific living thing (such as the kitten) more closely resembles its parents in appearance than it resembles other living things.

Social Studies: Some children may begin to think about the relationships of living things to nonliving things. Shelter and implements are among the uses of nonliving things that you can highlight. You may wish to have children begin to think about and discuss how nonliving things, such as volcanoes, violent weather, and landslides, affect the lives of humans.

What Is a Seed?

Objective	■ The children will be able to describe a seed as something capable of growth.

Science Processes Emphasized

Predicting	Interpreting data
Observing	Contrasting variables
Recording	

Materials for Each Child or Group

Large cardboard box cut 2 to 4 inches tall and lined with plastic
Soil or starting mixture (vermiculite plus soil)
Collections of seeds and other small things ("red-hot" candy, marbles, pebbles)
Chartpaper
1 index card per student

Motivation

Ask the children to bring in seeds and other small items for some science experiments. When the candy comes in, tell them they will begin their study of seeds and discover whether the candy will grow.

Directions

1. Begin by setting out samples of the small things that have been brought in. Ask the students to describe the items while you list their observations on the chartpaper.
2. Have each group record in pictures and in words the appearance of each item at the start of the experiment. In addition, each group can glue an item to an index card and then use the index card to record observations from the activity.
3. Have each group decide how many of each item should be planted and the depth of planting. Explain that the amount of water, light, warmth, and so on should be the same for each item. These things will be easy to control if the samples are planted in the same box.
4. Have each group label each row with the name of the item planted. Then, set aside a short period of time each day for maintenance and data gathering. Encourage the children to keep a daily log of what they see.

Young children enjoy bringing in their own seeds and observing how they grow.

5. Some children may want to peek at the seeds during the experiment. If they do this, they need to think about the number of each item that was planted and how they can make their inspection without disturbing the others. One way to observe germination without disturbing the seeds is to place moist paper toweling in a glass jar and "plant" the item between the toweling and the glass. Such a jar will allow students to see what is going on in the soil in the boxes, but perhaps it can be kept a secret until the students have had the pleasure of digging up a few of their own seeds.

6. When the seeds have been growing for awhile, have the children dig up samples of each type of seed. They can make observations, record them, and compare their new observations with the observations they made at the start of the experiment.

7. After some items have sprouted, it would be useful to divide the original set of items into growers and nongrowers. With this set to examine, students should begin to investigate where the items come from and develop a general definition of a *true seed*.

Key Discussion Questions

1. In what ways are all these items alike? *They are all small.*
2. How many items of each type should be planted? *More than one or two, since some might die before they come up and can be seen.*
3. How deeply should they be planted? *Answers will vary based upon gardening experience, but common sense usually prevails.*
4. What should be done about the amount of water, sunlight, temperature, and so on that the items receive? *They should be kept the same so that all seeds have the same chance of living.*
5. What is the biggest difference among the items at the end of the experiment? *Some grow and some don't.*
6. What did some seeds become? *They grew into new plants.*

Science Content for the Teacher

Seeds come in all sizes, from those as small as the period at the end of a sentence to others as big as a walnut. Shape can also vary dramatically, from round and smooth to pyramidlike. Seeds have protective shells (seed coats) that keep the embryonic plant alive. Stored food will provide the energy for the seedling to reach the soil surface and begin producing food of its own.

In order to survive, some plants produce *great* numbers of seeds, and others produce seeds with structures (such as the hooks on burrs and the "wings" on maple seeds) that enable them to be dispersed. Some seeds even look like insects, which discourages seed-eating birds from consuming them.

Even with this great diversity, seeds differ significantly from all the nonseed items in this activity by being able to *grow* and reproduce their own kind (much to the despair of some candy lovers!).

Extensions

Science: You may wish to cut open some fruits and vegetables and have the children find and describe the seeds. Some students may then wish to produce a poster or bulletin board with as many kinds of seeds as can be collected. The seeds can be grouped by size, shape, or color.

Math: Some students may be interested in collecting seeds to be used as "counters." These students can sort the seeds into sets and arrange them in order from smallest to largest.

Who Goes There?

Objective	■ The children will be able to match pictures of common animals with the animals' footprints.
Science Processes Emphasized	Observing Inferring
Materials for Each Child or Group	Set of pictures of the animals for which you have footprints Set of pictures showing the various environments in which the animals live Set of animal name cards Construction paper headband Paper feathers of various colors
Motivation	Hand out the animal pictures and a headband to each group. Suggest that they pretend they are teams of animal trackers, and explain that each team will be awarded one feather for each animal they successfully track.

Directions

1. Before beginning this activity, you will need a set of unlabeled animal footprints and a set of pictures illustrating environments in which the animals are likely to be found. *Note:* A good source of information on tracks is the ESS unit *Animal Tracks* originally published by McGraw-Hill but now available from Educational Resources Information Center: Clearinghouse for Science, Mathematics, and Environmental Education; Ohio State University, Columbus, Ohio.
2. Hold up pictures of the animal track and its environment. After some discussion, have the children try to think of the animal being described. The group members can discuss the possibilities among themselves before the group suggests an animal. Each group should elect a chief to be their spokesperson.
3. When all the teams are ready, have each chief hold up the picture of the animal his or her group selected. Encourage each chief to tell why his or her group's choice is the correct one.
4. Staple a paper feather to the headband of each chief that is correct. The job of being chief is then rotated to the next person in each group, and the game continues.

Key Discussion Questions

1. Which of the tracks comes from the biggest animal? *Answers will depend on the tracks and the pictures you are using.*
2. Which of the tracks comes from the smallest animal? *Answers will vary.*
3. Which of the tracks comes from an animal with claws that stick out? *Answers will vary.*
4. Which of the tracks belongs to an animal that can climb trees? *Answers will vary.*
5. Hold up the pictures of various environments (e.g., a treetop for squirrels and an open plain with trees in Africa for elephants), and ask which of the animals might be found in them. Ask the students to try to guess which footprint might be found in most environments. (Be sure to have the teams explain why they decided on particular footprints.)

Science Content
for the Teacher

Footprints hold clues about the lives and environments of the animals that made them. Very large footprints often belong to large animals or to animals that travel over soft terrain. For example, the relatively large feet of the snowshoe rabbit support its weight on snow, thus allowing it to travel well on terrain that hinders most other animals. Most animals that live on the open range have evolved smaller feet with hooves that allow them to run fast on fairly smooth, hard land. Some footprints show evidence of claws used for defense as well as climbing. Retractable claws are an obvious benefit to animals that must be able to run quickly and silently before catching their prey.

Extensions

Science: Obtain or reproduce pictures of various tracks showing something happening (e.g., animals walking and then running). Have the teams determine what happened.

Some students may wish to research the topic of fossils, especially fossilized tracks, and what scientists have learned about the animals that made them. Other students may enjoy making answer boards on which others try to match pictures of animals with pictures of their footprints.

Art: Students may want to make pictures from a set of linoleum printing blocks of footprints.

For Middle-Level Learners [LS 5]

Male and Female Guppies: What's the Difference?

Objective

■ The children will observe the physical characteristics of male and female guppies.

Science Processes
Emphasized

Observing
Classifying

Materials for Each
Child or Group

Male and female guppies
2 clean liter- or quart-size jars filled with aquarium water
Dry fish food
Hand lens

Motivation

Ask the children if they know what a guppy is. If possible, have them describe guppies without the benefit of guppies to observe. Now display the guppies you will be using for the activity, and tell the children that they will have a chance to make careful observations of male and female guppies.

Directions

1. Distribute a jar containing aquarium water, a female guppy, and a hand lens to each child or group.
2. Ask each child or group to observe the external characteristics of the guppy and make a drawing of it, labeling the body parts. Encourage them to shade in parts of their drawing to show the guppy's markings.
3. Once the drawings are completed, distribute a jar containing aquarium water and a male guppy. Have the children observe the male guppy and then make a labeled drawing of it.

4. Allow the children to visit with one another to see if their male guppy resembles other male guppies and if their female guppy resembles other female guppies.
5. Circulate around the room and sprinkle a small amount of dry fish food on the surface of each container. Ask the children to observe the feeding behavior of the guppy.

Key Discussion Questions
1. How can you tell the difference between a male and a female guppy? *The female is usually larger, with a gray color and a fan-shaped fin; the male is smaller, with patches of color and a tubelike part at the base of its tail.*
2. How does the location of the guppy's mouth make it easier and safer for the guppy to feed? *It's at the top of its head, which lets it feed on surface food without having to lift its head out of the water; this makes it easier for it to sneak up on food.*

Science Content for the Teacher
Guppies are tropical fish. The male is smaller than the female but has a larger tail. It is also more lightly colored. The female is usually a uniform gray. The female has a fan-shaped anal fin. The male's anal fin is pointed and tubelike.

Extensions
Science: The demonstration on the birth of guppies, described later in this chapter (pages 162–163), is an effective follow-up to this activity.

Art: Some children may wish to create larger drawings of the guppies they have observed. Drawing paper and a supply of pastels will assist them in such a project. Encourage the children to reproduce nature's coloration faithfully by using the appropriate colors and shades of pastels. You may wish to spray fixative on the children's finished drawings to preserve them.

For Middle-Level Learners [LS 6]

Do Mealworms Like or Dislike Light?

Objectives
- The children will set up and carry out an experiment to determine how a mealworm responds to light.
- The children will collect, summarize, and interpret the data they gather.

Science Processes Emphasized
Observing   Interpreting data
Recording data

Materials for Each Child or Group
Live mealworm (available in a petstore)
Small flashlight
20 cm (about 8 in.) circle of paper divided into 8 pie-shaped sections

Motivation
Ask the class how they can find out what people like. The children will suggest that they can ask people or try something and see if people smile, frown, or become angry. Some children may suggest that the number of times a person does something could be used to determine what the person likes. Tell the children that they will be finding out how well mealworms like being in the dark and that since mealworms do not talk, the children will have to do an experiment to find the answer.

Directions
1. Display the mealworms, and discuss some strategies that the children could use to find out what a mealworm likes. Show the circle that has been divided into eight parts, and explain that it is the tool they will use to find out whether a mealworm likes light.
2. Have the children prepare their own circles and divide them into eight parts. They should number the sections from 1 to 8.
3. Place the flashlight about 30 centimeters from section 1 on the circle. Direct the light toward the center of the circle, darken the room, and have the children observe your setup.
4. Have the children place a light source near their section 8 and the mealworm in the center of the circle where all the lines intersect. The children should record the number of the section toward which the mealworm moves. This should be repeated 10 times.
5. Have the children develop charts or graphs to summarize their findings. Finally, have the class suggest a strategy for combining the results from all the groups so that conclusions can be drawn.

Science Content for the Teacher
Mealworms usually avoid lighted areas. They are frequently found in bins of old grain or meal, which provide dark, dry environments. A mealworm that enters a lit area will lose touch with its food supply and possibly fall prey to birds or other predators.

Key Discussion Questions
1. Why should you do this experiment many times before concluding that a mealworm likes or dislikes light? *Mealworms don't always move in the right direction. It takes the mealworm a few tries before it figures things out.*
2. What other things might make a mealworm respond by moving? *They might be afraid of us. They might not like the heat that comes from the light. They see light from other parts of the room.*
3. Why might a mealworm avoid light? *It likes dark. The light may mean danger to the mealworm.*

Extensions
Science: Some children may wish to design and conduct experiments to see how mealworms respond to heat, cold, moisture, dryness, loud sounds, and different kinds of food.

Language Arts: Have the children pretend that they are mealworms and write stories describing their adventures in a land of giants.

For Middle-Level Learners [LS 7]

How Does Light Affect the Growth of Plants?

Objectives
- The children will design and conduct an experiment to test the effect of light on the growth of grass.
- The children will observe and record the color and length of grass grown under two conditions: light and dark.

Science Processes Emphasized
Formulating hypotheses	Experimenting
Interpreting data	

Materials Needed

2 paper cups
1/4 tsp. of grass seed
Potting soil or synthetic plant-growing material
Light source that can be placed about 25 cm (about 10 in.) above the cup
   (a fluorescent grow-light fixture would be best)
Ruler
Graph paper
Easel paper for class data

Motivation

Tell the class that they are going to observe and measure the effect something has on plants. Display the grass seeds and related materials. Ask the children to guess what they will be investigating.

Directions

1. Distribute the materials, and have the children label one cup *light* and one cup *dark*. They should also record the date on each cup. Tell them to fill each cup two-thirds full of soil, scatter a pinch of seeds across the surface, and then lightly cover the seeds with more soil. Tell the children to punch a few holes into the bottom of the cup to allow excess water to drain.
2. Ask each group to predict what will happen if one cup is placed in a dark location and one cup is placed in a light location for three days. Have the groups record their predictions. This would be a good time to have a class discussion about the range of predictions that are made.
3. Have the children add the same amount of water to each cup and then put their cups in the appropriate environments. *They should plan to observe the cups every three days.*
4. When the groups make their observations, they should record the appearance, color, and average length of plants. The determination of length will be challenging because the groups will need to invent a strategy that does not require the measurement of every plant. One strategy might be to measure five plants from different parts of the cup and average the measurements. Another would be to simply record the total height of the sample. The length measurements as well as other observations should be recorded on a data sheet, which should be maintained for about two weeks.

Key Discussion Questions

1. If we want to see if the seeds need light to grow, what must we do to the water and temperature of the plants? *We have to keep the water and temperature the same for both cups.*
2. Why did all the seeds start to grow equally well? *Seeds don't need light to sprout.*
3. Why did the plants in the dark stop growing and turn yellow after awhile? *They ran out of food. They needed light to grow.*

Science Content for the Teacher

Grass seeds contain a small amount of stored food in their cotyledons, which allows them to begin growing. When the food is used up, the plant must rely on sunlight for the energy required for further growth.

Extension

Science/Nutrition: Some students may wish to obtain seeds at a health food store that are appropriate for sprouting (mung beans, alfalfa, lettuce). Once the seeds have sprouted, the class can have a feast while discussing the nutrients found in the sprouts.

DEMONSTRATIONS

The Curious Gerbils

Note: This demonstration is a long-term classroom project that involves proper care of living organisms. You must face many questions if you embark upon it, not the least of which is what you will do with the gerbils that are born in the classroom. You will quickly run out of appropriate living space for these creatures, as they are capable of reproducing at an alarming rate. The children will undoubtedly volunteer to take excess gerbils. However, do not assume that every child who wants a gerbil will be able to provide appropriate care or that his or her family will want to have a new addition to the household. Also be aware that some of the children who may want gerbils may be allergic to them. You should spend time thinking about both the benefits and problems associated with raising animals in the classroom before beginning this project.

Objective
- The children will observe the characteristics of gerbils.
- The children will provide appropriate care for gerbils in the classroom.
- The children will observe the birth of gerbils in the classroom.

Science Processes Emphasized
Observing
Inferring

Materials
Male gerbil   Gerbil food
Female gerbil   Supply of lettuce
Gerbil cage with exercise wheel, water bottle, nesting material
   (cedar shavings, newspaper, cloth, and so on)

Motivation
Keep the presence of the gerbils and the cage supplies secret. Tell the children that they are going to have an opportunity to meet some classroom pets. Do not divulge what kind of animals the pets are. Ask the children if they think they can be responsible for the care of some pets in the classroom. Assuming the answer is yes, proceed with the demonstration.

Directions
1. Display all the materials and the male and female gerbils.
2. Place the nesting material, food, and exercise wheel in the cage and fill the water bottle. Have the children discuss the purpose of each object in the cage.
3. Before placing the male and female gerbils in the cage, allow the children to observe them.
4. Discuss the importance of proper care of the gerbils. Talk about the children's responsibilities and appropriate rules for the gerbils' care.
5. If you are fortunate, within a month or two you may have a litter of gerbils. In this event, have the children observe the changes that occur as the tiny creatures begin to appear more and more like their parents.

Key Discussion Questions	1. Are gerbils mammals? *Yes. They are alive, they drink their mother's milk, and their bodies are covered with hair/fur.*

1. Are gerbils mammals? *Yes. They are alive, they drink their mother's milk, and their bodies are covered with hair/fur.*
2. What do you think gerbils need in order to survive and stay healthy in the classroom? *Answers will vary but may include food, water, nesting material, air, exercise, and some peace and quiet.*
3. Various other questions concerning the children's responsibilities for the continuing care and feeding of the gerbils should be asked. Such questions should focus upon what the responsibilities will be, how they should be carried out, and who will carry them out.

Science Content for the Teacher

Gerbils are small animals that are easy to care for in the classroom. They are covered with hair, give birth, and suckle their young; they are true mammals. Young female gerbils may bear young every six to eight weeks.

Extensions

Science: Students may be interested in learning about the care of puppies, cats, guinea pigs, hamsters, and other animals.

Art: The class may want to make drawings of both the male and female gerbil and any babies. The children can use commercially available crayonlike pastels to reproduce the coloring of the animals.

For Young Learners [S&T 3]

Is It Alive?

Objective
- The children will observe and describe the differences between living and nonliving things.

Science Processes Emphasized

Observing   Inferring
Communicating

Materials

Living animal (fish, insect, mouse)
Living plant
Nonliving thing (shoe, pencil, book)
Wind-up toy that makes sounds (or nonelectric ticking clock with second hand)
Cardboard box with fitted top

Motivation

Prior to class, place the mechanical toy or ticking clock in a box with a fitted top. Do not tell the children what is in the box. Have volunteers come forward to listen to the toy or clock in the box. Tell the children that they are going to discover some things about the object in the box and how to tell the difference between things that are alive and things that are not.

Directions

1. Hold up for observation the animal, the plant, and the shoe, book, or pencil. Display each object one at a time so that the children can focus their observations.
2. On the chalkboard, create a chart on which to record the children's observations. Provide a space at the bottom of the chart to write their guesses about the object in the box and whether or not it is alive.

3. Once all the observations have been recorded, play a game of 20 questions with the children to help them refine their thinking. Suggest that they use their observation when asking questions. *Hint:* Actually peek into the box after each question. A little acting on your part will help maintain interest in the game.

4. Finally, display the object in the box and engage the children in a discussion of the differences between living and nonliving things.

Key Discussion Questions

1. In what ways are living and nonliving things the same? *Answers will vary and may include such observations as living and nonliving things can be the same color or size. They can both be soft or hard.*

2. In what ways are living things and nonliving things different? *Answers will vary and may include the idea that nonliving things stay the same, last a long time, don't change very much; living things like plants have seeds; animals have baby animals.*

Science Content for the Teacher

Living things and nonliving things may share some common characteristics. They both may move; they both may make noise; they may be the same color or weight. However, things that are alive grow, change, or develop from infant to adult and are able to reproduce their own kind.

Extension

Health: Discuss the special responsibilities involved in caring for living things that are different from the responsibilities involved in caring for nonliving things. Some children may want to make drawings or posters that show how to care for pets or other living things.

For Middle-Level Learners [LS 5]

The Birth of Guppies

Note: This demonstration can be used as a follow-up to the discovery activity on male and female guppies described earlier in this chapter (pages 156–157).

Objectives

- The children will observe the construction of an aquarium.
- The children will describe the roles of male and female guppies in the reproductive process.

Science Processes Emphasized

Observing
Inferring

Materials

Fish aquarium	Thermometer
Aged tapwater at room temperature	Small container with 2 male guppies
Aquarium sand and gravel	Small container with 4 female guppies
1 dip net	Light source (a reading lamp can be used)
2 or 3 nursery traps	Dry fish food
Assorted freshwater plants, including *Anarchis,* duckweed, and eelgrass	

Motivation

Ask the children if they have ever seen the birth of guppies. After a discussion of any observations they have made of guppies reproducing, tell them that within the next few weeks they may be able to see guppies being born. Display the aquarium and other materials.

Directions   1. Have the children observe all the materials that you have placed on display.
2. Begin assembling the aquarium by placing a 5-centimeter (2-inch) layer of sand on its floor. Plant eelgrass in the sand. Now add the aged tap water; do it gently so as to avoid stirring up the sand. Float the duckweed and *Anarchis* in the water.
3. Put the thermometer in the water and place the light source nearby. The light source will need to be moved back and forth during the demonstration so as to maintain the water temperature at 25°C (75°F).
4. Place the male and female guppies in the aquarium.
5. Float the nursery traps in the aquarium, and sprinkle some fish food on the water's surface.
6. Maintain the aquarium over a two- or three-week period, and encourage the children to make observations of any changes that occur in the shape of the female guppies. A pregnant female will develop a bulging abdomen. Use the dip net to place each pregnant female in its own nursery trap. This increases the chances that the soon-to-be-born babies will survive, for the traps will protect the new guppies from hungry adult fish.

Key Discussion Questions   1. Why did we plant eelgrass and other aquarium plants in the aquarium? *Answers will vary. They may include: So that some living things in the aquarium would have plants to eat.*
2. What does the male guppy do in the reproductive process? *Places sperm in the female guppy.*
3. What does the female guppy do in the reproductive process? *Produces the eggs that get fertilized; has a place inside her body where the new guppies begin to develop.*

Science Content for the Teacher   For this demonstration, you must know how to assemble and maintain a simple freshwater aquarium. The preceding directions provide some of the basic information. If you wish to increase the likelihood of maintaining a healthy aquarium for more than one or two weeks, it would be worthwhile to talk with a knowledgeable salesperson in a petstore to learn the details of raising and caring for tropical fish in general and guppies in particular. Additional materials—such as water heaters, pumps, and filters—are necessary if you wish to keep the aquarium functioning all through the year. This equipment is commonly available at petshops.

For Middle-Level Learners [LS 7]

The Insect Aquarium

Note: This demonstration should be done in the spring.

Objectives   ▪ The children will observe the construction of a freshwater insect aquarium.
▪ Children will infer the reasons for the placement of various materials in the aquarium.

Science Processes Emphasized   Observing
Inferring

Materials   4 liter wide-mouth jar (about a gallon) or a small plastic or glass aquarium
Source of fresh pond or stream water
Collection of live water plants and insects from a pond or stream
Small twigs from the pond or stream
Pebbles and rocks found at the water's edge
Clean aquarium sand (available from a petshop)
Fine mesh screening to cover the top of the aquarium

Motivation   Tell the children that you have gathered a variety of materials to use to construct a freshwater aquarium. Discuss the difference between freshwater and saltwater. Tell the children that the aquarium you are going to build will not contain fish but may contain other interesting creatures. Their job will be to give you ideas as you construct it.

Directions   1. In the spring prior to the demonstration, gather freshwater and a variety of plants and aquatic insects from a local pond or stream. Keep the specimens fresh and take them to class.
2. In the classroom, fill the bottom of the container with about 5 centimeters (about 2 inches) of sand, and root the water plants in the sand. Place a few large twigs at the side of the jar in a way that roots their ends in the sand, and put some rocks and pebbles on the surface of the sand.
3. Gently add freshwater until the water level is about 12 centimeters (about 5 inches) from the top. Float some twigs on the surface so that any insects emerging from the water have a place to stay. Cover the top with the mesh, and put the aquarium where it can receive sunlight and benefit from air circulation.
4. Encourage the children to make daily observations of the aquarium and to infer the reasons for some of the changes they observe.

Key Discussion Questions   1. Why do you think we are doing this demonstration in the spring? *Answers will vary and may include the idea that insects hatch in the spring.*
2. Why do you think we put the aquarium in the sunlight? *Answers will vary and may include the idea that the plants need sunlight to make food.*

Science Content for the Teacher   Insects you may be able to find in a pond are the nymphs of dragonflies, water boatmen, mosquito larvae, mayflies, and water beetles. Insects are easily found in the shallow water at the edge of a pond or stream.

Extension   *Science/Language Arts:* After about a week of observation, ask the children to write a poem entitled "Changes" that will include at least three observations they have made of the aquarium.

6A

The Human Body

Content

The Body's Systems

In the cold gray light of dawn, a runner moves briskly along the pavement. The row houses look quietly on as her footsteps echo off their walls. Her stride is steady and firm. Her breathing barely reflects the strain of four miles of running. Her gaze is clear and her ears are sensitive to the sounds of the neighborhood awakening. The blood courses through her arteries, bringing oxygen and nourishment to her body's cells and carrying away by-products produced by the cells. The runner's body systems are functioning well when she arrives home. Within minutes, her body has recovered from this morning's ritual run. She feels refreshed and alive.

The well-functioning systems of the runner's body enable her to concentrate on the things that matter in her life. The discipline of her body is matched by the discipline of her mind, which wills her to rise early each day to run. To understand fully how the human body is able to perform, we need to consider its basic systems. *Body systems* are groups of organs that work together to carry out a particular function. For example, the heart, arteries, and veins each perform specific tasks that together enable the blood-stream to transport oxygen, nutrients, and waste products. This system of heart, arteries, and veins is called the *circulatory system.* The other basic body systems are the *digestive, skeletal-muscular, respiratory, nervous, excretory,* and *reproductive systems.* To understand them, you need to know both their structures and their functions.

The Digestive System

Thinking a thought, blinking an eye, and taking a step are not possible without energy. The basic source of this energy is the food we eat. The process of digestion changes food from its original form to a fuel that can release energy when it reacts with oxygen. Digestion also releases and transforms proteins—the materials necessary for building new cells and repairing old ones. The hamburger, french fries, and ear of corn on your plate at a late-summer picnic are the raw materials for the conduct of life itself.

Structure and Function

Digestion is the process through which the body breaks down the molecules that make up the food that has been eaten and prepares them to react with oxygen to produce energy. Digestion begins in your mouth. As you chew food, glands in your mouth secrete *saliva,* a digestive juice that mixes with the food particles. Saliva contains water, mucus, and an enzyme that begins the process of breaking down the food.

As food moves through the digestive system, *enzymes* continue to act on it. Each enzyme breaks down a particular material found in food. The seeds of certain fruits, the cellulose in vegetables, and some meat tissues are indigestible. Such material passes into the large intestine and is eventually excreted.

FIGURE 6A.1
This food guide pyramid illustrates
the recommended daily requirements
for a well-balanced diet.

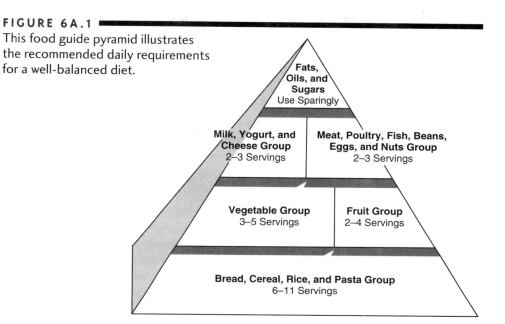

Food and Nutrition

All food contains *nutrients,* specific substances that provide the energy and materials the body requires to function properly. The nutrients in the food we eat are used in one of two basic ways by the body. Some are converted into energy and used immediately. Others are used to build new cells. Six specific nutrients are necessary for health and growth: carbohydrates (starches and sugars), fats, proteins, minerals, vitamins, and water. The foods we eat contain different amounts of these nutrients.

The United States Department of Agriculture recommends that we all eat more grains, fruits, and vegetables and less meat, fat, and sweets. To convey this view of appropriate nutrition, the Department of Agriculture has created a food guide pyramid that can help you make wise decisions about what you eat (see Figure 6A.1).

The Skeletal-Muscular System

Bones: Structure and Function

Your bones and muscles work together to give your body its form and structure. The bones provide support, protection for vital organs, a place in which red blood cells and some white blood cells are produced, a storage area for minerals, and surfaces to which muscles are attached. Although many people think that bones are hard, dry objects within the body, they are really alive.

Bone tissue is composed of living bone cells, which require food and oxygen, just as other body cells do, the products of bone-cell respiration, and deposits of minerals. Most bones in the human body originate from softer bonelike structures, or *cartilage*. As you age, the cartilage present in your body when you were very young becomes strong bone. This process continues until you are 20 to 25 years old.

A *joint* is a place where two bones meet. There are five types of joints in the human body: immovable, hinge, ball-and-socket, pivot, and gliding. Each provides flexibility of movement. In some joints—such as the one that connects the upper arm to the shoulder—bands of strong connective tissue, called *ligaments,* hold the bones of the joint together.

Muscles: Structure and Function

The muscles in your body provide you with the ability to move. This results from the ability of muscle cells to contract. There are three types of muscles in your body: smooth muscle, cardiac muscle, and skeletal muscle. *Smooth muscles* are those that act involuntarily. For example, the muscles that line the stomach and intestinal walls and the arteries are all involuntary muscles. This means they are able to operate quickly and without the direct control of the brain.

The involuntary muscle found in your heart is called *cardiac muscle.* When the fibers in this muscle contract, the chambers of the heart are squeezed and blood is forced out through blood vessels. If the cardiac muscle was not involuntary, your brain would have to tell your heart to beat each time blood needed to be pumped through your circulatory system.

Skeletal muscles are voluntary muscles. They work because the brain tells them to bend or flex or stretch. Skeletal muscles attach directly either to bones or to other muscles. *Tendons* are bands of connective tissue that attach the ends of some skeletal muscles to bones. When a skeletal muscle such as one in your upper arm contracts as a result of a message your brain gives it, it pulls on the muscles of your lower arm. The movement of the lower arm results from the contraction of the voluntary skeletal muscle.

The Respiratory System

The food you eat supplies your body with energy through a series of chemical reactions that take place in the body's cells and require oxygen. Without oxygen, the food molecules could not be broken down and energy would not be released. While some of this energy is released as heat, much of it is stored in chemical form. Carbon dioxide and water are given off during this energy-producing process. The stored energy is used by body cells, tissues, organs, nerves, and other body organs. This simple equation shows the process by which energy is produced in your body cells:

food + oxygen → carbon dioxide + water + energy

The Diaphragm, Windpipe, and Lungs: Structure and Function

The oxygen your body needs to produce energy from food is contained in the air you breathe. Air is about 21% oxygen and about 78% nitrogen. When you inhale, both oxygen and nitrogen enter your lungs. The nitrogen, however, is not used by the body. The in-and-out action of your lungs is controlled by the *diaphragm,* a large curved muscle that lies underneath them. As the diaphragm contracts, it moves downward. At the same time, the rib muscles separate the ribs and move them forward. These actions increase the amount of space in your chest and allow the lungs to expand.

After the air space in your chest has been enlarged, outside air pressure forces air through your nose and throat, down your windpipe, and into your lungs. After you have inhaled air, the action of your diaphragm and rib muscles increases the pressure within your chest and pushes air out through your windpipe, throat, and nose. This occurs each time you exhale.

The *windpipe* is a tube that stretches from your throat to your lungs. At your lungs it divides into two branches. Each of these branches subdivides into smaller and smaller branches within the lungs. These small branches end in tiny air sacs, each of which is surrounded by tiny blood vessels called *capillaries.* The air sacs have very thin walls, which permit the oxygen to pass through them and into the capillaries.

Oxygen Transport

Once oxygen has entered the air sacs of the lungs and diffused into the capillaries, it is picked up by red blood cells and carried to all parts of the body, where it reacts chemically with food to produce energy, carbon dioxide, and water. Carbon dioxide produced in the cells enters the bloodstream and is carried back to the air sacs in the lungs. There it leaves the bloodstream, enters the lungs, and is exhaled. The paper-thin walls of the air sacs are continually allowing oxygen to pass from the lungs to the bloodstream and carbon dioxide to pass from the bloodstream to the lungs.

The Nervous System

A chirping bird catches your attention during a quiet morning walk along a wooded path. You stop and turn your head in an attempt to locate the source of this early morning joy. Your ears help focus your attention on the uppermost branch of a nearby tree. The song seems to come from somewhere behind a clump of leaves and twigs attached to the branch. Suddenly, your eyes pick out a slight movement and come to rest on a brownish head that pokes its way over the nest top and looks directly at you.

Your sight and hearing are precious gifts that, along with your other senses, gather information about the surrounding world. These sense organs are the farthest outposts of your nervous system. It is your nervous system that permits you to see, hear, touch, smell, taste, and, of course, become aware of and enjoy the existence of chirping birds on quiet morning walks through the woods.

Nerves: Structure and Function

The nervous system consists of the brain, the spinal cord, and many nerve cells. A *nerve cell* has three parts: a cell body, short, branchlike fibers that receive impulses from the brain, and long thin fibers that carry impulses away from the cell body. Bundles of either short or long fibers are known as *nerves*. Nerves carry messages from the brain to other parts of the body and from other parts of the body to the brain. Messages are carried by nerve impulses, chemical changes that cause electrical charges to be transmitted through the nervous system.

Twelve pairs of nerves directly connect the brain to the eyes, ears, nose, and tongue. These nerves are called *cranial nerves*. Branches of some of these nerves leave the head and connect with the variety of muscles and other internal organs in other parts of your body.

The principal way in which messages are sent from the brain to the body is through the *spinal cord,* a column of nerves that extends from the base of the brain down through the backbone. Thirty-one pairs of nerves directly connect the spinal cord with such organs as the lungs, intestines, stomach, and kidneys. These organs usually function without voluntary control. Thus, the nerves that control these functions make up what is known as the *autonomic nervous system.* Actions over which the individual has some control or awareness of are controlled by the *somatic nervous system.*

A *reflex* is another type of automatic action controlled by the nervous system. A reflex, the simplest way in which your nervous system operates, occurs when some part of the body is stimulated. The knee-jerk reaction is a good example of a reflex. If a person taps your kneecap with an object, your lower leg swings upward. The tapping of the kneecap stimulates a nerve cell in your lower leg. The nerve impulse travels along nerves to the spinal cord. When the impulse reaches the spinal cord, a message is immediately sent to the leg muscle, which causes the jerking movement. In this and many other reflex reactions, the response is not controlled by the brain. Reflex reactions are completed well before the brain is aware of their occurrence. Other reflexes are coughing, blinking, and laughing when you're tickled.

The Senses

The sense organs, the farthest outposts of the human nervous system, contain specialized nerve cells that receive stimulation from the outside world and carry messages to the brain. Nerve cells that are capable of receiving information from the external environment are called *receptors.* Each of your sense organs has special receptors.

The Skin Sensors

Your skin is able to sense a variety of stimuli, including touch, pressure, pain, heat, and cold. Whenever a receptor is stimulated, an impulse, or nerve message, begins traveling along the nerve to which the receptor is connected and eventually arrives at the central nervous system. Receptors for the various skin senses are distributed at different locations and different depths in the skin. The touch receptors are close to the surface of the skin. Your fingertips contain many touch receptors. Pressure receptors are deeper in the skin.

Taste

Your ability to taste results from specialized nerve receptors on your tongue. The areas containing these receptors are called *taste buds*. There are specialized taste buds for each of the following flavors: sour, sweet, salt, and bitter. What you interpret as taste is actually a combination of taste and smell, for when you chew food, vapors from it reach your nose. Thus, you simultaneously taste and smell the food you're eating. You may have noticed that when you have a cold, food does not taste as good as usual. This is due to the fact that you cannot smell it as you eat it.

Smell

The principal nerve that carries information about smell to the brain is the *olfactory nerve*. Branches of this nerve are contained in a cavity in your nasal passage. Vapor from the food you eat enters your nasal cavity, is dissolved in a liquid, and stimulates the endings of the olfactory nerve.

Hearing

The ear is the principal organ through which sound waves enter the body. Sound waves enter the opening in your external ear and travel through a tube called the *auditory canal*. This canal ends at a membrane called the *eardrum*. The sound waves stimulate the eardrum, causing it to vibrate. On the other side of the eardrum a group of tiny bones—the hammer, the anvil, and the stirrup—transmit vibrations from the eardrum to the cochlea and the semicircular canals, located in the inner ear. These organs relay the vibrations to the sensitive receptors at the end of the auditory nerve, which carries them to the brain.

Sight

Your eyes receive information in the form of light from the external world (see Figure 6A.2, page 172). Light passes through a transparent covering called the *cornea* and enters the *pupil*, a small opening at the front of the eyeball. The size of the pupil is controlled by the opening and closing of the *iris,* the colored portion of the eyeball. Directly behind the pupil is the *lens,* which focuses your sight. Focusing is achieved by a muscular contraction that changes the shape of the lens. Between the lens and the cornea is a watery liquid known as the *aqueous humor*. Within the eyeball is a thicker, transparent substance called the *vitreous humor.* The structures at the front of the eyeball all serve to focus light on the *retina,* the rear portion of the eyeball containing light receptors. These receptors are of two types: cones and rods. The cones are responsible for color vision; the rods produce a material that helps you see in dim light. Focused light rays, or images, that reach the retina stimulate the receptors, which in turn transmit information about them to the brain via the optic nerve. In interpreting these messages, the brain gives us the sense we call sight.

FIGURE 6A.2
The human eye receives
information from the
external environment.

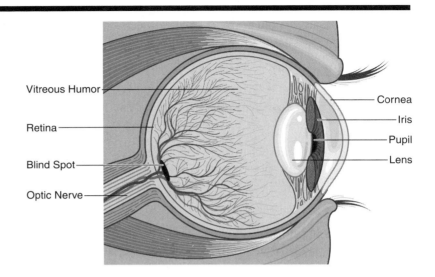

FIGURE 6A.2
The human eye receives
information from the
external environment.

Vitreous Humor

Retina

Blind Spot

Optic Nerve

Cornea

Iris

Pupil

Lens

The Excretory System

The process by which your body rids itself of wastes is called *excretion*. Virtually all forms of energy production create waste by-products. The human body produces both energy and an abundance of gaseous, liquid, and solid wastes. These wastes result from the production of energy and the process through which complex food materials are changed to simpler, more usable ones. If, for some reason, wastes cannot leave the body, sickness and death are certain to follow. The human body is able to rid itself of wastes by means of a very efficient group of organs.

The Kidneys: Structure and Function

Wastes from your body's cells enter the bloodstream and are carried to specific excretory organs. The major excretory organs are the kidneys and the skin. The kidneys lie on each side of the spine in the lower back. Each kidney is protected by a layer of fat. Waste-containing blood enters the kidneys and is divided into smaller and smaller amounts as the arteries transporting it branch into capillaries. From the capillaries, the blood flows through filters that separate the wastes from the blood and combine them into urine. *Urine* is a liquid that contains, in addition to the body's waste by-products, water and excess mineral salts that have also been filtered from the blood by the kidneys. Tubes called *urethras* carry the urine from the kidneys to the *urinary bladder*. This muscular organ then expels the urine from the body through the *urethra*. Meanwhile, the cleansed blood exits the kidneys through the renal veins.

The Skin and Lungs: Function

You may be surprised to learn that your skin is an important excretory organ. Its principal role is the removal of excess heat. When the body becomes too warm, blood vessels in the skin open wide, increasing the flow of blood to the capillaries, which allows heat to be given off to the air. Through pores in the skin exit water, salts, and small amounts of *urea,* a waste found principally in the urine. The liquid that contains these body wastes is *perspiration.* As perspiration evaporates, it helps cool the body. The lungs are considered part of the excretory system because they rid the body of carbon dioxide and excess water in the form of water vapor.

The Liver and Intestines: Function

Although the liver is principally a digestive organ, it is also able to form urea and secrete it into the bloodstream. Bacteria, some drugs, and hormones are removed from the blood in the liver and converted into less harmful substances. These substances are returned to the blood and eventually excreted from the body by the kidneys.

The large intestine performs an important excretory function by removing from the body food that has not been digested by the small intestine. Solid waste that moves through the large intestine is composed largely of undigested food and bacteria. It is eliminated from the body through the *anus*—the end of the digestive tract. The *rectum* is that portion of the large intestine that lies directly above the anus.

The Circulatory System

A complex system consisting of a pump and conducting vessels keeps you alive. This system, known as the circulatory system, operates efficiently whether you are sitting, standing, walking, running, or sleeping. The circulatory system is an extraordinarily complex system but so efficient and automatic that you are able to carry out the activities of living without even an awareness of its existence.

The Heart and Blood Vessels: Structure and Function

The heart is the powerful pump that moves blood through your body's blood vessels. It has four chambers: a right atrium, a left atrium, a right ventricle, and a left ventricle. Blood enters this marvelous pump through the *atria* (the upper chambers) and is pumped out of the heart by the *ventricles* (the lower chambers). Between the atria and the ventricles are *valves* that prevent the blood from flowing backward. Once blood passes from the atria to the ventricles, it is impossible for it to return through these controlling valves. The opening and closing of the heart valves produce the sound that a physician hears when he or she uses a stethoscope to listen to your heart. The "lub-dub, lub-dub" is simply the opening and shutting of the valves. If the heart valves are damaged and blood is able to leak backward from the ventricles to the atria, a health problem results. Physicians can usually detect this problem by listening through their stethoscope for the sound produced by blood moving in the wrong direction. This sound is called a *heart murmur.*

The vessels that carry blood from the ventricles to various parts of the body are called *arteries.* The vessels that return blood to the heart are called *veins.* Within the body tissues the major arteries branch into smaller and smaller arteries and small veins merge to form large veins. A series of microscopic *capillaries* connect small arteries and veins and permit the exchange of dissolved nutrients, oxygen, wastes, and other substances.

The right side of the heart receives blood from the body cells and pumps it to the lungs. This blood contains the carbon dioxide produced by the cells as they converted nutrients to energy. In the lungs, the carbon dioxide is removed from the blood, and oxygen from inhaled air is added. The oxygen-rich blood is then carried to the left side of the heart, which pumps it to the remaining organs of your body (see Figure 6A.3). To understand the circulatory system, you must remember that the heart seems to act like two pumps. On the right side, blood that contains carbon dioxide is pumped to the lungs. On the left side, blood that is rich in oxygen, as a result of having passed through the lungs, is pumped to all parts of the body.

Blood

Human blood is made of a variety of materials. One such material is *plasma,* which is 90% water and 10% various dissolved substances. Among the most important of these substances are *antibodies,* which help your body fight diseases.

Red blood cells are another component of blood. They contain *hemoglobin,* the iron-rich substance that receives oxygen from the lungs and carries it to the tissue cells.

Another type of cell found in the bloodstream is the *white blood cell.* White blood cells do not contain hemoglobin. Rather, they are your body's first line of defense against infection. If you have an infection, the number of white cells in your blood increases very rapidly. White blood cells are able to surround disease-causing bacteria and kill them.

Fibrinogen, which makes possible the process of clotting, is found in plasma. If you cut yourself, substances called *platelets* release a chemical that causes fibrinogen to turn into needlelike fibers that trap blood cells and form a clot. It is this clotting process that allows the bloodstream to repair itself in the event of a cut. It simply restricts the flow of blood to an open cut or puncture.

As blood passes through the body, it picks up many things. In the capillaries of the small intestine, it absorbs dissolved food, which it then carries to the liver, an organ that is able to store sugar. Other nutrients in the blood are carried to the various body cells, where, in combination with oxygen, they are converted to energy. This energy production results in carbon dioxide, water, and other waste by-products. These wastes leave the cells and are carried by the bloodstream to organs that are able to rid the body of them.

FIGURE 6A.3   The human heart consists of two pumps lying side by side to form a single organ. The right side of the heart sends oxygen-poor blood to the lungs; the left side of the heart sends oxygen-rich blood to the rest of the body.

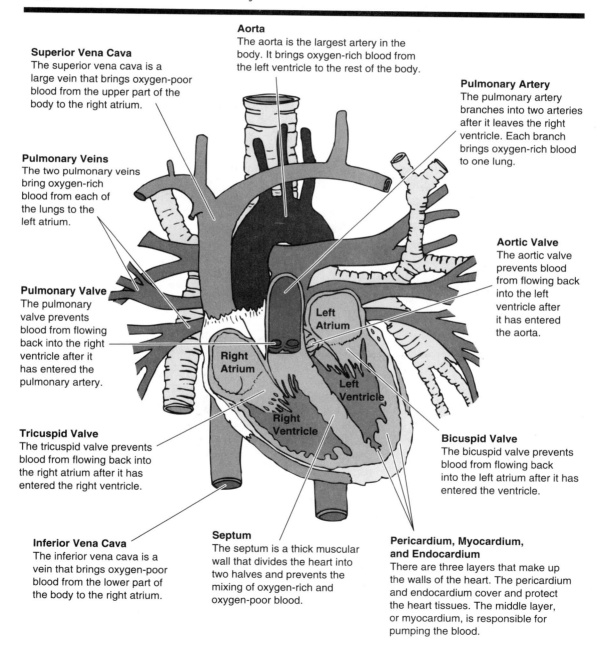

Superior Vena Cava
The superior vena cava is a large vein that brings oxygen-poor blood from the upper part of the body to the right atrium.

Aorta
The aorta is the largest artery in the body. It brings oxygen-rich blood from the left ventricle to the rest of the body.

Pulmonary Artery
The pulmonary artery branches into two arteries after it leaves the right ventricle. Each branch brings oxygen-rich blood to one lung.

Pulmonary Veins
The two pulmonary veins bring oxygen-rich blood from each of the lungs to the left atrium.

Aortic Valve
The aortic valve prevents blood from flowing back into the left ventricle after it has entered the aorta.

Pulmonary Valve
The pulmonary valve prevents blood from flowing back into the right ventricle after it has entered the pulmonary artery.

Tricuspid Valve
The tricuspid valve prevents blood from flowing back into the right atrium after it has entered the right ventricle.

Bicuspid Valve
The bicuspid valve prevents blood from flowing back into the left atrium after it has entered the ventricle.

Inferior Vena Cava
The inferior vena cava is a vein that brings oxygen-poor blood from the lower part of the body to the right atrium.

Septum
The septum is a thick muscular wall that divides the heart into two halves and prevents the mixing of oxygen-rich and oxygen-poor blood.

Pericardium, Myocardium, and Endocardium
There are three layers that make up the walls of the heart. The pericardium and endocardium cover and protect the heart tissues. The middle layer, or myocardium, is responsible for pumping the blood.

Aorta

Left Atrium

Right Atrium

Left Ventricle

Right Ventricle

The Reproductive System

The egg or sperm cells within your body are so tiny that they can be seen only with a microscope, yet within each reposes half of a blueprint for a new human being, who may one day contribute one of its own reproductive cells to the process of creating a new person. We are bound backward in time to our parents, grandparents, and all those who have preceded us.

Structure and Function

The male reproductive organs produce *sperm,* or male reproductive cells. The female reproductive organs produce female reproductive cells, or *eggs.* Through sexual inter-course, a sperm cell and an egg cell may unite to form a human embryo. The embryo has the potential for becoming a new human being.

Sperm are produced in an organ called the *testis.* A pair of testes are contained in a pouch called the *scrotum.* Since this scrotum is outside the body wall, the temperature of the testes is somewhat lower than the body temperature. However, the production of healthy sperm cells requires this lower temperature. Within each testis are numerous coiled tubes. The cells that line the walls of these tubes produce sperm. These tubes merge to form a larger tube, the *sperm duct.* The sperm duct carries sperm and fluids produced by other glands (Cowper's gland, the prostate gland, and the seminal vesicles) into the body and then through the external sexual organ, the *penis.* The penis is used to fertilize egg cells in a female (see Figure 6A.4).

FIGURE 6A.4
The human male reproductive system

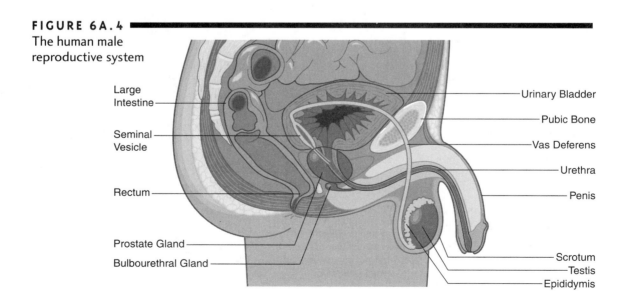

Human egg cells are produced in a pair of *ovaries* in the female body. During a human female's lifetime, about 500 eggs, or *ova,* will mature and be released by the ovaries. Usually one ovum matures and is released at one time. A mature ovum leaves the ovary and passes into a tubelike organ known as an *oviduct,* where it is pushed along by hairlike projections to a large muscle-lined tube called the *uterus.* If the egg is fertilized by a sperm, it will become attached to the uterus wall and develop into an embryo (see Figure 6A.5).

The *vagina* is a tube that connects the uterus with the outside of the body. During intercourse, sperm cells placed here may swim through the uterus and reach the oviducts. If a healthy sperm cell reaches a healthy, mature egg cell, fertilization occurs. The nucleus of the female egg cell and the nucleus of the male sperm unite to form the beginning of a new human being.

Within one week of fertilization, the cell produced by the union of the sperm and egg will divide into about 100 cells. Nine months later, the embryo will consist of more than 200 billion cells, each designed to carry out a particular life function.

The developing embryo gets its food through a membrane called the *placenta.* Nutrients and oxygen in the mother's bloodstream pass from the uterus into the blood vessels of the placenta and from there into the embryo, by way of blood vessels in an umbilical cord. The belly button, or *navel,* marks the place where the umbilical cord entered the developing embryo's body. Wastes produced by the cells of the developing embryo enter the embryo's bloodstream and are eventually carried by the placenta to the mother's bloodstream. However, the blood of the mother and the embryo do not mix.

FIGURE 6A.5 ■
The human female
reproductive system

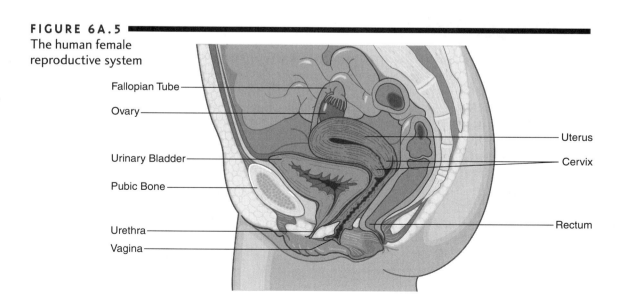

Fallopian Tube

Ovary

Urinary Bladder

Pubic Bone

Urethra

Vagina

Uterus

Cervix

Rectum

When the embryo reaches maturity, birth occurs. At birth, the embryo is forced through the vagina and out of the mother's body as a result of contractions of the uterine wall. The umbilical cord that had connected the embryo with its mother is cut. The baby is born.

Reproduction and Heredity

Heredity is the transmission of the physical traits of the parents to their offspring. Your physical traits result from the transmittal of hereditary information that occurred when a sperm and egg united to produce you. The nucleus of the sperm cell and the nucleus of the egg cell contain material that determines the embryo's physical traits. The part of the nucleus that contains hereditary information is the *gene*. Genes occupy distinct places on ribbonlike structures called *chromosomes*. The nuclei of all human cells contain chromosomes. Although the nuclei of most cells contain 46 chromosomes, the nucleus of a human sperm cell and the nucleus of a human egg cell contain only 23 chromosomes. When a sperm cell and an egg cell unite, the resulting cell has 46 chromosomes. Twenty-three carry genes from the male parent, and 23 carry genes from the female parent. The genes on the chromosomes of the first complete cell and the particular order in which they are located on the chromosome give the offspring its inherited traits.

Identical twins result when an embryo splits in two. The two halves develop into individuals who have the same physical traits. *Fraternal twins* are the result of two ova being fertilized by two sperm. They are simply siblings who happened to be conceived and born at the same time.

Summary Outline

I. The digestive system converts food into energy or cell-building material.

II. The skeletal-muscular system provides the body with its shape and structure and gives it the ability to move.

III. The respiratory system secures the oxygen necessary for the conversion of food to energy and eliminates carbon dioxide.

IV. The nervous system receives stimuli and carries them to the brain; it then transmits the brain's messages to various parts of the body by means of nerve impulses.

V. The excretory system rids the body of gaseous, liquid, and solid wastes.

VI. The circulatory system moves a variety of substances from place to place in the body.

VII. The reproductive system of a male produces sperm cells capable of fertilizing an ovum, the reproductive cell of a female.

6B The Human Body

Attention Getters, Discovery Activities, and Demonstrations

ATTENTION GETTERS

For Young Learners [S&T 1]

How Can We Help People See Us at Night?

Materials   1 sheet of dark construction paper   Transparent tape
1 small mirror   1 flashlight
Silver glitter   Bicycle reflector (optional)
Glue

Motivating
Questions
- Is it hard or easy to see people who are walking or riding bikes at night?
- What should people who are out at night do to keep themselves from being hit by a car?

Directions   1. Darken the room, and ask the children if it would be hard or easy to see a person on a bicycle at night wearing a shirt that is the color of the construction paper. *Note:* This would be an excellent time to have a brief discussion of bicycle safety.
2. Shine the flashlight near the paper, and have the children pretend that the light is an automobile headlight. Ask how visible the person would be if the children were in a car. Tape the mirror to one side of the paper, and repeat the demonstration. Be sure the children notice that mirrors do not help if the light beam does not shine directly on them.
3. Draw a circle on the paper, fill the circle with glue, and sprinkle it with silver glitter. Try to produce some layers of glitter so that not all the glitter is flat on the paper. Your intent is to replicate a bicycle reflector. Have the children compare the extent to which the paper is lit without anything on it, with the mirror on it, and with the glued-on glitter. If you are able to obtain a bicycle reflector, attach that to the paper, as well.

Science Content
for the Teacher   How well we see something depends on how well light is reflected from the object. A bicycle reflector contains many tiny mirrorlike objects that reflect light from many directions so it is easy to see at night.

For Young Learners [SPSP 1]

When Do We Do Things That Keep Us Healthy and Strong?

Materials   1 large clock with hour and minute hands
Easel paper and marker

Motivating
Questions
- What things do you do before, during, and after school that help keep you healthy and strong?
- What things could you do that you are not doing now?

Directions
1. Begin by explaining to the children that they are going to discuss what an imaginary child named Pat might do to stay healthy and strong. Tell them that you are going to make a chart on which you will record their ideas.
2. Set the hands of the clock to 7:00 A.M., review or teach time telling, and have the children give their ideas about what Pat might be doing. For example, 7:00 A.M. might be the time for washing, 7:15 A.M. might be the time that Pat eats a healthy breakfast, 7:30 A.M. might be the time that Pat brushes her or his teeth, and 7:45 A.M. might be the time that Pat puts on a seat belt for the bus ride to school. Carry this through the school day.

Science Content for the Teacher
Children do many things in the course of a day that contribute to their health and well-being. The sequence of activities is relatively constant. By thinking about what more they could do and by trying to fit new ideas into their sequence, they can improve their health.

For Young Learners [LS 3]

How Do Your Ears Help You Learn Things?

Materials
1 small rubber ball
1 sheet of newspaper
1 empty soda bottle
1 empty glass
1 glass of water
Movable room divider or other object to use as a visual screen

Motivating Questions
- Which sounds are easy (hard) to guess?
- Why are some sounds easy to guess and some sounds hard to guess?

Directions
1. Keep all materials behind a screen for the duration of the demonstration. Ask for volunteers to sit in front of the screen facing the class.
2. Use the newspaper, ball, soda bottle, and glass of water to produce various sounds—such as the crumpling of paper, the bounce of a ball, the noise of water poured from glass to glass, or the sound made blowing across the soda bottle—and have the volunteers try to identify them. Discuss what factors make it easy or difficulty to recognize the sources of sounds.

Science Content for the Teacher
The human senses are important because they allow us to take in information about our surroundings. The sense we make of the sounds we hear depends on a variety of factors, including our previous experience, whether the sound is clear or muffled, how loud the sound is, and the sensitivity of our ears.

For Middle-Level Learners [LS 4]

How Does Light Affect Your Eyes?

Note: This Attention Getter can be done as a cooperative group activity, if you have a flashlight and drawing paper for each group.

Materials
1 flashlight
Drawing paper

Motivating
Questions

- Why do people sometimes wear dark glasses?
- Does your vision change when you go from a well-lit room to a dark room?

Directions

1. Distribute the drawing paper to the children. Have the children carefully observe one another's eyes and make drawings that show the iris (the pigmented part of the eye) and the pupil (the entryway of light into the eye).
2. Darken the room somewhat so that the children can observe changes in the pupil, and have them note additional changes when the lights are turned on.
3. Ask for a volunteer to come to the front of the room, and then select two observers. Have the observers look into the volunteer's eyes and tell the rest of the class how large the pupils are.
4. While the observers are studying the volunteer's eyes, briefly shine the flashlight perpendicular to the volunteer's eyes. Have the observers describe any changes they see. *Safety Note:* Do not shine the light into the volunteer's eyes. Light coming from the side will be sufficient to cause the pupils to dilate.

Science Content
for the Teacher

Our capacity to see depends on how much light enters the pupil and reaches the retina. It is difficult to see when too little light enters. Too much light can cause severe damage to the eyes. Muscles in the iris of the eye cause the pupil to become larger or smaller, depending on the availability of light. It is interesting to note that both eyes will react to changes in light intensity even if the changing light conditions occur for one eye.

For Middle-Level Learners [SPSP 6]

What Is in That Cereal?

Materials

2 or 3 large cereal boxes, including at least one heavily sweetened cereal
1 small cereal box for each group
1 transparency made from a cereal nutrition label

Motivating
Questions

- Which of these boxes of cereal do you think has the most calories per serving?
- Which of these boxes of cereal do you think has the most vitamins and minerals?

Directions

1. Project the cereal nutrition label, and review the categories of information on the label.
2. Distribute one cereal box to each group, and ask the groups to interpret the information on the nutrition labels. Be sure they note the number of calories per serving, the suggested serving size, and the percentage of sugars and fats in the cereal as well as the types and amounts of vitamins and minerals.

Science Content
for the Teacher

While cereal can provide some of the carbohydrates the body needs, many cereals have added sugar, which is not good for you. The nutrition information provided on a food label can be very helpful to consumers. As children study the labels, they should note the differences between various cereals and the contributions made by milk to the nutrient values of the cereals.

What Is in Cream?

Materials	1 pt. of pasteurized heavy whipping cream 1 mixing bowl Electric hand mixer or eggbeater

Motivating Questions
- How is cream the same or different from milk?
- What do you predict will happen if we beat cream with a hand mixer?

Directions
1. Ask the children how cream differs from milk. Pour the cream into the bowl, and have children make observations about its consistency and color.
2. Ask for volunteers to take turns using the mixer or eggbeater to churn the cream. Have some children act as observers who describe to the class the changes they observe as the cream is beaten.
3. In time, butter will begin to form and the bowl will contain butter and buttermilk. Ask for volunteers to taste the buttermilk and butter.

Science Content for the Teacher

Cream has a very high fat content. When it is shaken vigorously, the fat begins to form granules. These granules gradually clump together, making butter. Although the color of butter we buy in the store is yellow, in some cases this color is due to the addition of food coloring. The actual color of butter varies greatly and depends on the type of cows that produced the milk and the type of food the cows consumed.

The Mystery of Galen, Harvey, and the Heart

Note: Use this Attention Getter to motivate interest for a unit on human body systems or the circulatory system, in particular.

Materials	Access to the Internet Science resource books and encyclopedias Posterpaper and markers Assorted art materials Assorted fabric pieces

Motivating Questions
- Lightly touch your heart to feel it beating. People sometimes say your heart is like a pump. What do you think they mean by that?
- Do you think arteries and veins are similar?
- Do you think that people's ideas about how the heart works have stayed the same over the years?

Directions
1. Give half of the groups the task of researching the life and theories of Galen and the other half, the life and theories of William Harvey.
2. Once each group has the needed information, they should select and prepare one of the group members to play the role of its scientist: Galen or Harvey. That "scientist" will explain his theories about the heart and circulatory system to the class.
3. Have each "scientist" speak to the class for 3 or 4 minutes, telling about his life and theories.
4. Keep track of questions and comments that class members have, and use them to structure a later discussion on human body systems.

Science Content for the Teacher The Greek physician Galen believed that the right side of the heart squeezed blood into the left side through tiny holes in the "wall" between the chambers. About 1,400 years later, William Harvey proposed a detailed theory about bloodflow, in which he specified the locations and functions of arteries and veins and identified one-way valves in veins. Harvey's theory serves as the basis for much of our present understanding of the circulatory system.

DISCOVERY ACTIVITIES

For Young Learners [S&T 3]

The Mystery Bag

Objectives
- Using their sense of touch, the children will name assorted objects.
- The students will match objects that they see with ones that they feel.

Science Processes Emphasized
Observing
Inferring

Materials for Each Child or Group
Assorted objects, including pencils, erasers, paper clips, rubber bands, wooden blocks, marshmallows, and coins of various sizes
Boxes for the objects
Large paper bags with two holes (large enough for a hand to fit through) cut near the bottom of each bag
2 paper clips to close the tops of the bags

Motivation
Before class begins, place one of the objects in a bag. Explain to the children that they are going to discover how their sense of touch can help them identify things. Begin the activity by placing your hand in one of the holes in the bag to feel the object inside. Describe the object to the children. Have various children come to the front of the room to feel the object in the bag. On the chalkboard or easel pad, record what they think the object is.

Directions
1. Form two-person cooperative learning teams, and give each team a box containing the objects listed for this activity. Have the teams decide who will go first in each team, and have that person close his or her eyes. At the front of the room, hold up the type of object for the other team member to place in the bag.
2. Have the children who have had their eyes closed put one hand through each hole and feel the mystery object.
3. Ask the children to identify the object. If they are unable to name the object, hold up an assortment of objects and have the children vote for the one they think is correct.

Key Discussion Questions
1. What part of the body do we use most to feel things? *The hands.*
2. What are some of the things that the hands can feel? *How hot or cold things are. Whether objects are sharp, smooth, rough, soft, hard, and so on.*
3. What are some things that hands can't tell? *What color an object is, how shiny or bright it is, and so on.*

Science Content for the Teacher

The skin has sense receptors that are sensitive to touch, warmth, cold, pain, and pressure. These sense receptors are not evenly distributed. Pressure is felt most accurately by the tip of the nose, the tongue, and the fingers. Sense receptors in our hands give us our awareness of heat, cold, pain, and pressure.

Extension

Math: You may want to place a set of rods of different lengths in the bags and ask the children to select the biggest rod, the smallest, the second biggest, and so on.

Art: Some children may want to build a "feely board" collage out of materials of various textures, shapes, and sizes.

For Young Learners [LS 1]

Sniff, Snuff, and Sneeze

Objectives

- The students will use their sense of smell to determine the contents of closed paper bags.
- The students will be able to identify various common odors (those of an onion, vinegar, an apple, and an orange).

Science Processes Emphasized

Observing
Inferring

Materials for Each Child or Group

Paper bags (lunch size)	Peppermint oil	Vinegar
25 cm (10 in.) of string for each bag	Wintergreen oil	Onion
Plastic sandwich bags	Camphor oil	Apple
Paper towels	Lemon extract	Orange

Motivation

Place a small amount of one of the odor-producing substances in one of the bags. Tie the bag loosely with string so that odors are able to escape but the students cannot see into it. Invite the students to identify the scent in the bag without looking in it and without using their hands.

Directions

1. Distribute the paper bags and string, and have the children write their names on the bags. Have them select one of the odor-producing foods (apple, orange, or onion), place a small piece of it on a small piece of paper toweling in the bag, and loosely tie the bag.
2. Divide the children into cooperative learning groups, and have the members of the groups try to identify what is in each bag without looking.
3. Have each group select one bag to share with another group. Each group should discuss their observations and reach some agreement about what is in the other group's bag.
4. Place one or two drops of each oil and the vinegar on a small piece of paper towel, and seal it in a plastic bag.
5. Give each group a set of bags. Tell them to smell all of the bags and then identify and classify the scents any way they can.

Key Discussion Questions

1. How can we tell what is in the bag without opening it or touching it? *By smell.*
2. What are some words that can be used to describe odors? *Good, bad, strong, sour, sweet, medicine-smelling, food-smelling.*

3. How does smelling help animals survive? *By helping them track prey. By helping them sense enemies.*

Science Content for the Teacher   When we smell something, we sample the air by inhaling it and having it move over receptors deep in our nasal cavity. These receptors analyze the chemicals in the air sample with great precision and transmit the findings to our brain for analysis and storage. Minute odors can trigger vivid memories.

Extension   *Art:* Some children may want to produce a collage of pictures of good- and bad-smelling things. The children may be able to scent portions of the collage, such as pictures of flowers.

For Young Learners [LS 1]

Using Your Senses to Classify Things

Objective   ■ The children will use their senses of sight and touch to classify seeds.

Science Process Emphasized   Classifying

Materials for Each Child or Group   Paper plate   Hand lens
Small plastic bag containing a variety of dried seeds, including
    sunflower seeds, kidney beans, lima beans, lentils, and so forth

Motivation   Display a bag of seeds, and tell the children that they are going to see how well they can sort through such a bag. Explain to them that they are to sort the seeds into different groups on their paper plates.

Directions   1. Distribute a bag, paper plate, and hand lens to each group, and have the groups classify the seeds by placing them in like piles on a paper plate. *Safety Note:* If you are doing this activity with very young children, caution them not to eat any of the seeds or to put them in their nose, ears, or mouth.
2. After the groups have begun their work, display the hand lenses and ask how they could be used to help classify the seeds.

Key Discussion Questions   1. How did your sense of sight help you group the seeds? *Answers will vary but might include references to color or shape.*
2. If I asked you to group the seeds by how smooth or rough they were, what sense would you use? *Touch.* (After you ask this question, have the groups reclassify their seeds on the basis of smoothness and roughness.)

Science Content for the Teacher   Our senses provide us with detailed information about our surroundings. Even something as simple as calling a person by name requires us to first use our senses to identify the person and then to decide whether we know the person or not. We can identify the person by sight or by the sound of her or his voice.

Extension   *Science/Health:* You may want to bring in a variety of healthy foods and have the children group them according to taste: sweet, salty, sour, or bitter.

How Does Smell Affect Taste?

Objectives
- The children will predict the effect of the smell of a substance on its taste.
- The children will observe how the ability to smell affects taste.
- The children will infer the relationship between the senses of smell and taste.

Science Processes Emphasized

Observing   Inferring

Predicting

Materials for Each Child or Group

Onion slice in a closed container
Apple slice in a closed container
White potato slice in a closed container
5 packs of small hard candies, such as Lifesavers or Charms,
    each of a different flavor
2 glasses of water   2 blindfolds

Motivation

Keep the materials out of sight, and ask the children if they have ever noticed that they sometimes lose some of their ability to taste foods. Some children may note that food lost some of its taste when they had colds. Tell the children that in this activity, they will discover how the smell of a substance affects its taste.

Directions

Note: This activity has two parts. Begin by doing steps 1–5 as a demonstration. Then have the children work in groups to try the experiment using a volunteer from their group.

1. Tell the children that you need a volunteer for a taste test of hard candies. Blindfold the volunteer, and have the class predict how well the volunteer will do.
2. Give the volunteer one of the candies, and have him or her taste it and tell its flavor. Have the class record the accuracy of the result.

By observing how smell affects taste, middle-level learners can infer the relationship between these two senses.

3. Have the volunteer take a drink of water to rinse the taste from his or her mouth, and repeat the taste test with a different flavor of candy. Continue repeating the taste test until all the flavors have been tested. Be sure the volunteer rinses his or her mouth after each test and that the class records the results of each test.
4. Blindfold the volunteer, hold an apple slice under his or her nose, and have him or her take a small bit of the potato slice. Ask the volunteer what kind of food was eaten.
5. Have the volunteer take a sip of water before beginning the second test. Place an onion slice in front of the child's nose, provide an apple slice for him or her to chew on, and ask him or her to identify the food.
6. Now have the class form cooperative learning groups to carry out steps 1–5 with a volunteer from each group.

Key Discussion   1. Were you surprised at any of the things you observed during this activity? Why?
Questions   *Answers will vary.*
                   2. How do you think the way something smells affects its taste? *When we taste some-
                      thing our brain also discovers how it smells. The taste of food depends in part on how it
                      smells.*

Science Content   Substances must be dissolved in liquid before sensory nerves are able to detect their
for the Teacher   presence. The nerve endings in the taste buds are stimulated by the dissolved sub-
                   stances and send information about them to the brain. The nerve that carries infor-
                   mation about smells to the brain branches into receptors that line the nasal cavities.
                   Particles of food that enter the air as gases are dissolved in the liquids on the surface
                   of the nasal cavities and stimulate the smell receptors. A cold or allergic reaction that
                   produces large quantities of mucus in the lining of the nasal cavities limits the ability
                   of the olfactory nerve to receive information.

Extension   *Art:* Have the children discover the relationship between what we see when we look
                   at food and how we think the food is going to taste. Using food colorings, they can
                   prepare cookies, bread, and fried eggs in different colors and investigate why some
                   people may not wish to sample them.

For Middle-Level Learners [SPSP 6]

How Does Rest Affect Tired Muscles?

Objectives   ▪ The children will gather data about the number of exercises they can do within
                     a given period of time.
                   ▪ The children will determine the effect of rest on the amount of exercise they can do.

Science Processes Observing and gathering data
Emphasized   Inferring

Materials for Each Pencil   Chart with 10 columns
Child or Group   Paper   Watch or clock with a second hand

Motivation   Ask the children if they remember that in the lower grades, their parents or teachers
                   tried to make them rest or take naps. Have the children discuss why the adults
                   wanted them to rest. You may wish to point out that young children are very active
                   and tire quickly. Explain that rest gives muscles a chance to regain some strength.
                   Tell the children that in this activity, they will find out how rest affects their muscles.

Directions   1. Divide the class into two-member teams. One member will perform the exercise
                      while the other member records data. Have the member who is going to perform
                      the exercise make a clenched fist with one hand and then extend his or her
                      fingers. Have the other member count how many times this exercise can be
                      completed within 15 seconds. He or she should then enter the number in the
                      first column of the chart.
                   2. Have all teams repeat this procedure four times, with no rest between trials. After
                      the first member has completed five trials, have him or her rest for 10 or 15 min-
                      utes. During this rest period, have the other member of the team do the exercise.

3. After the other member has completed five trials, have the teams repeat the activity but this time with a minute of rest between trials. Have the partners record the data as they did before.

Key Discussion Questions

1. How did resting for a minute between trials affect the results? *When I rested between trials, I was able to do more exercises during the trials.*
2. How can you use what you learned in this activity? *If I want to improve how well my muscles work when I play a sport or a game, I should rest as much as possible during time-outs or between innings.*

Science Content for the Teacher

Skeletal muscles are voluntary muscles. They contract because we tell them to do so. When they contract, they cause various body parts to move. The energy that produces this movement comes from food that is digested in our body. As the cells produce energy, wastes accumulate. When too much waste has accumulated in the muscle cells and tissues, the cells are no longer able to contract normally. If this occurs, we experience muscle fatigue. One way of dealing with muscle fatigue is to allow muscles to rest. This permits the bloodstream to remove excess wastes that have built up in the muscle tissue.

Extension

Math: You may wish to have some students synthesize all the data from this activity and prepare a classroom graph showing the average number of exercises performed during each trial for both the first part of the activity (exercises without rest periods) and the second part of the activity (exercises with intervening rest periods).

For Middle-Level Learners [LS 7]

Are You Part of Any Food Chains?

Objectives

- The children will trace the locations of foods they have eaten in the food chain and discover their own location in the food chain.
- The children will communicate orally or in writing information about the factors that may affect the quantity and quality of the food that reaches them.

Science Processes Emphasized

Inferring
Communicating

Materials

Potato   Magazine picture of a hamburger

Motivation

After a brief discussion of what the children's favorite meals are, ask whether they have ever thought about how the food was produced. Hold up a potato and a picture of a hamburger, and tell the children that they are going to discover how they receive energy from the sun through each of these foods.

Directions

1. Distribute a small potato and a magazine picture to each group. Ask the groups to make food chain charts that relate the foods to them. The chart for the potato, for example, would simply show the potato and a human. The chart for the hamburger would identify grass or grain, beef cattle, and humans.

2. Challenge some of the students to create a food chain that includes a human and a great white shark. When they are done, ask them to look at their food chain to see if they have shown the complete sequence of events that leads from the sun's energy to the energy the shark needs to survive to their own needs for energy.

Key Discussion Questions

1. How would changes in soil, water, air, or amount of sunlight affect the food you eat? *Answers will vary but should note that poor soil, limited water or sunlight, and air pollution can affect plant growth and thus affect animals that eat the plants and people who eat the plants and animals.*
2. If you are a vegetarian, is your food chain longer or shorter than the food chain of a person who is a meat eater? Why? *Shorter because the energy from the sun that is captured through photosynthesis goes directly from the vegetables to the person.*

Science Content for the Teacher

Photosynthesis, the process by which the sun's energy is captured by plants, depends on the quantity and quality of the soil, water, sunlight, and air. Meat eaters as well as vegetarians require access to this captured energy in order to carry out life processes.

Extension

Science / Social Studies: Encourage the children to identify the specific geographic locales where some of their favorite foods are produced. Have them describe and illustrate the various modes of transportation used to move the food products to them.

DEMONSTRATIONS

For Young Learners [SPSP 1]

What Can Change Bones?

Objectives
- The children will observe two changes in bones.
- The children will infer the presence of minerals and water in bones.

Science Processes Emphasized

Observing
Inferring

Materials

4 small chicken bones   Paper label
Jar of white vinegar
Alcohol or propane burner (if one is not available in your school,
    you may be able to borrow one from a high school science teacher)

Motivation

Tell the children that this demonstration will help them understand what bones are made of. Display the bones, vinegar, and burner. Ask the children to guess how these materials could be used to discover some things about bones.

Directions

1. Place two of the bones in the jar of vinegar. Put a label on the jar, and write the date on the label. Tell the children that you are putting the jar aside and will remove the bones from the jar in about a week. Encourage the children to make observations of the contents of the jar each day during the week.

2. Compare the flexibility of the two remaining bones by bending each slightly.
3. Heat one of the bones over the burner. After the bone has been dried by this process, allow it to cool and then try to bend it. If it has been thoroughly dried, it will break in two easily. *Note:* Be sure the room is well ventilated, since heating the bone will produce some strong odors.
4. After a week has passed, retrieve the bones that were placed in the vinegar. Show the children that these bones bend easily.

Key Discussion Questions

1. How did heating affect the bone? *It made the bone break easily.*
2. How were the bones that were placed in vinegar changed? *They could be bent very easily.*

Science Content for the Teacher

Vinegar is a weak acid that is able to react with the calcium in bones. Calcium gives bones the strength to support weight. Bones contain living cells as well as calcium and other minerals. Heating a bone dries out the water contained in the cells. Without water, the bone becomes brittle.

Extension

Art: You may wish to have some of the children research how artists use their knowledge of bone structure in animals and humans in creating paintings and sculptures.

For Young Learners [LS 1]

Your Nose Knows

Objectives

- The children will observe how long it takes for them to notice a substance introduced into the air in the classroom.
- The children will infer how the scent of a substance travels to their noses.

Science Processes Emphasized

Observing
Inferring

Materials

| Perfume | Oil of citronella | Oil of peppermint |
| Ammonia cleaner | 4 saucers | |

Motivation

Pinch your nostrils closed, and ask the children if they have ever done this. Tell them that they are going to discover how much their sense of smell tells them about their world.

Directions

1. Have the children sit around the room at various distances from the table you will use for the demonstration. Open one of the containers, and pour a few drops of one of the substances on a saucer. Tilt the saucer to spread the liquid over its surface.
2. Ask the children to raise their hands when they smell the substance.
3. After you have repeated the process for each substance, ask the children to try to explain how the smell got from the substance on the saucer to their noses. This is an opportunity for you to discuss the idea of particles entering the air from the substance and gradually spreading out, or diffusing.

Key Discussion Questions	1. Would opening a window or turning on a fan help us notice the smell more quickly or less quickly? *Answers will vary. If the movement of air directs molecules of the substance toward the children, they will smell the substances more quickly than they will if the window is closed or there is no fan.*
	2. Do you think dogs have a better sense of smell than humans? *Answers will vary. Some children may have seen television programs or movies showing dogs used to track crime suspects.*
Science Content for the Teacher	Sense organs gather information about our surroundings and send the information to the brain. Our sense of smell, or olfactory sense, results from the stimulation of olfactory cells in the nose by odors in the air. Nerve impulses carry information from the olfactory cells to the brain. What we know as smell is in fact the brain's response to the information it receives.
Extension	*Science/Health:* Engage the children in a discussion of the possible safety advantages provided by the ability to smell odors. Ask: Does your nose help keep you safe? As the children respond, be sure to comment on how the smell of food going bad gives our brains important information.

For Middle-Level Learners [LS 4]

What Is Your Lung Capacity?

Objectives	■ The children will estimate the capacity of the teacher's lungs.
	■ The children will measure the capacity of the teacher's lungs.
Science Processes Emphasized	Observing Using numbers
	Predicting Measuring
Materials	4 liter (1 gallon) glass or translucent plastic jug
	1 liter container of water
	1 m (about 3 feet) of clear plastic tubing (available for purchase in any hobby store)
	Bucket large enough for the jug to be totally immersed
	Source of water
	Reference book that has a diagram of the human lungs and upper torso
Motivation	Tell the children that this demonstration will give them an idea of the amount of air that can be contained by the lungs. Display the drawing of the lungs. Ask the children to estimate how many liters of air the lungs can hold. Have the children write down their predictions.
Directions	1. Involving the children as assistants, fill the bucket to a depth of 10 centimeters (about 4 inches) with water. Fill the jug completely with water.
	2. Cover the mouth of the jug with your hand, invert the jug, and place it in the bucket. When the mouth of the jug is under water in the bucket, carefully remove your hand. The water in the jug will remain in place. Have a child hold the inverted jug in position.

3. Place one end of the tube inside the jug, at least 10 centimeters (about 4 inches) up from its mouth. Leave the other end of the tube free.
4. Take a deep breath and exhale as much of the air in your lungs as possible through the free end of the tube. This air will displace some of the water in the jug.
5. Cover the free end of the tube with your thumb, and have a child cover the inverted end of the jug with his or her hand. Now extract the tube and have the child completely seal the mouth of the jug.
6. Turn the jug upright. The jug will be partly empty. This empty region represents the amount of water displaced by your exhaled air and, therefore, represents your lung capacity.
7. Have the children determine the number of liters of air that were exhaled. To do this, have them pour water into the jug from the liter container.
8. The children can compare the resulting figure with their predictions.

Key Discussion Questions

1. How could we make a jug that would tell us the amount of air that was exhaled? *Fill the jug with liters of water, and make a mark on the out side of the jug to show where the water level is for each liter of water. When the jug is turned upside down and used, measure the amount of air in it by seeing how many liters of water were pushed out.*
2. How did your prediction of lung capacity compare with the lung capacity we measured? *Answers will vary.*
3. What are some things that might shrink a person's lung capacity? *Answers will vary but may include any injury or disease that affects one or both lungs.*

Science Content for the Teacher

Each time you breathe, the diaphragm muscle (located under your lungs) contracts, enabling the rib cage to expand. This expansion allows the lungs to expand to full capacity. As this occurs, air is taken into the lungs. As the diaphragm returns to its normal state, the contents of the lungs are expelled. The capacity of the lungs depends on a variety of factors, including general body size, the condition of the diaphragm and lung tissues, and the health of the respiratory system in general.

Extension

Art: You may wish to encourage some children to make a series of large labeled drawings that show the location and size of the lungs in a variety of animals. These children will need access to reference books in order to carry out this activity.

For Middle-Level Learners [LS 6]

How Fast Is Your Reaction Time?

Objectives
- The children will gather, graph, and interpret reaction time data.
- The children will suggest strategies for decreasing their reaction time.

Science Processes Emphasized
Interpreting data
Controlling variables

Materials
Penny   Meterstick

Motivation   Display the materials, and ask the children to guess how you will use them. Explain that the demonstration will deal with reaction time, and ask them to suggest techniques that you could use to assess reaction time with a penny and with a meterstick.

Directions   1. Ask for several volunteers. Have one volunteer extend his or her hand with the thumb and forefinger separated. Hold a meterstick by one end, and have the other end dangle between the volunteer's thumb and forefinger. Tell the volunteer that you are going to let go of your end of the meterstick, and ask him or her to catch it with his or her thumb and forefinger. The distance that the meterstick drops before it is caught is an indicator of reaction time. Repeat this exercise a number of times, and have the children create and interpret a graph of the data gathered.

2. Hold a penny above the outstretched hand of one of the volunteers. Tell the volunteer to try to move his or her hand away from the penny as it falls. Hold the penny at various distances above the child's hand. When the penny is close to the child's hand, it will be difficult for the child to move his or her hand away before the penny hits.

3. Ask the children what variables might affect reaction time. For example, a penny dropper might inadvertently signal a forthcoming drop with a facial gesture. Encourage them to invent ways to control some of the variables.

Key Discussion Questions   1. Can you think of an invention for a bicycle that might decrease the time between seeing a danger and braking? *Answers will vary. One example would be a radarlike device that would automatically engage the brakes when it sensed an object directly in the rider's path.*

2. What can an automobile driver do or avoid doing to improve his or her reaction time? *Answers will vary. Responses might include never driving while impaired by alcohol or drugs, keeping windshields clean, or playing the automobile radio at moderate volume levels so horns or sirens can be heard.*

Science Content for the Teacher   Reaction time is the time between the receipt of sense information by our brain and the movement of muscles in response to the information. In everyday life, this movement can have important safety consequences. Alcohol is one example of a substance that can increase reaction time.

Extension   *Science/Language Arts:* Have the children create a story about a superhero or -heroine whose principal advantage is the speed of his or her reaction time. Have the children focus on developing a central incident in which this advantage leads to the capture of a villain.

PART THREE

The Physical Sciences and Technology

What makes that arching band of colors appear from nowhere in the distant sky and then, in the blink of an eye, disappear? What are *you* really made of? How can I speak to someone in Hong Kong, half a world away, and not be connected by a telephone wire? How can a cardiac surgeon tell exactly where my elderly uncle has a blocked coronary artery?

The answers to these questions and more come from the most fundamental of the sciences: the physical sciences. In fact, *all* science emerges from our knowledge of matter and energy. These topics are at the center of physics and chemistry.

Careers in the Physical Sciences

A range of career paths are open to those women and men who have the required knowledge, skills, and motivation to explore the nature of matter and energy. Here are a few of the possibilities:

- *Chemist.* The chemist's work, in general, involves assembling atoms to form new molecules or breaking down complex molecules to explore the numbers and types of atoms they contain. The results of this work include improved processed food products, cosmetics, fuels, household products, industrial chemicals, pollution control, weapons systems, and drugs.

- *Physicist.* Through careful experimentation, the physicist tries to find explanations for natural phenomena such as the action of forces on matter, as well as for the behavior of energy in all its diverse forms. *Theoretical physicists* explore phenomena that are impossible to represent on Earth, such as the nature of space and time, the formation of black holes, and the interactions that occur as stars pass through their life cycles.

■ *Engineer.* Engineers apply the knowledge produced by physicists and chemists to the development of products and procedures that solve human problems. The subspecialties of engineering include the development of electronic circuits on chips; the creation of machines to fabricate products; the design of bridges, aircraft, and satellites; and the creation of new drugs to improve our health and well-being.

Key Events in the Development of the Physical Sciences

500 B.C.E.	Sometime during the fifth century B.C.E., Empedocles proposes that everything comes from four *elements:* earth, air, fire, and water.
440 B.C.E.	Democritus observes and reflects upon the matter around him and concludes that it is made of fundamental particles he calls *atoms.*
260 B.C.E.	Archimedes uses mathematics to propose the principle of the lever. He also discovers the principle of buoyancy, which states that the upward force on an object in water is equal to the weight of the volume of water displaced by that object.
1490	Leonardo da Vinci observes and then describes capillary action in detail.
1581	Galileo Galilei observes that the movement of pendulums displays a time-keeping property.
1589	By observing rolling balls on an inclined plane, Galileo Galilei shows that objects of different masses fall with the same acceleration.
1687	Isaac Newton publishes *Principia Mathematica.*
1781	Joseph Priestly creates molecules of water by combining hydrogen and oxygen and igniting them.
1786	Luigi Galvani discovers what he refers to as *animal electricity* and concludes that the bodies of living animals contain electricity.
1808	John Dalton proposes the theory that each element has its own type of atom and that every compound is made of a particular combination of atoms.
1820	Hans Oersted observes that a current in a wire can affect a compass needle.
1852	James Joule and Lord Kelvin show that a gas that expands rapidly cools while it does so.
1873	James Clerk Maxwell concludes that light is an electromagnetic phenomenon.
1862	Dmitri Mendeleyev summarizes his research about the properties of elements by creating a chart known as the *periodic table,* which places elements into groups and rows. The elements of each group have similar properties.
1895	Wilhelm Roentgen discovers X-rays.

1897   Joseph Thomson discovers electrons and calls the particles *corpuscles*.

1897   Marie Curie begins research on so-called uranium rays, which eventually leads to the discovery of radioactivity.

1905   Albert Einstein explains the photoelectric effect.

1905   Albert Einstein states the theory of special relativity as well as the law of mass/energy conservation.

1907   Albert Einstein states that gravitation and inertia are the same and uses this to predict the gravitational red shift of starlight.

1907   Albert Einstein infers from his studies that time is slowed in a gravitational field.

1912   Albert Einstein concludes that the space/time continuum is curved and that gravity is caused by that curvature.

1913   Niels Bohr proposes that when electrons move from a high energy level to a lower energy level around an atom, photons ("packets") of light are released. He also states that the movement of electrons from a low energy level to a higher energy level is the result of photons being absorbed.

1915   Albert Einstein puts forth his complete theory of general relativity and also proves that the excess precession of the planet Mercury is a result of general relativity.

1871–1937   Ernest Rutherford conducts experiments that indicate that particular types of atoms radiate particles and discovers that alpha particles are helium atoms without electrons and beta particles are high-speed electrons.

1932   The first atom is split with a particle accelerator.

1934   Irene Joliot-Curie and Frederick Joliot-Curie bombard aluminum atoms with alpha particles and create artificially radioactive phosphorus-30.

1934   Leo Szilard concludes that nuclear chain reactions may be possible.

1939   Lise Meitner and her nephew, Otto Hahn, reveal that uranium nuclei can disintegrate through a process called *fission*.

1943   The first all-electronic calculating device (computer) is developed by a team led by Alan Turing and used to crack German codes during World War II.

1945   On July 16, the first atomic bomb is successfully tested in the United States.

1949   William Bradford Shockley and his research team invent the transistor.

1952   The first hydrogen bomb is tested.

1969   Murray Gell-Mann wins the Nobel Prize for physics for his work on classifying elementary particles.

1994   Kyriacos Nicolau and Robert Holton create a synthetic molecular form of the naturally occurring cancer treatment compound Taxol.

1997   Steven Chu, Claude Cohen-Tannoudji, and William D. Phillips win a Nobel Prize for developing a way to trap and study individual atoms using laser technology.

1998   Robert B. Laughlin, Horst L. Stormer, and Daniel C. Tsui win a Nobel Prize for discovering a new form of matter known as *quantum fluid.*

2001   Carle E. Wieman, Wolfgang Ketterle, and Eric A. Cornell win the Nobel Prize in physics for work on an exotic state of matter that results from cooling down an alkali gas to 0.00000002° above absolute zero.

2002   Raymond Davis, Jr., Mastoshi Koshiba, and Riccardo Giacconi win a Nobel Prize for their study of the nearly undetectable cosmic radiation that reaches Earth.

Women and Men Who Have Shaped the Development of the Physical Sciences

ISAAC NEWTON (1642–1727) is known as the founder of modern physics and mathematics. His studies of the natural world led to the laws of inertia, action and reaction, and the acceleration of a mass being proportional to force applied. He also proposed the universal law of gravitation and is considered to be the inventor of calculus.

COUNT ALESSANDRO VOLTA (1745–1827) was an Italian nobleman who conducted research into the nature of electricity. The unit of electricity known as the *volt* is derived from his name.

MICHAEL FARADAY (1791–1867) was a bookbinder whose intense curiosity led him to read every book that he bound, particularly those that dealt with energy. Later in life, he became a chemist and a physicist. His accomplishments included the separation of benzene from petroleum and experiments with electromagnetic induction (the production of current in wires moved through a magnetic field).

LADY AUGUSTA ADA BYRON, COUNTESS OF LOVELACE (1815–1851) wrote what we now refer to as the *code,* or the program to operate the first mechanical computer. The U.S. Navy named the computer language *Ada* in her honor.

THOMAS ALVA EDISON (1847–1931) was perhaps the greatest inventor in history. His patents led to development of the phonograph, the motion picture camera, electric lights, and power plants to produce electricity. He received over 1,000 patents in his lifetime.

LEWIS H. LATIMER (1848–1928) invented, among other things, a method for producing the carbon filaments used in the electric lamps of his time. He was an engineer at the Edison Electric Light Company and the only African American in Edison's engineering and invention group. Latimer authored *Incandescent Electric Lighting,* the first book describing the installation and operation of lighting systems.

GRANVILLE WOODS (1856–1910) was an African American whose early work as a fireman/engineer on railroads provided foundation for his later studies of electrical and mechanical engineering. His inventions included devices that could send telegraph messages between moving trains and an automatic airbrake system.

MARIE CURIE (1867–1934) was a Polish-born scientist whose work touched both physics and chemistry. An indication of her extraordinary contribution to the sciences is the fact that she won the Nobel Prize twice! She and her husband, Pierre, shared the Nobel Prize in 1903 for their discovery of radium and polonium, and in 1911, she won it by herself for the research that led to the isolation of pure radium.

ERNEST RUTHERFORD (1871–1937) was known for his exploration of many phenomena related to atomic structure, energy release, and the nature of particles, including alpha, beta, and gamma radiation and the proton and neutron. He is credited with discovering the nucleus of an atom and with proposing a model of the atom in which electrons orbited the central nucleus.

ALBERT EINSTEIN (1879–1955) stands as one of the true geniuses in the history of civilization. His theories shaped the development of modern science and have had profound implications on science and society. Among his many accomplishments, he explained Brownian motion and the photoelectric effect, and he developed both the special and general theories of relativity. Born in Germany, he emigrated to the United States while in his fifties. He joined the Institute for Advanced Study in Princeton, New Jersey.

NIELS BOHR (1885–1962), a Danish physicist, provided an explanation for the structure of the atom that included a description of how electrons absorb and lose energy. His theory provided the best explanation for experimental results gathered by atomic physicists from around the world. Bohr received the Nobel Prize for physics in 1922.

GRACE HOPPER (1906–1992) was an active-duty U.S. Navy lieutenant who was key in developing computer programs. Her programming skills were used in one of the earliest computers, the Univac I. She is credited with invention of the term *computer bug.*

CHIEN SHIUNG WU (1912–1997) received her Ph.D. in physics from the University of California, Berkeley. She is most well known for her work in developing an experiment that confirmed a theory related to particle physics proposed by T. D. Lee and C. N. Yang. Lee and Yang received the Nobel Prize for their work on the theory but Wu did not. She did receive the Comstock Award from the National Academy of Sciences in 1964 and was the first woman to do so.

ROSALIND FRANKLIN (1920–1958) received her doctorate in physics from Cambridge University in 1941 and developed great expertise in the study of crystals. Her analysis of the behavior of fine beams of X-rays through DNA (deoxyribonucleic acid) was the basis for her eventually sharing the Nobel Prize in medicine with James D. Watson and Francis H. C. Crick in 1962.

ROSALYN SUSSMAN YALOW (1921–) shared the Nobel Prize for medicine in 1977, which was awarded for development of a method to detect minute traces of substances in blood and other body fluids.

MURRAY GELL-MANN (1929–) is most famous for proposing a theory that grouped atomic particles into eight "families." This grouping was grounded in his belief that all particles are composed of smaller particles that he called *quarks*. He won the Nobel Prize for physics in 1969.

STEVEN WEINBERG (1933–) is known as one of the twentieth century's most talented theoretical physicists. He is best known for his work on a unified field theory, or a single explanation that ties together the laws of physics dealing with gravity, electromagnetism, the strong force holding the atom's nucleus together, and the weak force (which results in the breaking apart of the nucleus). He shared the Nobel Prize for physics in 1979 with Sheldon Glashow and Abdus Salam.

Personal and Social Implications of the Physical Sciences

Personal and Community Health

Maintaining your personal health depends, in large part, on the work of physicists and chemists. Does that sound a bit surprising? Just think about it for a moment. Every medication was most likely created by chemists, any instrument used to fix broken bones or repair other body parts uses metals and plastics that came from a physical scientist's laboratory, and many of the diagnostic procedures used to identify the causes of illnesses emerged from the laboratories of physical scientists. To be sure, scientists from other disciplines are obviously also heavily involved in the development and delivery of personal health care, but in many ways, chemists and physicists carry out the fundamental research upon which health-related work is done.

Your health, and that of those around you, also depends a great deal on the environment in which you live. And knowledge about that environment emerges, in part, from the work of physicists and chemists. The quality of land surfaces, oceans, and atmosphere is constantly being assessed (and hopefully improved) as a result of the basic research done by physical scientists and the engineering of diagnostic instruments and remedial equipment done by engineers.

Hazards, Risks, and Benefits

The degradation of natural resources—whether the land, water, or atmosphere—poses a severe threat to the health and well-being of *all* populations of living things. Many scientists work to acquire knowledge that will serve as the basis for inventing devices and systems to measure changes in environmental quality and to use chemical agents and physical processes to retard or correct problems that affect life in its many forms.

One example of work in this area is that done to stop or at least slow down depletion of the ozone layer, which is a part of the atmosphere that shields us from certain radiant energy. The free movement of ultraviolet radiation through the atmosphere and to the skin surfaces of living things can cause serious harm. The instrumentation for monitoring the ozone layer, the modification of industrial processes to slow down ozone depletion, and even the creation of chemicals to retard sunburn have all emerged from work done in the physical sciences.

Personal safety for workers as well as travelers can be increased by the use of certain technologies, such air pollution measurement devices, built-in sprinkler systems, and procedures and equipment that permit the rapid exiting of individuals from factories, businesses, homes, automobiles, trains, and airplanes. Technology has also brought us increased surveillance techniques that can be used to safeguard our personal and societal well-being. Of course, with these surveillance techniques comes the potential for risk to our privacy. As with any technology, we must carefully weigh the benefits against the risks.

Physical Science Technology: Its Nature and Impact

If you've eaten a slice of toast today or traveled in a car or turned on a light, you have used technology that came from the physical sciences. The study of matter and energy has not only revealed some of the deepest secrets of our natural world but has also provided the basis for most of the world's technology. Engineers have used the principles of physics and chemistry to produce items as varied as disposable diapers, long-lasting lipstick, palm-sized computers, and nuclear bombs.

Even your personal recreation possibilities have been affected by the technology that's rooted in the physical sciences. Plastic kayak hulls, indoor ice rinks, roller coasters, snowboards, specialized shoes, and, of course, the aluminum softball bat have all come from work in the physical sciences.

The Design of Physical Science Technology

The engineers who create technology based on the findings of the physical sciences develop measuring devices, materials, and tools whose design usually meets the following criteria:

1. It addresses a problem that has been clearly identified and for which data can reasonably be expected to be gathered.
2. It serves as a data-gathering tool to assist in physical science exploration or as a device to be used in the fabrication of a material or product.
3. It can withstand a wide range of external environmental conditions.
4. It presents data in a manner that is readily interpretable by chemists or physicists, as appropriate.
5. If it is a tool, it can be readily used.
6. It preserves the safety and health of individuals who use it.
7. It provides constant feedback about the accuracy of the data being represented or the efficiency of the tool.

Examples of Physical Science Technology

Many devices have been developed from the foundation of knowledge produced from work in physics and chemistry, and they can be used to produce further knowledge about the physical world or to improve the quality of life:

Radiation-measuring devices   Wind tunnels
Computers   Lasers
Circuit testers   Solar energy collectors
Particle accelerators
Chemical reagents (molecules that can split or combine other molecules)
Oscilloscopes (convert sound waves to electrical signals that can be viewed on a screen)
Spectrophotometers (identify the components of a substance)
Chemical indicators (for example, a solution that can identify the presence of hemoglobin)
Calorimeters (can measure the amount of energy released during a chemical reaction)

Long-Term Implications of Physical Science Technology

The technological implications of the physical sciences are profound. In the area of medicine, knowledge of the behavior of elements, including how they may be combined to form molecules, has led to the development of pharmaceutical agents that have done much to reduce pain and suffering. In the area of food production, the application of scientific techniques to the measurement of trace amounts of substances has provided government and other agencies with the capability of analyzing food products to determine if they meet certain standards of purity.

Technology has led to the creation of an amazing array of brand-new materials. In addition to some rather extraordinary synthetic materials—including plastic, nylon, and rayon—there are some very specialized materials used to construct recreational boats and automobiles, replacement devices for joints and organs, and even aircraft that are invisible to radar.

In this early part of the twenty-first century, we have seen how discoveries related to digital electronics have been used to develop widespread use of the Internet, computerized manufacturing, computing for personal and business uses, and the ubiquitous cellular phone. Looking ahead, we can see truly extraordinary technology emerging, including miniature robotic devices, made of only a few hundred or thousand molecules, that can be injected into the bloodstream and travel to specific sites, where they will repair damaged tissues or organs! And while this may sound like science fiction, is it really that hard to foresee?

Before you answer that question, consider all of the technological innovations that seemed like utter fantasy at one time but have become real—very real. It seems that what the human mind can imagine, the physical sciences can create!

7

The Physical Sciences and Technology

Unit, Lesson, and Enrichment Starter Ideas

203

The Letter

Her throat was hoarse, her eyes itched, and her feet ached. It had been one of those long, long school days. On her way out of the building, she stopped in the main office to check her mailbox. A pink envelope, which signified interoffice mail, was tucked in the back of the box. Fishing it out, she opened it and began to read:

> *Dear Elizabeth:*
>
> *You will recall that last year, our elementary science curriculum committee recommended that we revise our entire elementary science curriculum this year. In order to accomplish this, each teacher will be a member of a subcommittee responsible for making recommendations about various parts of the curriculum. I would like to ask you to serve on the subcommittee that will review the physical science units that are presently in the curriculum. Part of that review should include assessing the extent to which the units are correlated to the NSE Standards.*
>
> *Each subcommittee should be prepared to make recommendations concerning the appropriateness of various units, activities, and materials to the full elementary science curriculum review committee within three months. I would like to thank you in advance for your contribution to this very important effort.*
>
> *Cordially,*
>
> *Margaret Stephanson*
>
> *Margaret Stephanson*
> *Elementary School Curriculum Coordinator*

At the bottom of the page, there was a handwritten note: "P.S. Beth, would you mind being the chairperson for the subcommittee? Your principal and I both feel that you would be terrific for the job. Thanks. Margaret." A wry smile crossed Beth's face as she thought about her consistent avoidance of, and lack of interest in, physical science in high school and college and the irony of being appointed chairperson of a subcommittee that was going to focus on physical science units. She shook her head, tucked the letter in the pile of papers under her arm, and walked out the door.

Regardless of whether you enjoy learning about atoms, molecules, and energy, physical science topics make up a substantial portion of any curriculum or textbook series that you are likely to work with. If you enjoyed working with magnets, pushing on levers, playing with tuning forks, and making light bulbs light, you are going to have a lot of fun observing children's involvement in these activities. If you didn't enjoy physical science, you will discover how interesting it can be when approached with a child's sense of wonder.

Assessing Prior Knowledge and Conceptions

"But we learned all that in Mr. Greeley's class last year."

Have you ever been in a classroom and observed a teacher getting "ambushed?" That's what happens when teachers assume that children know little or nothing about a topic, only to discover too late that they know a lot. The results are also disastrous when teachers assume that children know a lot about a topic and, in fact, know very little. (Plus, valuable lesson-planning time will have been wasted.) Even assumptions about children's beliefs about phenomena in the natural world can stop teachers in their tracks. Children may have very strongly held beliefs that are totally incorrect, and that may not be discovered until the class is deep in a lesson or unit.

So, as a teacher in the real world of schools and classrooms, how can you quickly get a sense of what the children know, what skills they possess, and what they believe? Part of the answer is to use *probes:* basic questions and simple activities that get children thinking and talking about particular topics. The answers children give will provide very direct guidance about what you should include in science units and lessons.

The probes and sample responses that follow come from informal interviews that I or my students have done with children. I think you'll be amazed at some of the responses and motivated to develop probes that you can use *before* planning units and lessons.

Probe	*Responses That Reveal Prior Knowledge and Conceptions*
■ After showing a child an ice cube and a glass of water: *What is the difference between these two things?*	"Ice is frozen and water is plain." "One's colder, it's been frozen. Oh, and how fast the molecules are moving."
■ After putting a magnet on a metal file cabinet: *Why do you think the magnet sticks?*	"Because the drawer is metal and the magnet is a different kind of metal that sticks." "Because it's a magnet." "Because one has got negative charges and one has got positive—or something like that."
■ After showing some eyeglasses: *How do eyeglasses work?*	"I'm not sure. I think it has something to do with the shape and the way that they carved it."
■ *Why is it easier to bike down a hill than up a hill?*	"The gravity pulls on the bicycle when you are going down the hill."
■ *What are some ways that people could save energy?*	"Turn off the lights, radio, and TV. "Wear a sweater instead of turning up the heat." "Be careful of what you throw away."

(continued)

Probe	Responses That Reveal Prior Knowledge and Conceptions
■ After turning a desk lamp on for a minute: *Slowly move your hand toward the bulb, but don't touch it. How is it possible for you to feel the warmth from a fire, the sun, or a light bulb when you are not touching it?*	"Because they are so hot that it comes on so strong. It comes all the way down to the earth from the sun or comes to your hand from the light bulb."
■ *How is an airplane able to stay in the air?*	"The pressure from the air keeps it up somehow— it can dip up or down—I really don't know."

Unit Plan Starter Ideas

That great idea for a science-teaching unit may come from deep within your brain, your school curriculum guide, a state science curriculum framework, a science resource book, a course, a workshop, a discussion you have with children, or some other source. Unfortunately, a great idea (like a friend, an umbrella, and a good restaurant with cheap food) is sometimes hard to find when you really need one.

To make it easier for you to come up with great ideas for science units, I have prepared three different sources of unit starter ideas, which are presented as three lists:

1. The first is based on the National Science Education (NSE) Standards for science content. I created these starter ideas for standards related to grades K–4 and 5–8.

2. The second source of starter ideas is based on my study of physical science topics that commonly appear in school curriculum guides. These are shown by grade level.

I am certain that the unique compilation of starter ideas that follows will help you plan and create wonderful discovery-based teaching units.

Ideas Based on the NSE K–8 Content Standards

CONTENT STANDARD K–4: Physical Sciences [PS]
As a result of activities in grades K–4, all students should develop an understanding of:

> Properties of objects and materials
> Position and motion of objects
> Light, heat, electricity and magnetism[1]

■ Starter Ideas for Objects and Materials

UNIT TITLE: *Observe, Think, Sort*

UNIT GOAL: Children classify the objects in collections of marbles, blocks, small tiles, and pebbles into categories based on weight, shape, color, and size.

UNIT TITLE: *Tell Me about It*

UNIT GOAL: Children use tools such as rulers, balances, and thermometers to take, write down, and tell about measurements they make about the items in a collection of solid objects and containers of liquids.

UNIT TITLE: *Water Changes*

UNIT GOAL: Children observe and explain why water and other substances can be changed from a solid to a liquid to a gas and from a gas to a liquid to a solid.

■ Starter Ideas for Position and Motion of Objects

UNIT TITLE: *Where Is It?*

UNIT GOAL: Using three objects labeled "a," "b," and "c," children describe their relative positions using the terms *in back of, in front of, above, below*, and *beside.*

UNIT TITLE: *Forces Cause Changes*

UNIT GOAL: Children demonstrate to their peers how an object's change in position is related to the strength and direction of the applied force.

UNIT TITLE: *Vibrations Cause Changes*

UNIT GOAL: Using a variety of objects, children demonstrate that sound is produced by vibrating objects and that pitch can be changed by changing the object's rate of vibration.

■ Starter Ideas for Light, Heat, Electricity, and Magnetism

UNIT TITLE: *Paths of Light*

UNIT GOAL: Using mirrors, lenses, focused-beam flashlights, and pins to mark path positions, children compare the actual paths of beams of light to predicted paths.

UNIT TITLE: *Electrical Energy*

UNIT GOAL: Children identify the characteristics of a simple series circuit, build a circuit, and use it to produce light, heat, sound, or magnetic effects.

UNIT TITLE: *Magnets*

UNIT GOAL: Children use permanent magnets to demonstrate attraction, repulsion, the presence of poles, and the existence of magnetic fields.

CONTENT STANDARD 5–8: Physical Sciences [PS]

As a result of the activities in grades 5–8, all students should develop an understanding of:

Properties and changes of properties in matter

Motion and forces

Transfer of energy

■ Starter Ideas for Properties and Changes of Properties in Matter

UNIT TITLE: *It's Dense*

UNIT GOAL: Students calculate the densities of regular and irregular objects using tools such as a ruler, graduated cylinder, overflow container, and balance.

UNIT TITLE: *Matter Changes*

UNIT GOAL: Students gather, organize, and chart data about the changes in characteristics of sugar, cornstarch, baking soda, and flour as a result of testing each by heating, adding water, and adding vinegar.

UNIT TITLE: *Physical or Chemical?*

UNIT GOAL: Students observe teacher demonstrations of physical and chemical changes, make observations, and correctly group the demonstrations into those that show physical changes and those that show chemical changes.

■ Starter Ideas for Motion and Forces

UNIT TITLE: *Observe the Motion*

UNIT GOAL: Children gather and record data about the positions, directions of motion, and speeds of battery-powered toy cars moving across the classroom floor.

UNIT TITLE: *Graph the Motion*

UNIT GOAL: Children graph the positions, directions of motion, and speeds of battery-powered toy cars moving across the classroom floor.

UNIT TITLE: *Predicting Motion*

UNIT GOAL: Children predict the motions of objects acted upon by unbalanced forces that cause changes in speed or direction.

■ Starter Ideas for Transfer of Energy

UNIT TITLE: *Generators Small and Large*

UNIT GOAL: After classroom science activities and field work at a power station, children make labeled diagrams that compare the initial energy sources and the energy transfers that occur in a classroom hand-operated generator and at the power station.

UNIT TITLE: *Energy Changes*

UNIT GOAL: Children construct hands-on displays for a school science fair that demonstrate the transfer of electrical energy into heat, light, and sound.

UNIT TITLE: *Energy—The Space Traveler*

UNIT GOAL: After library research work and class discussions, children explain how energy is produced by the sun, transmitted through space, and captured by green plants.

UNIT TITLE: *Egg Saver*

UNIT GOAL: Using everyday materials, children design containers that can protect an uncooked egg dropped from the height of a stepladder to a school sidewalk.

UNIT TITLE: *Safest, Cleanest, Cheapest*

UNIT GOAL: After library research work, Internet research, field work, and classroom discussions, children compare three alternate forms of energy with respect to safety, pollution, and economy.

UNIT TITLE: *Who Are They?*

UNIT GOAL: After library research work, Internet research, and classroom discussions, children identify and write brief biographies of five women scientists who have had made significant contributions to the physical sciences.

Ideas Based on Typical Grade-Level Content

■ Starter Ideas for Kindergarten

UNIT TITLE: *Push It, Pull It*

UNIT GOAL: Children learn that forces cause things to move or change shape.

UNIT TITLE: *Hot and Cold*

UNIT GOAL: Children learn that heating and cooling things can change them.

UNIT TITLE: *What Is It?*

UNIT GOAL: Children learn how to describe and compare objects on the basis of their properties.

■ Starter Ideas for First Grade

UNIT TITLE: *Water Changes*

UNIT GOAL: Children learn that liquid water can be changed to a solid or a gas and that heating and cooling produce changes in form.

UNIT TITLE: *Like and Unlike*

UNIT GOAL: Children learn to compare material objects by using the terms *bigger, smaller, longer, shorter, heavier,* and *lighter* appropriately.

■ Starter Ideas for Second Grade

UNIT TITLE: *I Can Measure*

UNIT GOAL: Children learn how to use such measuring devices as clocks, metersticks, and scales to measure time, length, and weight.

UNIT TITLE: *Sounds Are All Around*

UNIT GOAL: Children learn the requirements for the production, transmission, and reception of sound waves.

Starter Ideas for Third Grade

UNIT TITLE: *Matter Can Change Its Form*

UNIT GOAL: Children learn that matter can exist as a solid, liquid, or gas.

UNIT TITLE: *Electricity: Where Does It Come From?*

UNIT GOAL: Children learn the alternate ways in which electrical energy is produced, the environmental effects of the alternatives, and the importance of conserving electrical energy.

Starter Ideas for Fourth Grade

UNIT TITLE: *Bending Light and Making Colors*

UNIT GOAL: Children learn how to use various lenses and prisms to affect the movement of light rays.

UNIT TITLE: *Simple Machines*

UNIT GOAL: Children learn how simple machines operate and are able to identify the effort force, resistance, effort distance, and resistance distance for a variety of simple machines.

Starter Ideas for Fifth Grade

UNIT TITLE: *Two Kinds of Electricity*

UNIT GOAL: Children learn the effects produced by static and current electricity.

UNIT TITLE: *Changes*

UNIT GOAL: Children learn to distinguish between physical and chemical changes.

Starter Ideas for Sixth Grade

UNIT TITLE: *Matter in Motion*

UNIT GOAL: Children observe and classify the everyday interactions of objects and forces in terms of Newton's laws of motion.

UNIT TITLE: *Chemical Reactions*

UNIT GOAL: Children learn the variables that can affect the rate of chemical reactions.

Starter Ideas for Seventh Grade

UNIT TITLE: *Energy of Position and Energy of Motion*

UNIT GOAL: Students learn the difference between potential and kinetic energy.

UNIT TITLE: *Atoms and Molecules*

UNIT GOAL: Students learn the fundamental structures of atoms and molecules.

■ **Starter Ideas for Eighth Grade**

UNIT TITLE: *Matter Is Conserved*

UNIT GOAL: Students learn that matter is neither created nor destroyed in ordinary chemical reactions.

UNIT TITLE: *Energy Is Conserved*

UNIT GOAL: Students learn that energy can be changed in form and that the total amount of energy in a system remains constant.

Lesson Plan Starter Ideas for Common Curriculum Topics

Sometimes, you will be responsible for teaching lessons that are part of units prepared by committees of teachers in your school district or units that are commercially available. You may wonder how to break these units into lessons. To help you come up with lesson ideas for the physical sciences, I have analyzed a variety of teaching units and prepared a list of lesson plan starter ideas based on topics usually covered in these units. The lesson descriptions are very specific, so each description may also be viewed as the lesson's principal objective.

■ **Starter Ideas for Characteristics of Matter**

- Identify, compare, and classify objects on the basis of touch, taste, smell, and emitted sounds.
- Describe objects using the characteristics of size, shape, and color.
- Infer the characteristics of a small object in a closed box without looking in the box.
- Name three forms of matter (gas, liquid, and solid), and give an example of each.
- Illustrate how the movement of molecules in solids, liquids, and gases differs using body movements.
- Create a diagram illustrating an imaginary experiment that shows that air expands when it is heated and contracts when it is cooled.

■ **Starter Ideas for Energy and Its Changes**

- Observe that sound waves are produced by objects vibrating in a medium.
- Use a stopwatch correctly during an outdoor activity to calculate the speed of sound.
- Identify light, heat, electricity, and magnetism as forms of energy, and prepare a two-column chart that shows a human use for each form.
- Evaluate three different light bulbs to determine which will provide the most light, which will last the longest, and which is the best value for the money.
- Given appropriate safe materials, construct a simple electromagnet.
- Make a graph that compares the speed of sound with the speed of light.

- Make a hypothesis about the ability of light waves to travel without the presence of a medium, and invent an experiment to test the hypothesis.
- Make a hypothesis to explain the formation of rainbows using the knowledge that water droplets can act as prisms.
- Make a labeled diagram that shows how convex and concave lenses differ in shape.

■ Starter Ideas for Forces and Motion

- Observe the operation of various machines, and then identify the effort, force, and resistance.
- Create an illustrated chart identifying the characteristics of six simple machines.
- Draw an imaginary "wake-me-up-and-get-me-out-of-bed" machine that uses at least six different simple machines.
- Make a labeled drawing of one frequently used object that is made up of at least two simple machines.
- Using simple instruments, measure direction, distance, mass, and force of gravity (weight).
- Describe the position of an object relative to another object using the terms *north, south, east,* and *west.*
- Construct a simple machine, and use it to do work.
- Make a hypothesis to explain how a pulley system is able to multiply force, and invent an experiment to test the hypothesis.

■ Starter Ideas for Airplane, Jet, and Rocket Motion

- Make a diagram of an airplane in flight, and label the forces of gravity, lift, thrust, and drag.
- Explain how a jet engine takes advantage of the law of action and reaction.
- Explain how gravity affects large objects and that the strength of attraction between objects depends on their masses and distance apart.
- Write a story about a boy or girl who lives on an imaginary planet that does not have gravity.
- Make a diagram of a rocket in flight, and label the action and reaction forces.
- After doing library research on the exploration of Mars, evaluate the likelihood of humans reaching the planet by the year 2020.

WebQuest Starter Ideas

Imagine the WebQuest possibilities for your students when you teach the physical sciences! They'll be able to use the vast resources of the Internet to discover fascinating information about the atoms and molecules that make up everything they see around them—including themselves, how matter and energy interact, and how the sun produces and releases the energy on which every living thing depends.

The starter ideas in this section will help you plan your own physical science WebQuests. As you study the ideas, please keep the following in mind:

1. The WebQuests are correlated with the NSE Standards for grades K–8 (which are printed inside the front cover).
2. In the WebQuest context, the term *reports* has a very broad meaning and includes poster preparation, skits, dance, video presentations, labeled diagrams, and, of course, traditional written reports, when and if appropriate.

■ Starter Ideas for WebQuests

WEBQUEST TITLE: *The Best Bubble-Making Recipe*

SUGGESTED GRADE LEVELS: 1, 2, 3 (to be done with an adult)

NSE CONTENT STANDARDS: PS 1 and 4; S& T 1

CHALLENGE—MOTIVATION: The King of Bubbledom has asked you to be his "Bubble Maker." He is going to have a birthday party next week and wants everyone there to make bubbles as part of the fun.

CHALLENGE—REPORTS: Go on the Internet and find three recipes for making bubble liquid. Try each recipe and list your observations about the bubbles it makes. Then . . .

KEY TERMS FOR SEARCH ENGINES: Bubble Recipe, "Bubbleology," Bubble Making

WEBQUEST TITLE: *How Can the Sun Help Heat Our School?*

SUGGESTED GRADE LEVELS: 2, 3

NSE CONTENT STANDARDS: PS 3; S&T 1 and 2

CHALLENGE—MOTIVATION: The fuel used to heat your school and to make hot water is too expensive. Your principal wants your ideas on how to use the sun's energy to heat the school.

CHALLENGE—REPORTS: Make a sketch of the outside of your school. Then use the Internet to find out how the sun's energy could be used for heating. Now make a new sketch of your school that shows . . .

KEY TERMS FOR SEARCH ENGINES: Solar Homes, Solar Energy, Home Greenhouse

WEBQUEST TITLE: *Simple Machines in a Bicycle*

SUGGESTED GRADE LEVELS: 4, 5, 6

NSE CONTENT STANDARDS: PS 1, 2, 5, and 6; S&T 1, 2, 4, and 5

CHALLENGE—MOTIVATION: Your teacher has asked you to do a science demonstration on simple machines. To keep the other students' attention, you bring your bicycle to school for it.

CHALLENGE—REPORTS: Make a poster that has a labeled picture of a bicycle and the simple machines it contains. Show your classmates where each machine is on the bicycle. Also . . .

KEY TERMS FOR SEARCH ENGINES: Bicycle Physics, Wheel and Axle, Simple Machines

MAKE THE CASE   *An Individual or Group Challenge*

■ **The Problem**

Children need science experiences that range across the earth/space, life, and physical sciences. Teachers may tend to include those topics they feel most comfortable with and thus inadvertently limit the scope of the children's learning.

■ **Assess Your Prior Knowledge and Beliefs**

1. When comparing your knowledge of the physical sciences to your knowledge of the earth/space sciences and life sciences, do you believe you have acquired more, less, or the same amount of basic science content in each?

	More	Less	Same
Earth/space sciences	_____	_____	_____
Life sciences	_____	_____	_____

2. When you were a student in grades K–8, would you say you were exposed to more, less, or the same amount of physical science content as you were to life science content and earth/space content?

	More	Less	Same
Earth/space sciences	_____	_____	_____
Life sciences	_____	_____	_____

3. Gravity is a common physical science topic for children. Identify five discrete items of knowledge that you now have about gravity.

_____

_____

_____

_____

_____

4. Now identify five things about gravity that you think you should know but do not.

_____

_____

_____

_____

_____

■ **The Challenge**

You are part of a team of teachers planning a unit on gravity. Give examples of physical science activities you might include.

WEBQUEST TITLE: *What Is an Atom?*

SUGGESTED GRADE LEVELS: 4, 5, 6

NSE CONTENT STANDARDS: PS 1 and 4

CHALLENGE—MOTIVATION: Kelly just told you that atoms are small bits of matter. Kelly also said that there is nothing smaller than an atom. Do you think Kelly is right?

CHALLENGE—REPORTS: Find out if Kelly is right or not. Then write a short poem that tells whether atoms have parts. If they do, tell what they are called . . .

KEY TERMS FOR SEARCH ENGINES: Atom Parts, Atom Model, Proton, Neutron, Electron

WEBQUEST TITLE: *Famous African American Inventors*

SUGGESTED GRADE LEVELS: 4, 5, 6

NSE CONTENT STANDARDS: S&T 1 and 2; HNS 1, 2, 3, and 4

CHALLENGE—MOTIVATION: Do you know who these people are? Dr. Charles Richard Drew, Percy Julian, Lewis Latimer. Do research to find how who they are and what they did as . . .

CHALLENGE—REPORTS: Select any three African American scientists or inventors and study their lives. Then write a one-minute speech that each might give if he or she could visit your class.

KEY TERMS FOR SEARCH ENGINES: African American Scientists, African American Inventors, Science Biographies

WEBQUEST TITLE: *How Do Birds Fly?*

SUGGESTED GRADE LEVELS: 4, 5, 6

NSE CONTENT STANDARDS: PS 5 and 6; LS 4

CHALLENGE—MOTIVATION: Isn't it strange that birds can fly but people can't? You can wave your arms really fast, but you'll never get off the ground!

CHALLENGE—REPORTS: Find out how a bird's body and wings are adapted to make flying possible. Then make two or three labeled drawings of a bird in flight to show . . .

KEY TERMS FOR SEARCH ENGINES: Bird Flight, Bird Wings, Flight Feathers

WEBQUEST TITLE: *How Does a Light Stick Work?*

SUGGESTED GRADE LEVELS: 4, 5, and 6

NSE CONTENT STANDARDS: PS 4, 5, and 6; S&T 4 and 5

CHALLENGE—MOTIVATION: Have you ever had a light stick—one of those plastic tubes that produces light after you bend it? Sometimes, children have them at celebrations and sporting events. Have you ever wondered how light can come from a plastic tube?

CHALLENGE—REPORTS: Get a light stick at a toy store and do research on the Internet to find out how it works. Demonstrate and explain how a light stick works to your class. Make a diagram that includes the part of the light stick that has the chemicals and . . .

KEY TERMS FOR SEARCH ENGINES: Light Stick, Fluorescent, Chemiluminescence

WEBQUEST TITLE: *How Does a Battery Work?*

SUGGESTED GRADE LEVELS: 4, 5, 6

NSE CONTENT STANDARDS: PS 4, 5, and 6; S&T 4 and 5

CHALLENGE—MOTIVATION: Your hand-held computer game has batteries, CD players have batteries, and so do many other things you use. Have you ever wondered how a battery produces electricity?

CHALLENGE—REPORTS: Make a collection of small batteries to show your class. Then make a labeled overhead transparency that shows how all of the battery parts make electricity. Use the transparency and battery to explain how a battery works to your class. Also, . . .

KEY TERMS FOR SEARCH ENGINES: Battery Chemistry, Battery Technology, Dry Cell Chemistry

Classroom Enrichment Starter Ideas

In-Class Learning Centers

A well-prepared in-class learning center offers children many opportunities to make their own discoveries. In order to be well prepared, such a center must provide a wide range of materials that encourage hands-on, discovery-based learning, ranging from print and audiovisual resources to art supplies and games. In addition, the learning center must be located where children have ready access to it yet can also be somewhat removed from the larger classroom setting while doing independent activities.

The following starter ideas for in-class learning centers should get you thinking about how to create centers in your own classroom. Note that the relevant NSE Standard is identified for each starter idea and that asterisks indicate those that are particularly suited for young children.

■ Starter Idea for a Learning Center

CENTER TITLE: *Energy Savers*

NSE CONTENT STANDARD: PS 6

IDEA: Try to locate the center in an area that has enough space for writing, game-playing, dramatizing, and constructing activities. Be sure to provide construction paper, cardboard boxes of various sizes, foam packing peanuts, ice cream buckets, and a scrapbook. Have the children sign up to work for a half-hour on one activity per day in the center. If you have computer software or videos related to energy, make them available in this center, too.

So that students will know what to do in the center, prepare activity cards (cards that give directions for activities you develop) based on the following ideas:

■ *Feltboard* * Have the children make figures out of paper or cardboard. Glue strips of felt to the backs of the figures, and give them names such as "Walter Waste Energy," "Conni the Conserver," and so forth. Have the children invent and dramatize the adventures of these characters and their friends.

- *Ice Cube Race* Challenge the children to build ice cube "keepers." Provide foam packing peanuts, ice cream buckets, cardboard, tape, and small cardboard boxes. Have the children use baby food jars to hold ice cubes that are allowed to melt at room temperature to get data for a control.
- *Energy Scrapbook** Have the children cut out pictures and articles from newspapers and magazines on such energy issues as nuclear power and solar energy. Then have them prepare scrapbook pages for an energy scrapbook that will be kept in the center.
- *Power Play* Have the children invent and construct a board game that employs a die, tokens, and a set of "chance" cards that say such things as "You left the TV on; go back two spaces" and "You took a 30-minute shower; go back four spaces" and "You put on a sweater instead of turning up the heat; go ahead ten spaces." The children can use file folders or construction paper to make the board.

■ Additional Starter Ideas for Learning Centers

CENTER TITLE: *Matter Can Change**

NSE CONTENT STANDARD: PS 1

IDEA: Carry out activities that reveal properties of matter, such as melting, freezing, and evaporating.

CENTER TITLE: *Pushes and Pulls**

NSE CONTENT STANDARDS: PS 1 and 2

IDEA: Use a toy car to show how pushes and pulls can affect the positions and motions of objects, such as starting, stopping, moving with constant speed, speeding up, and slowing down.

An in-class learning center like this one, called Energy Savers, can encourage students to discover more about the physical sciences.

CENTER TITLE: *Magnet Time**

NSE CONTENT STANDARDS: PS 2 and 3

IDEA: Using bar and horseshoe magnets, do activities to identify the poles and show attraction and repulsion.

CENTER TITLE: *Conductors and Insulators*

NSE CONTENT STANDARD: PS 6

IDEA: Build a working simple series circuit with batteries, wire, a bulb, and a switch; then test a variety of materials to determine how much each is an electrical insulator or conductor.

Bulletin Boards

Good bulletin boards have the potential to be something that children can both look at and learn from. There are many ways to use classroom bulletin boards to enhance physical science units and extend your teaching to nonscience areas. The following list offers a few starter ideas for you. Again, asterisks indicate activities that may be particularly appropriate for young children.

■ Starter Ideas for Bulletin Boards

BULLETIN BOARD TITLE: *Matter and Its Composition*

IDEA: Divide the bulletin board into 16 squares: four rows going down and four columns going across. Leave the top of the first column blank, but label the next three columns *Solid, Liquid,* and *Gas.* Label the four rows going down *Object,*

This bulletin board, Matter and Its Composition, invites students to apply what they have learned.

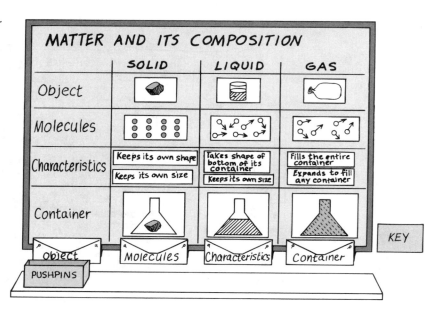

Molecules, Characteristics, and *Container.* Set aside three cards and draw a rock on one, a vial filled with colored water on another, and an inflated balloon on the third. Create three cards illustrating the organization of molecules in solids, liquids, and gases; three cards illustrating a solid, a liquid, and a gas in flasks; and six cards listing the characteristics of solids, liquids, and gases. Place the cards in manila envelopes labeled *Object, Molecules, Characteristics,* and *Container.* After discussing the characteristics of solids, liquids, and gases and demonstrating how matter can change from one state to another by melting ice and boiling water, have the children take the cards from the envelopes and arrange them in the appropriate rows and columns, using pushpins to hold the cards in place. Children should do this in their free time; they can check their work using an answer key that you provide.

BULLETIN BOARD TITLE: *Sound and Light**

IDEA: Divide the bulletin board into three sections, and label each *Light, Heat,* or *Sound.* Subdivide each section allowing space for children to attach pictures, and add the following subtitles: *Where does it come from? How does it move? How do we use it?* Provide magazines, scissors, drawing paper, and markers so children can locate or create pictures to place in each subsection.

BULLETIN BOARD TITLE: *Find the Forces**

IDEA: Place the title "Find the Forces" across the top of the bulletin board. Have children locate magazine pictures of people actively participating in gymnastics, dancing, or sports. Each week, place one of the pictures on the bulletin board; have children attach index cards with the words *push* and *pull* near the pictures to identify where forces are acting.

BULLETIN BOARD TITLE: *Temperature and You**

IDEA: Draw three large thermometers on the bulletin board showing the following temperatures: 0°C (32°F), 20°C (68°F), 35°C (95°F). Challenge the children to attach magazine pictures or their own drawings depicting outdoor activities that could be done at each temperature.

BULLETIN BOARD TITLE: *The Simple Circuit*

IDEA: Create a three-dimensional bulletin board that is, in fact, a working circuit. Temporarily mount and hook up a dry cell, wires, switch, and bulb holder with bulb. Have children create a label for each item. (*Safety Note:* You must use insulated wire and make sure that neither the bulb nor any bare ends of wire touch any surface. Also be sure that the circuit is switched off after each use.)

BULLETIN BOARD TITLE: *Find the Machine*

IDEA: Create a three-dimensional bulletin board to display items such as a scissors, doorknob, wood chisel, nutcracker, wood screw, clay hammer, and hand-operated egg beater. Encourage children to attach a label on or near each object that identifies the type of simple machine the item is or the name and location of a simple machine within the item.

Field Trips

Field trips provide amazing opportunities for discovery learning, as they take children out of the classroom and immerse them in the real world. Whether you teach in a city, suburban, or small-town school, you can find ideas for field trips all around you. To understand just how true that is, think about how you could tailor each of these topics to the resources of the community in which you teach:

Forces and machines
The electric company
The telephone company
Types of transportation

The field trip may be to the regional airport or the train depot down the street, but either way, children will be eager to see what the day will hold. After all, children *love* field trips!

Here are starter ideas for field trips for all schools. Note that asterisks indicate activities that may be particularly appropriate for young children:

■ Starter Ideas for Field Trips

FIELD TRIP TITLE: *The Telephone Company**

IDEA: A trip to the local telephone company will be a memorable science lesson that has many language arts, geography, and art applications. When you make the initial contact, find out what the facility contains; repair services are often in a different location and could be considered for a separate field trip. During the actual visit, children can discover how long-distance and overseas calls are made, how records of calls are kept, the many styles of phones, and the latest advances in communication technology.

FIELD TRIP TITLE: *Force, Motion, and Machines*

IDEA: The study of friction can be the basis for various field trips. Contact the showroom of a car, boat, airplane, or snowmobile dealership or the repair facility at a bus station, garage, or airport to arrange the excursion. Alert the individual who will serve as your tour guide that the children will be interested in how the design of the vehicle minimizes air and surface friction, how it's propelled, and what type of energy it uses. As a follow-up to the trip, have children draw diagrams and then build models of what they have seen. They can also invent modifications to the vehicle that would further reduce friction.

FIELD TRIP TITLE: *Energy-Conserving Home**

IDEA: Look around the community for a building or home that was constructed or retrofitted to save energy. One with an active or passive solar system, windmill, off-peak power storage system, or underground design would be especially interesting. Installers of alternative energy systems and building contractors are good sources of information on energy-efficient building techniques and places to visit. After the visit, children can study the school and their homes for energy-efficient features as well as improvements needed.

Many of the factors that make the city an interesting and exciting place to live also make it a place that overflows with field trip possibilities. Here are some additional ideas that should stimulate your thinking about field trips for children in city schools:

■ Starter Ideas for Field Trips

FIELD TRIP TITLE: *Shadow Study*

IDEA: Children track changes in the shadows they see on a sunny day.

FIELD TRIP TITLE: *Simple Machines on the Playground*

IDEA: Children locate and classify playground equipment according to the simple machines incorporated in them.

FIELD TRIP TITLE: *Temperature Here, Temperature There*

IDEA: Children use thermometers to discover if the temperatures at various places on the school grounds are the same.

FIELD TRIP TITLE: *Getting from Here to There*

IDEA: During a walk around the block, children gather data about the numbers of cars, trucks, buses, and bicycles observed traveling on a street. On returning to the classroom, children graph the data they have collected.

FIELD TRIP TITLE: *Count the Passengers*

IDEA: After observing and gathering data about the number of people riding buses, children draw inferences regarding energy savings brought about by the use of public transportation.

FIELD TRIP TITLE: *Harbor Machines*

IDEA: If your city is on an ocean, lake, or river, children can observe machines at work in the harbor.

FIELD TRIP TITLE: *Building Going Up*

IDEA: From a safe distance, children can observe the machines in use at a building construction site to identify the sources of energy for the machines and the simple machines that make up the more complex machines at work.

Additional Field Trip Destinations

Airport control tower
Cellular phone service provider
Chemistry or physics department at a local college
Computer repair facility
Electrical power station (hydroelectric)
Electrical power station (fossil fuel or nuclear powered)
Electronics company
Eyeglass preparation facility
Internet service provider
Oil refinery
Photographic film-processing plant
Radio station
Television station

Cooperative Learning Projects

As you consider the following starter ideas for cooperative learning projects, keep in mind the importance of stressing the three key aspects of cooperative learning:

1. Positive interdependence
2. Individual accountability
3. Development of group process skills

■ Starter Ideas for Cooperative Learning Projects

PROJECT TITLE: *The Living Machine*

IDEA: After doing activities or observing demonstrations related to the three types of simple machines, challenge groups to use their bodies to demonstrate each type. Various members of each group can represent resistance, fulcrum, and effort. Groups can also use their bodies to create and demonstrate a complex machine that uses all three types of simple machines. After the groups have practiced, they should present their machines and have the rest of the class identify the simple machines and locations of the resistance, fulcrum, and effort.

PROJECT TITLE: *Fancy Flyers*

IDEA: This project should occur over a period of days. Provide the groups with a wide assortment of materials (e.g., plastic wrap, paper of different weights, cardboard, strips of balsa wood, glue) that can be used to build model gliders. Have the groups do research to learn about various designs for gliders. After they have studied the topic, encourage each group to prepare three gliders for display and demonstration. If weather permits, have the groups display and demonstrate their gliders outdoors. If this is not possible, the gym or cafeteria might serve as an acceptable environment.

PROJECT TITLE: *Density Detectives*

IDEA: After discussing the concept of density (density = mass/volume), have each group develop a way to find the density of an irregular object and explain its method to the class. (*Hint:* The volume of an irregular solid can be found by determining the volume of water it displaces when it is submerged.)

PROJECT TITLE: *School Energy Survey*

IDEA: Have each group evaluate how the school building loses heat to the outside environment or how heat from the outside environment enters the school. Have groups observe such things as how fast the front doors close, how airtight the windows are, and how well weather stripping seals around door jambs. After organizing their observations, groups should report the results of their studies and their recommendations for slowing down heat loss or heat gain to the class and, if appropriate, to the school principal.

■ Additional Starter Ideas for Learning Groups

- Provide groups with flashlights, cardboard tubes, wire, "C" or "D" batteries, flashlight bulbs, and other materials, and encourage them to create their own working flashlights.
- Challenge groups to use cardboard tubes, straws, rubber bands, balloons, tape, and so forth to create air-powered rockets that will move along a length of fishing line stretched across the room.
- Challenge groups to create bridges using straws, paper, cardboard, and tape that will support one or more school books. If you use this idea, be sure that each group gets the amount of each material you provide and that the bridges must all span a fixed distance, such as 25 centimeters (about 10 inches).

RESOURCES FOR DISCOVERY LEARNING

Internet Resources
Websites for Physical Science Units, Lessons, Activities, and Demonstrations

Bill Nye Demo of the Day

www.nyelabs.com

This site showcases ideas from popular educational television personality Bill Nye, "The Science Guy." When you reach this site, select "Home Demos," which provides a daily demonstration that can be done with inexpensive, readily available materials. Most of these demonstrations are related to some aspect of the physical sciences. To receive each demonstration automatically, change your Internet browser's default startup page to this one.

The Atoms Family

www.miamisci.org/af/sln/

This site, sponsored by the Miami Museum of Science, presents information about energy concepts, the power of the sun, energy conservation, energy transformation, electricity, and fossil fuels. You and your students will find physical science activities in places with rather interesting names, such as "Dracula's Library," "Frankenstein's Lightning Laboratory," and the "Phantom's Portrait Parlor."

Explorer Web

unite.ukans.edu

This is an extremely comprehensive resource for teachers of science and mathematics at all grade levels. To teach children topics in the physical sciences, first select "Natural Sciences Curriculum" and then select from among the physical sciences entries on the next page that appears. You'll find complete lessons, including objectives, related process skills, as well as downloadable files you'll be able to use with the lessons. This is an extraordinary collection!

Science Try Its

www.ktca.org/newtons/tryits

This site, sponsored by the *Newton's Apple* television program, is a collection of physical science activities that students can try at home. When you reach this page, select any of the "Science Try Its." Each activity has an accompanying illustration to help you and your students assemble the materials and equipment needed. A brief presentation of the science concepts that explain each activity is also included.

The Science Explorer

www.exploratorium.edu

Teachers and students who visit this site, sponsored by the world-famous Exploratorium in San Francisco, California, will find many adventures. This URL will take you to the part of the site that provides science activities students can do at home or school. Each is well illustrated and in a consistent format that includes "What do I need?" "What do I do?" and "What's going on?" The latter subsection explains the science concepts that are part of each activity.

Kids Web: Science

www.npac.syr.edu/textbook/newkidsweb

Selecting the "Sciences" option at this site will bring up more options for such physical science–related topics as "Chemistry," "Physics," and "Computers." This is a very comprehensive site, so you should be able to find resource ideas appropriate for any grade level. Those resources will include projects and activities as well as science subject matter presentations.

 ## Print Resources
Articles from Science and Children and Science Scope

Burns, John, et al. "Solving Solutions." *Science Scope* 24, no. 2 (October 2000): 30–33.

Cavallo, Ann M. L. "Convection Connections." *Science and Children* 38, no. 8 (May 2001): 20–25.

Cox, Carole. "Isaac Newton Olympics." *Science Scope* 24, no. 8 (May 2001): 18–22.

Frazier, Richard. "Rethinking Models." *Science Scope* 26, no. 4 (January 2003): 29–33.

Galus, Pamela. "Reactions to Atomic Structure." *Science Scope* 26, no. 4 (January 2003): 38–41.

Hammrich, Penny L., and Kathleen Fadigan. "Investigations in the Science of Sports." *Science Scope* 26, no. 5 (February 2003): 30–35.

Harris, Mary E. "Slurper Balls." *Science Scope* 25, no. 4 (January 2002): 22–27.

Hechtman, Judith. "The Science of Invention." *Science and Children* 40, no. 5 (February 2003): 16–18.

Lucking, Robert A., and Edwin P. Christmann. "Tech Trek: Technology in the Classroom." *Science Scope* 26, no. 4 (January 2003): 54–57.

Proto, Christopher, and Edmund A. Marek. "Disecting Light." *Science Scope* 23, no. 7 (April 2000): 14–16.

Radhe, Sue Ellen, and Lynn Cole. "Star Trek Physics." *Science Scope* 25, no. 6 (March 2002): 52–57.

Roy, Ken. "Safety Is for Everyone." *Science Scope* 26, no. 5 (February 2003): 16–17.

Sarow, Gina A. "Miniature Sleds, Go, Go, Go." *Science and Children* 39, no. 3 (November/December 2001): 16–21.

Shaw, Mike. "A Dastardly Density Deed." *Science Scope* 26, no. 4 (January 2003): 18–21.

Stroup, Diana. "Balloons and Newton's Third Law." *Science Scope* 26, no. 5 (February 2003): 54–55.

Villano, Diane D. "Classroom Catapults." *Science Scope* 24, no. 5 (February 2001): 24–29.

Weimann, Kimberly. "Blue Solids, Red Liquids, and Yellow Gases." *Science Scope* 23, no. 5 (February 2000): 17–19.

Wetzel, David R. "Fan Car Physics." *Science Scope* 23, no. 4 (January 2000): 29–31.

NOTES

1. This standard, as well as the others identified in later sections, are excerpted with permission from the National Research Council, *National Science Education Standards* (Washington, DC: National Academy Press, 1996), pp. 104–171. Note that the bracketed symbol to the right of each standard was prepared by this author. See also the list of all the K–8 content standards inside the front cover of this book.

2. Note that I have related this sampling of NSE Standards E, F, and G to the physical sciences.

8A Matter and Motion

Content

From Atoms to Rockets and Other Technological Wonders

Imagine the thrill of driving in the Indy 500. Now imagine doing so in a solar-powered car, like that shown in Figure 8A.1. In the not-too-distant future, we may all be trading in our gas-guzzling cars for newer models powered by other forms of energy, such as solar energy or electricity.

Our ability to accomplish such amazing things as faxing a document across the world or microwaving a meal in only a matter of minutes is the result of the technology available to us. We can have full-color photographs in a minute; we have drugs that can prevent or cure illnesses; we have automobiles, airplanes, unbelievable weapons of destruction, and, wonder of wonders, sonic toothbrushes. The rapid pace of technological development is a direct result of our increased knowledge of the nature of matter, our ability to release energy from it, and our ability to predict and control the motion of objects.

Matter

Silly Putty, a chicken, and pistachio ice cream all have something in common. They are all *matter*. Anything that occupies space and has weight is matter. The earth, the planets, the sun, and everything else in our universe that has weight and occupies space are composed of matter. This definition allows us to distinguish matter from energy. *Energy* is defined as the capacity to do work or to produce change. Electricity, light, sound, heat, and magnetism are all considered forms of energy. Matter and energy are related. Under very special circumstances, matter can be changed into energy, and energy can be changed into matter.

FIGURE 8A.1
This solar-powered car may seem an oddity today, but it's quite likely the car of the future.

Scientists have found that all matter in the universe exerts an attractive force on all other matter in the universe. The matter in this book is exerting an attractive force on you, and you are exerting an attractive force on the matter in the book. This attractive force is called *gravitation,* and it exists regardless of the location of the matter. The strength of the force depends on the amount of matter in both you and the book, for example, and your distance from the book. The force that the earth exerts on matter is called *weight.* The weight of an object is a measurement of the extent to which the earth pulls on the object and the object pulls on the earth.

There are many different types of matter. The earth is itself a vast storehouse of matter. Here is a list of some of the common types of matter found in the earth's crust (and next to each is the symbol that scientists use to refer to it):

	Symbol	Percent by Weight
Oxygen	O	47.3
Silicon	Si	27.7
Aluminum	Al	7.9
Iron	Fe	4.5
Calcium	Ca	3.5
Sodium	Na	2.5
Potassium	K	2.5
Magnesium	Mg	2.2
Hydrogen	H	0.2
Carbon	C	0.2
All others		1.5

The Physical Properties of Matter

We usually describe matter by its physical properties. We say various types of matter are *solids, liquids,* or *gases.* These forms of matter are known as *states,* or phases, of matter. Rocks and soils are solids. Water may be found as a solid, a liquid, or a gas. The state that matter is in can be determined by observation. A solid has a definite shape. A liquid takes the shape of its container. Both solids and liquids have a definite volume: They occupy a certain amount of space. A gas takes the shape of its container, but it also expands to fill all of the container. Thus, gases do not have a definite volume: Their volume is the volume of the container.

We can also describe matter by describing its color, how hard or soft it is, the extent to which it dissolves in liquid, and whether it is easily stretched or broken. Another specific physical property of matter is its *density.* Unlike units of weight, which represent a gravitational attraction for that matter, units of mass, such as grams and kilograms, represent the amount of matter in something. Density is commonly measured as mass per unit of volume and is expressed in grams per cubic centimeter. To find the density of something, we can simply divide its weight by its volume. Density may also be found by dividing mass by volume.

Molecular Theory

Matter can be changed from one state to another. A cold, crystal-clear icicle receives morning light from the sun and begins to change—to melt into water. A child wanting to draw a "happy face" without paper and pencil breathes on a cold mirror, creating a thin film on which to draw. All these changes in matter are physical changes. The matter has undergone a change, but the original substance remains. Some of the water in the solid icicle has changed to a liquid; the water vapor exhaled by the child has become the tiny droplets of water that formed the "canvas" for the drawing. No new substances were produced in any of these cases. They were all physical changes. This can happen, scientists have concluded, for several reasons:

1. Matter is made up of small particles called *molecules.*
2. Spaces exist among the molecules.
3. The molecules of matter are in constant motion.

Changes in the state of matter, then, can be explained by the motion of molecules. A solid has a definite shape because its molecules are arranged in a pattern. Although the molecules hold this pattern, they also vibrate. If heat is applied to a solid, the rate at which its molecules vibrate becomes so fast that they break away from one another in the pattern. If we add sufficient heat, the solid melts and becomes a liquid. If we add even more heat, the molecules in the liquid may move fast enough to escape from the surface of the liquid and enter the air. These molecules have gone from the liquid state to the gaseous state—the process known as *evaporation.*

If we reverse this process, if we take the heat from gas, its molecules may slow down sufficiently to form a liquid. If we take away more heat, the molecules may begin forming the patterns in which they exist in their solid state. These types of changes in matter are physical changes. No new matter is created.

The molecular theory of matter can be used to explain the expansion and contraction of matter. When the speed of the molecules in matter increases, they bump into one another more and tend to spread apart. *Expansion* of matter thereby occurs. If heat is removed, the molecules move more slowly and tend to come closer to one another. When this occurs, matter *contracts.*

Chemical Changes in Matter

Some types of matter are capable of uniting with one another to form very different types of matter. This characteristic is known as a chemical property of matter. A chemistry teacher holds a piece of magnesium with tongs and places it in the flame of a Bunsen burner. Bright light is produced, and the metallic magnesium changes to a white powder: magnesium oxide. Changes resulting in substances that differ from the original substance are known as chemical changes. The rusting of iron and the burning of wood or paper are other examples of matter changing and combining to produce new forms of matter.

Although we can describe these changes in many ways, to fully understand the chemical properties of matter it will be helpful to think about specific chemical changes. The roasting of a marshmallow and the phenomenon of fire are two good examples.

The Roasting of a Marshmallow

A marshmallow is made of sugar. Sugar contains carbon, hydrogen, and oxygen. You've probably noticed that when you heat a marshmallow over an open flame, the surface of the marshmallow darkens. It does so because the sugar undergoes a chemical change. The heat added to the sugar breaks the sugar into carbon, hydrogen, and oxygen. The dark material on the outside of the marshmallow is carbon. Hydrogen and oxygen leave the heated marshmallow in the form of water.

Fire

The flickering candles atop a birthday cake, the ring of blue flame on a stovetop, and a raging forest fire are all examples of matter that is undergoing a rapid chemical change that gives off both light and heat. In each case, three things are present: (1) a material that will burn (a fuel), (2) oxygen, and (3) something that heats the fuel to a temperature at which it will burn. The temperature at which a fuel will begin to burn is known as its *kindling temperature.*

All common fuels contain carbon. When these fuels burn, they undergo various chemical changes. The carbon within them combines with oxygen to form the gas carbon dioxide. If there is insufficient oxygen, however, carbon monoxide, a very dangerous gas, is released. If the fuel contains hydrogen as well as carbon, during *combustion* (another word for "burning"), oxygen in the air also combines with the hydrogen in the fuel to form water vapor. In each of these examples, matter undergoes chemical changes to become a new type of matter, and in each example, it is the presence of oxygen that allows the changes to occur quickly.

Elements, Compounds, and Mixtures

An *element* is a substance that cannot be separated into simpler substances by chemical changes. Carbon, hydrogen, and oxygen are elements and the basic building blocks of all matter. Through chemical changes, elements can be combined into *compounds.* Table salt is a compound composed of the elements sodium and chlorine. Its chemical name is *sodium chloride.* Elements and compounds can be represented as *formulas.* The formula for table salt, for example, is NaCl. This combination of symbols indicates that there is one part sodium (Na) and one part chlorine (Cl) in salt. The formula H_2O stands for a combination of two parts of hydrogen and one part of oxygen.

If we broke down a molecule of water or a molecule of salt, we would produce hydrogen and oxygen or sodium and chloride. These parts of a molecule are called *atoms.* When we write the chemical formula H_2O, we are indicating that a molecule of water contains two atoms of hydrogen and one atom of oxygen. When we write CO_2, we are saying that one molecule of carbon dioxide contains one atom of carbon and two atoms of oxygen. The number written below the line in the formula tells us how many atoms (if more than one) of the preceding element are present in the molecule.

Chemists use chemical equations to describe chemical changes in matter. Let's see how this is done. If we place a clean iron nail in a solution of copper sulfate, a chemical change will occur: The iron nail will become coated with a reddish covering, which is copper. As this occurs, the blue color of the copper-sulfate solution becomes less intense. In the chemical change that occurs, iron in the nail changes places with some of the copper in the copper sulfate. The equation that describes this reaction is as follows:

$$Fe + CuSO_4 \rightarrow FeSO_4 + Cu$$

Fe represents iron. $CuSO_4$ represents copper sulfate. The arrow means "forms" or "yields." On the right side of the arrow are the products of the chemical change: $FeSO_4$ (iron sulfate) and Cu (copper). Notice that the number of atoms on each side of the arrow is the same. No atoms are gained or lost during a chemical change.

Not all combinations of elements form compounds. The principal test is whether the various substances can be separated from one another. For example, if you were to mix a small amount of sand with a small amount of salt, no chemical change would occur. If you had patience and a strong lens, you could probably separate the two materials. It would take time, but it could be done, since the salt and sand do not chemically unite with each other. Any combination of materials that can be separated from one another is known as a *mixture*. The air we breathe is a mixture of various gases. The soil we walk on is a mixture of various rocks and minerals.

The Parts of an Atom

Scientists know a great deal about the way in which atoms interact with one another as well as the way in which they absorb and release energy. With this knowledge, scientists have constructed a model of what they believe an atom to be. Keep in mind that the protons, neutrons, and electrons that make up an atom are not really the round objects they are depicted to be in diagrams. Even so, diagrams can help us understand atomic interaction. Figure 8A.2 illustrates six different atoms. The electrons in these atoms exist in the outer rings, or shells. Electrons are negative electrical charges that orbit around the atom's nucleus. A *shell* is an energy level on which an electron exists.

The center of an atom is called the *nucleus*. This is the place where *protons*, heavy particles having a positive electrical charge, and *neutrons*, heavy particles having no electrical charge, are found. It is the protons and neutrons that make up most of the atom's mass. An *electron* has only $^1/_{1837}$ the mass of a proton. Atoms are electrically neutral. That is, an atom contains as many positive charges (protons) in its nucleus as there are negative charges (electrons) around the nucleus. Some atoms do not have

FIGURE 8A.2
Models like these are used to keep track of the number and placement of protons, neutrons, and electrons in atoms.

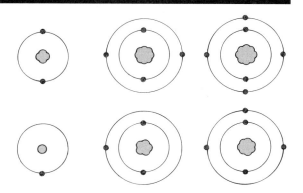

neutrons. The hydrogen atom, for example, has one proton and one electron but no neutrons. The helium atom consists of two protons and two neutrons in the nucleus surrounded by two orbiting electrons.

The *atomic number* of an element is the number of protons it contains. The *atomic weight* of an element is the weight of its protons plus the weight of its neutrons. An element's atomic weight is also determined in relation to the weight of a carbon atom, which is 12 units. A hydrogen atom has about $1/12$ the weight of a carbon atom. Therefore, hydrogen has an atomic weight of about 1. Magnesium is about twice as heavy as carbon; its atomic weight is 24. Here are the atomic weights of some elements:

Aluminum	27.0
Carbon	12.0
Chlorine	35.5
Copper	63.5
Gold	196.9
Hydrogen	1.0
Lead	207.2
Oxygen	16.0
Silver	107.0
Sulfur	32.1

Some atoms of an element are slightly heavier than most atoms of the same element. These atoms are known as *isotopes.* For example, the most common sulfur atom has an atomic weight of 32. However, some sulfur atoms have a weight of 36. Both types of atom are sulfur atoms, since they have an atomic number of 16. The average atomic weight of sulfur atoms is about 32.1. The 0.1 results from the atoms that have slightly different atomic weights. These isotopes of sulfur have the exact chemical properties of the element sulfur. Their physical properties, however, may differ from those of the predominant sulfur atoms. There are at least three isotopes of hydrogen in nature: hydrogen 1, hydrogen 2, and hydrogen 3. Study Figure 8A.3 and note that most hydrogen atoms have one proton and one electron. However, hydrogen isotopes may have one proton, one electron, and one neutron (hydrogen 2) or one proton, one electron, and two neutrons (hydrogen 3). The atomic weight of hydrogen represents the average weight of all hydrogen atoms, including the isotopes.

FIGURE 8A.3 The nuclei of these hydrogen isotopes have the same number of protons but not the same number of neutrons. Because the number of neutrons is different, each isotope has slightly different physical properties.

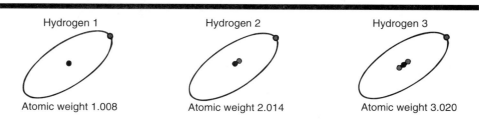

Hydrogen 1	Hydrogen 2	Hydrogen 3
Atomic weight 1.008	Atomic weight 2.014	Atomic weight 3.020

Quarks and Other More Fundamental Parts of Matter

The preceding discussion of the fundamental parts of matter is intended to provide you with background knowledge for teaching the science content commonly covered in elementary and middle school materials. Although these materials seldom carry their descriptions much further, you should be aware that there are even more fundamental particles than protons and neutrons. Scientists have hypothesized the existence of these particles as a result of experiments carried out with powerful atom-smashing devices. Two of the many laboratories involved in this type of work are the Stanford Linear Accelerator Center in California and the European Laboratory for Particle Physics in Geneva, Switzerland.

At the present time, it is believed that the most fundamental particle of matter is the *quark*. There are six kinds, or *flavors,* of quarks that are known as *up, down, strange, charm, bottom,* and *top.* Each kind of quark has three varieties, or *colors: red, blue,* and *green.* (The terms *flavor* and *color,* of course, bear no relationship to our everyday use of the words flavor and color.) Scientists believe that protons and neutrons are composed of quarks.

Obviously, a discussion of quarks is not likely to occur in elementary school. However, you should be aware of the term, as your students will undoubtedly come across it. You may want to encourage some children to pursue independent reading on this and other more advanced subjects.

Nuclear Energy

When matter undergoes chemical change, some of the electrons of the various atoms involved may be exchanged or shared. In doing this, energy is released. Energy can also be released through the nucleus of the atom. Such release of energy is brought about not by an ordinary chemical change but by a change in the nucleus of the atom. Atoms of some elements, such as radium and uranium-235, are naturally unstable: They have the potential to break up spontaneously. When they break up, they throw off some of their particles and a great amount of energy. The energy that is given off is known as *radiation.* Radioactive materials are too dangerous to be handled directly, since they may discharge rays that can damage human cells. This special property of radioactive materials is used by doctors to treat cancer patients. Focused radiation can destroy cancer cells; unfortunately, healthy cells also may be destroyed in the process.

Some uranium isotopes break down spontaneously, releasing energy and particles of matter that form radium. The nucleus of the radium atom can break down further to form a stable atom of lead. The breakdown of the nucleus of an atom is called *fission.* The amount of energy released in this process can be calculated by multiplying the amount of matter that is seemingly destroyed (actually it's converted to energy) by c (the speed of light) squared. If one gram of matter is changed directly to energy, the amount of that energy is equal to the amount produced by the burning of about 3,000 tons of coal. When scientists control these reactions, they harness great amounts of energy. A controlled flow of chain reactions occurs in nuclear power plants. In detonated atomic bombs, on the other hand, uncontrolled chain reactions take place.

Matter can also be changed by a different type of nuclear reaction: *fusion*. In this process, just as in the fission process, small amounts of matter are changed to large amounts of energy. Hydrogen bombs operate as a result of fusion. The sunlight that reaches you each day, as well as the light from the other stars in the universe, is all produced by nuclear fusion. At present, controlled fusion has been accomplished only in the laboratory.

Motion

"How long till we get there?"

This question commonly punctuates long family drives to distant destinations, regardless of the frequency of the parents' response. The driver, if he or she is patient enough, will try to give the child a response that is based on the speed of the automobile, its present location, and the location of the destination.

The *speed* of an automobile is determined by the distance it travels in a given unit of time. The units commonly used to express the speed of automobiles are *kilometers per hour* and *miles per hour*. We can use our knowledge of speed to answer the child's question about how long it will take to reach a destination fairly easily. Since speed is the distance divided by the time, we can multiply the speed of the object by the time available to find how far we will travel in that time. If you know the destination is 100 kilometers (about 60 miles) away and the average speed during the journey will be 50 kilometers (about 30 miles) per hour, you can divide the speed into the distance and remark calmly that the journey will take about 2 hours.

If you specify the speed of an object and the direction in which it is traveling, you are talking about an object's *velocity*. We call changes in velocity *acceleration*. An automobile speeding up is accelerating. The rate of acceleration is equal to the change in velocity divided by the time it took for the change. If your car stops at a red light during your trip and then gains a speed of 50 kilometers per hour (about 30 miles per hour) in 10 seconds, traveling in a straight line, the change in velocity is 50 kilometers per hour and it occurs in 10 seconds. Therefore, the rate of acceleration of the car is 5 kilometers per hour per second (about 3 miles per hour per second).

Since scientists define velocity as both speed and direction, an object that moves with constant speed yet changes direction is accelerating. For example, a racing car traveling around a track at a constant speed is accelerating because its direction is constantly changing.

With this information in mind, we can now consider objects in motion. To understand why objects in motion behave as they do, we need to understand the laws that govern them.

Newton's Laws of Motion

Have you ever blown up a balloon, held its end shut, and then released it to watch it rocket around the room? You may not have realized it, but you were demonstrating a phenomenon described about 300 years ago by Isaac Newton. Newton's observations of the motion of objects led him to reach conclusions that we now refer to as *laws of motion.* Newton's three laws of motion help us explain the motion of objects that are subjected to forces.

Newton's first law of motion, sometimes called the *law of inertia,* states that an object at rest will remain at rest and a body moving with a constant velocity in a straight line will maintain its motion unless acted upon by an unbalanced external force. This law tells us that in order to change the position of an object at rest, we must apply a force to it. Similarly, if we wish to change the velocity of an object, we must apply a force. To move a golf ball from the grass of a putting green to the hole, we apply a force with the putter. To increase the speed of an automobile, we cause the engine to increase the forces that turn the wheels. To slow down a bicycle that is moving along at a constant velocity, we apply frictional forces by using the brakes.

Newton's second law of motion states that the amount of acceleration produced by a force acting on an object varies with the magnitude of the force and the mass of the object. If the force on an object is increased and no mass is added to or taken away from the object, the object's acceleration will increase. Specifically, this law tells us that an object will accelerate in the direction in which an applied force is acting and that the acceleration will be proportional to the applied force. For example, when we begin to push or pull a child in a wagon that was stationary, the wagon moves in the direction of the push or pull and increases its acceleration as the force we apply increases.

Newton's third law of motion states that for every action, there is an equal and opposite reaction. The air escaping from the blown-up balloon mentioned earlier moves in one direction; it is the action force. The balloon moves in the opposite direction as a reaction to the action force.

Gravity and Motion

Whether you live in Beijing, China, or Paramus, New Jersey, you know that what goes up must come down and the downward path is always the same: All objects fall toward the center of the earth. After studying the behavior of falling objects, Newton concluded that the cause for the path of a falling object was the attractive force that exists between masses. This force of attraction depends on two variables: the mass of each attracting object and the distance between them.

Very precise scientific instruments have revealed that Newton was correct in his conclusion that all masses exert attractive forces. Newton's conclusion is called the *law of universal gravitation,* and it is a fundamental law of the universe. Every mass in the universe attracts every other mass with a force that varies directly with the product of the masses of the objects and inversely with the square of the distance between them. This law can be written as an equation:

$$F = G\, m_1 m_2 / r^2$$

Although it may not look it, this is actually an easy equation to understand. The *m*'s represent the masses of the two objects. The *r* is the distance between the centers of the objects. The *G* is a constant. In other words, the same value of *G* is used every time the equation is solved. *F* stands for the actual force of attraction between objects. As noted earlier, the force of attraction between an object and the earth is the object's weight.

The earth's gravitational pull causes falling objects to accelerate at the rate of 9.8 meters per second per second (32 feet per second per second). This means that an object increases its speed 9.8 meters per second (32 feet per second) during each second it falls. Strictly speaking, this rate applies to objects falling through a vacuum, since the presence of air retards the acceleration of objects that have a large surface area compared with their mass.

Jet and Rocket Engines

Rockets and jet airplanes are designed to capitalize on Newton's third law of motion. Both utilize engines that discharge hot gases in one direction (an action force) so as to produce thrust (a reaction force). In both engines, chemical energy is changed to the energy of motion.

The jet engine uses kerosene fuel to heat air that is taken into the engine. The products of the combustion of kerosene reach a high temperature and pressure and leave through the rear of the engine. This produces the reaction force, or *thrust*. In the turbojet, turning compressor blades take in air through the front of the engine and force it into the combustion chamber. At this point, kerosene is sprayed into the air and ignited. The hot exhaust gases expand and move out the back of the engine, turning the turbine blades in the process. The turbine blades are connected to the compressor blades and cause them to turn and bring in more air.

The engine of a rocket is designed to operate in outer space in the absence of oxygen. To provide the fuel that is burned with the oxygen needed for burning, tanks of liquid oxygen are carried near the engine. Some rocket fuels do not require oxygen. Instead, they use a chemical known as an *oxidizer.*

Flight

"Just pull the yellow oxygen mask toward you.
Now cover your mouth and breathe normally."

Each time a flight attendant says that prior to takeoff, I begin to wonder: How exactly do you breathe *normally* when an aircraft is having a serious problem that may soon give it the aerodynamic characteristics of a rock? I understand the physics of flight, but I am always astonished that masses of metal can become airborne. It is most amazing!

What causes an airplane to rise? The answer is a force called *lift*. A plane's wings are shaped so that air going across the upper surface moves at a higher velocity than the air going across the bottom surface. This causes a region of low pressure to form above the wing. The air pressure below the wing is greater than the air pressure above the wing, causing an unbalanced upward force.

The lifting force on a wing can be varied in several ways. For example, the faster a plane moves, the more lift is created. The angle that the front of the wing makes with the oncoming air also affects lift. This angle is known as the *angle of attack*. In fixed-wing aircraft, the pilot varies the angle of attack by using movable portions of the wing called *wing flaps*, or ailerons. Extending the wing flaps also increases the surface area of the wing. A larger surface produces more lift than a smaller surface.

FIGURE 8A.4
Each of these controls can change
an airplane's direction.

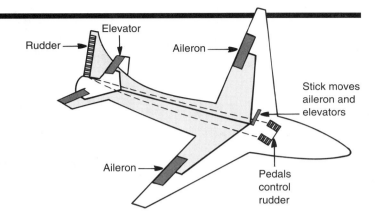

While the forward motion, or thrust, of a jet is a reaction force to hot exhaust gases expelled from the rear of the engine, propeller-driven planes move forward because of the propeller, which is designed very much like a miniature wing. The pressure on the rear surface of the propeller pushes the plane forward. Pilots use the term *drag* to describe a force that retards the forward motion of an aircraft. It results from the friction between the air and the surfaces of the aircraft.

The direction in which an airplane moves is controlled by the pilot's use of the ailerons, elevator, and rudder (see Figure 8A.4). The *elevator* (the movable flap on the horizontal part of the tail) causes the aircraft's nose to move up or down. The *rudder* (the movable flap on the vertical portion of the tail) causes the nose of the aircraft to move left or right. The *ailerons* change the lift on the wing surfaces. The pilot uses all these surfaces in combination to turn the plane.

Summary Outline

I. Anything that occupies space and has weight is matter.
  A. A change in matter from one state, or phase, to another is a physical change.
  B. Molecular theory is used to explain a variety of changes in matter.
  C. A change in matter that produces a new substance is a chemical change.
  D. Matter exists as elements, compounds, and mixtures.
  E. Atoms are composed of smaller particles.
  F. Under special conditions, portions of the matter in an atomic nucleus can be converted to energy.

II. Matter can be caused to move from place to place.
  A. Newton's laws of motion describe how the motion of an object will change as a result of the application of a force.
  B. The law of universal gravitation states that all masses are attracted to all other masses by a force that varies directly with the product of the masses and inversely with the square of the distance between them.
  C. The motion of jet planes and rockets can be explained by Newton's third law of motion, which states that for every action there is an equal and opposite reaction.
  D. Airplanes fly as a result of the action of two forces: lift and thrust.

8B

Matter and Motion

Attention Getters, Discovery Activities, and Demonstrations

ATTENTION GETTERS

Why Do We Need to Wear Safety Belts?

Materials
1 small toy wagon or truck
1 doll that can ride in or on top of toy wagon or truck
2 large rubber bands

Motivating Questions
- What direction will the doll move when the wagon suddenly stops?
- If the doll were wearing a safety belt, would it still move?

Directions
1. Display the wagon or truck without the doll. Gently roll it into the wall.
2. Put the doll in the wagon, gently push the wagon, and have the children predict in what direction the doll will move when the wagon strikes the wall.
3. After they have observed the wagon striking the wall, relate the wagon and doll to a car and passenger. Discuss the likelihood of the passenger striking or going through the windshield if the car hits something or stops suddenly.
4. Use the rubber band to restrain the doll, and repeat the demonstration. Ask the children for their observations.

Science Content for the Teacher
A fundamental law of motion is that an object at rest or in uniform motion tends to continue in that condition. An unrestrained passenger in a forward-moving automobile continues to move forward if the car stops, since he or she is not connected to the car.

Where Does the Water Go?

Materials
1 sponge   Bowl of water
Paper towels   3 dishes
1 clean, dry dishcloth   Pan balance (optional)

Motivating Questions
- How will the sponge (paper towel, cloth) change when we dip it in water?
- Where do you think the water goes when something dries?

Directions
1. In this demonstration, the children will observe a sponge, paper towel, and cloth when dry and when wet. The children will already know that when they dry themselves after a bath or shower, the towels they use become wet, but they may not have connected this knowledge with the concept that some materials can absorb water.
2. Dip the sponge, paper towel, and dishcloth in the bowl of water. Have the children make observations that you record on the board.

3. After wringing out the objects, place them on plates so that further observations can be made. If a pan balance is available, the children can check changes in mass as the objects dry.

Science Content for the Teacher   Many materials are capable of absorbing water. They retain this water as a liquid. The liquid that is in contact with the surrounding air evaporates and enters the air as water vapor.

For Young Learners [PS 2]

Where Are Wheels?

Materials   Easel paper and markers
Pack of index cards

Motivating Questions
- Is it easier to pull something with wheels or something without wheels?
- Do wheels all have the same shape or size?

Directions
1. Take the children for a walk around the school, both inside and outside the building. Challenge them to find as many wheels as they can. As they search, model how a scientist keeps track of information by writing notes about each wheeled vehicle observed on an index card. Use a different index card for each vehicle. Look for such things as automobiles, bicycles, cafeteria and custodial carts, wagons, and trucks. Don't miss the wheels under audiovisual carts and movable chalkboards or room dividers.
2. When you return to the room, prepare a three-column chart that includes a drawing of each vehicle and the number of wheels on it. Have the children discuss how wheels help move objects.

Science Content for the Teacher   Friction is a force that acts against the forward-moving wagon. If the force is large enough, it can slow down or stop the wagon. Wheels reduce the friction between objects and the ground. As a wheel turns, only a small amount of it touches the ground, which reduces the friction between the object and the ground and makes the object easier to move.

For Middle-Level Learners [PS 5]

Why Do Mothballs Rise and Fall?

Materials   1 unopened 2 liter bottle of club soda
6 mothballs

Motivating Questions
- Where do the bubbles in soda come from?
- What is in the bubbles?
- Why do the mothballs go up and down?

Directions
1. Have the children make some observations of the club soda before you open the cap.
2. Open the cap, have the children observe the bubbles that form throughout the soda, and then display the mothballs.
3. Drop the mothballs into the club soda, and have the children make observations about the motion of the mothballs.

Science Content for the Teacher
Club soda is water to which carbon dioxide has been added under pressure. Mothballs have a density that is close to the density of water. Thus, they will almost but not quite float. The carbon dioxide bubbles coat the surface of the mothballs, increasing the volume of the mothballs but only minimally increasing their mass. The mothballs and attached bubbles move toward the surface of the soda. When they reach the surface, the bubbles burst and the mothballs sink. This process continues as long as carbon dioxide gas is released in the soda.

For Middle-Level Learners [PS 4]

Can You Separate Sugar and Sand?

Materials
1 empty, clear 2 liter soda bottle   1/4 cup of sugar
1/4 cup of sand   1 saucer

Motivating Questions
■ When you mix sugar and sand, are you making a physical or chemical change?
■ How could we separate the sugar and sand?

Directions
1. Fill the bottle half full of water, and keep it out of sight. Display the sand and sugar. Mix both together on the saucer, and challenge the children to invent a way to separate them.
2. After a discussion of alternative strategies, show the bottle containing water. Ask the children if they have any ideas on how the bottle could be used to separate the mixture.
3. Add the mixture to the bottle, and shake it vigorously. The sand will settle to the bottom, and the water will dissolve the sugar. Challenge the children to think of a way to get the sugar back.

Science Content for the Teacher
Sugar, sand, and water do not chemically react to produce a new substance. The dissolving of sugar in water is a physical change, since the sugar can be recovered by evaporating the water.

For Middle-Level Learners [PS 5]

What Causes Lift?

Materials
2 textbooks of equal thickness   1 sheet of notebook paper

Motivating Questions
■ What do you think will happen if we blow under the paper?
■ What does the movement of the paper tell us about how an airplane is able to fly?

Directions
1. Align the books on a table top so they are about 10 centimeters (about 4 inches) apart. Lay the notebook paper across the tops of the books.
2. Ask the children to predict what will happen if you blow under the paper. Blow under the paper, and then ask the children for their observations.

Science Content for the Teacher
According to Bernoulli's principle, if we cause a fluid to move, the pressure in the fluid is reduced. Think of air as a fluid. By causing the air under the paper to move, you reduce the air pressure under the paper. Because the air pressure under the paper is slightly lower than the air pressure above the paper, the paper moves down. An airplane wing has a shape that forces air to move faster across the top than across the bottom. This lowers air pressure at the top and causes the wing to rise. The unbalanced force that moves the wing up is called *lift*.

For Middle-Level Learners [HNS 2, 3, and 4]

Marie Curie: Scientist and Humanitarian

Materials
Access to the Internet
Assorted art materials

Science resource books and encyclopedias
Assorted fabric pieces

Motivating Questions
- What do you think the word *humanitarian* means?
- Have you ever heard of Marie Curie and what she discovered?

Directions
1. Ask each group to research one of the following sets of questions (but more than one group can work on a given set):
   a. Where and when was Marie Curie born? What was her home life like? Where did she go to school? What subjects did she study? What research did she and Pierre Curie do? What was dangerous about it?
   b. What prize did Marie Curie win? What prize did she and Pierre win?
   c. How did the Curies' scientific work eventually help others? What other work did Marie Curie do to help people?
2. Each group should select and prepare someone to play Marie Curie. She will speak to the class for 2 or 3 minutes and answer questions about her group's research information. "Marie Curie" may wear some primitive costuming and use props.

Science Content for the Teacher
Marya Sklodowska, later known as Marie Curie, was an extraordinary physicist who, with her husband, Pierre, received the Nobel Prize for discovering natural radioactivity. Marie received another Nobel Prize on her own for her study of radium. The Curies' work led to the development of X-ray technology and the use of radiation to treat cancer. In addition to Marie Curie's scientific achievements, she devoted much of her attention to ways of relieving human suffering.

DISCOVERY ACTIVITIES

Matter and Changes¹

Objectives
- The children will identify a substance as a solid or a liquid.
- The children will describe changes in the color, shape, size, and state of samples of matter.

Science Processes Emphasized
Observing
Communicating

Materials for Each Child or Group
1 ice cube   Paper and pencil
3 saucers   Source of hot water
1 cube of butter the same size as the cube of clay
1 cube of modeling clay 2.5 cm × 2.5 cm × 2.5 cm (about 1 inch on edge)

Motivation
Put an ice cube in a glass, and tell the children that you are thirsty. Pretend to drink from the glass, and ask the children why you are having trouble getting a drink. The children will indicate that the ice cube must melt before you can have water to drink. Have the children discuss whether an ice cube is really water. Suggest that ice cubes might be made of "smush," a clear solid that changes to water. After some discussion of ways in which they could check to see if there is such a thing as "smush," begin the activity.

Directions
1. Have the children compare the size, shape, and color of the butter, clay, and ice cubes.
2. When this is done, have the children heat the plates in the hot water and then place the cube of butter on one plate, the cube of clay on another plate, and the ice cube on the third plate.
3. Have the children keep a record of the changes they observe.
4. After the butter and ice cubes have changed in form, discuss the states of matter, using the following questions to focus the children's thinking.

Key Discussion Questions
1. Which cubes were solid when you started the activity? What changes did you observe? *All three. The butter and the ice cubes started to melt.*
2. Did the color or shape of the cubes change? *The color didn't but the shape did.*
3. What would happen if we put the saucers in a freezer before the activity? How would the changes have been different? *The butter and ice cubes would not have melted as fast.*
4. What do you think caused the changes? *Heat.*

Science Content for the Teacher
Matter is commonly found in one of three forms or states: solid, liquid, or gas. In this activity, three substances that display the essential observable characteristics of solids are observed as heat from the air in the room and preheated sources cause a change in state. The flow of energy from these sources causes the molecules in the substances to increase their motion. In the case of the butter cube and the ice cube,

this increased energy causes the molecules to begin to flow past each other, and melting is observed. The change is a physical change because the substance remains the same but changes in form.

Extensions   *Science/Art:* Have some children make drawings of various changes, such as an icicle melting, water in a pond freezing, and a pond drying up during the summer.

Science/Physical Education: Some children may wish to make drawings of various sports that utilize water or ice. The children can discuss their drawings with the class and consider what would happen if the water depicted in them changed to ice or the ice changed to water.

For Young Learners [PS 3]

From Gas to Liquid

Objective
- The children will observe the result of water changing from gas to liquid.
- The children will infer the source of the water that condenses on the outside of a can.

Science Processes Emphasized   Observing
Inferring

Materials for Each Child or Group
1 shiny metal can or container   Paper towel
Supply of crushed ice

Motivation   Display an ice cube and a glass of water, and ask the children if they think that the ice is water. After some discussion of the possibility that water can be in a liquid form or in a solid form, explain to the children that water can be in still another form: a gas. Tell them that in this activity, they will make the invisible water in air become visible.

Directions
1. Distribute a can and paper towel to each group, and ask the children to polish the outside of the can with the towel. Have the children describe what they observe when they examine the outside of the can.
2. Have each group add crushed ice to the can.
3. Have the children again observe the outside of the can. In a short time, a thin film of water will appear on the can.

Key Discussion Questions
1. Where do you think the water that formed on the outside of the can came from? *The air.*
2. How could we get the water that formed on the outside of the can to go back into the air? *Answers will vary. Some children will suggest that they remove the ice from the can and add hot water.*

Science Content for the Teacher   Air contains water vapor, which is water in a gaseous state. The amount of water vapor that air can hold depends on various factors, including its temperature. If the temperature of air is lowered sufficiently, the water vapor in it will condense on any available surface. The temperature at which this occurs is called the *dew point*. The cold can causes air near its surface to condense and form a film of liquid water.

Extension   *Science/Health:* Ask the children to breathe on a mirror or windowpane and observe the surface. The film of water they see on the surface results from the condensation of the water vapor that is contained in the breath they exhale. The water is a by-product of the process by which food is converted to energy in the body.

For Young Learners [PS 1]

What Is Your Squeezing Force?

Objective   ■ The children will measure the amount of squeezing force they can apply.

Science Processes   Measuring
Emphasized   Interpreting data

Materials for Each   1 bathroom scale thin enough for children to grip
Child or Group

Motivation   Display the bathroom scale, and explain that it provides a measurement of the amount of pull the earth exerts on our bodies. Tell the children that they will use the scale to see how much pushing force they can exert with their hands.

Directions   1. Divide the class into groups, and have each group member squeeze the top and bottom of a bathroom scale together. The children should use both hands. As each child concentrates on squeezing the scale, another member of the group should write down the reading on the scale's weight display.
2. Have each group make a graph that shows the name of the person and the squeezing force he or she applied.

Key Discussion   1. Is the force you used to squeeze the scale a push or a pull? *The children should*
Questions   *realize they are exerting two pushes with each hand. They are pushing the top of the scale down and the bottom of the scale up.*
2. When we weigh ourselves, what is pulling us down on the scale? *The earth is pulling on us.*

Science Content   A bathroom scale has a spring system that reacts in response to the pull of gravity
for the Teacher   on any mass placed on the scale. Some scales include electrical devices that convert the movement of the springs to electrical information that is displayed in the form of a digital display.

Extension   *Science/Health:* Since young children experience rather steady growth in their skeletal/muscular system, they may find it interesting to measure their squeezing force at the beginning, middle, and end of the school year and prepare a simple graph of the results.

Secret Messages and Chemical Changes

Objectives
- The children will observe physical and chemical changes.
- The children will describe the characteristics of physical and chemical changes.

Science Processes Emphasized

Observing   Making a hypothesis
Communicating

Materials for Each Child or Group

Cotton swab   Roll of masking tape
Sheet of white paper   Plastic container of water
Iron nail   A few sheets of paper toweling
Desk lamp with incandescent 100 watt light bulbs
Access to a small container of freshly squeezed lemon juice
Small, clear plastic containers (such as disposable glasses) containing copper-sulfate solution. *Safety Note:* The containers of copper sulfate should remain under your supervision in a central location. The groups will place their iron nail in the container and simply observe the changes. At the end of the activity, you are responsible for disposing of the solutions. *At no time should the children handle copper sulfate.*

Motivation

This activity should be done following activities or discussion on physical changes. Ask the children to review the characteristics of a physical change with you, and discuss the possibility that some changes may result in the production of new substances. Tell the children that they will be doing some activities that may help them think about such changes.

Directions

1. Distribute the lemon juice, cotton swabs, and paper. Have the children write secret messages on their paper, using the swabs and lemon juice.
2. Have the children allow the paper to dry. While it is drying, have them record their observations of the lemon juice patterns on the paper.
3. Under your supervision, have the children exchange messages and take turns heating them over the reading lamps.
4. Ask the children whether they think a physical or a chemical change has occurred.
5. Distribute an iron nail to each group. Have the children clean the nails with paper towels.
6. Tell each group to make a small identifying tag out of masking tape for its nail and affix it to the top of the nail.
7. Have each group place its nail in one of the containers of copper sulfate and make observations every few hours (if this is convenient) or every time science class begins.
8. After some changes have occurred, discuss whether the changes observed are physical changes or something else.

Key Discussion Questions

1. When the secret writing became visible, do you think that there was a physical change in the lemon juice? *No, the lemon juice changed to something else. It got darker; we probably couldn't make it turn back into lemon juice.*

2. What were some changes you observed after the iron nail was placed in the blue liquid? *The blue color of the liquid got less; red stuff started to cover the nail.*

3. Do you think you saw a physical change? *No. Some new things formed. The color of the liquid changed, and the red stuff wasn't there when we started.*

Science Content for the Teacher

When matter undergoes a physical change, it changes in form but remains the same substance. Physical changes are usually easy to reverse. In contrast, this activity shows two chemical changes. In the first case, heat added to the lemon juice caused the formation of molecules that absorb light, giving the juice a dark color. In the second case, the copper that was part of the solution left the solution and accumulated on the surface of the nail as iron from the nail entered the liquid. The iron reacted with the copper sulfate to form a new substance: iron sulfate. The copper atoms that left the solution were observed in their metallic form on the surface of the nail.

Extensions

Science: You may wish to have some children observe an additional chemical change. Have them wedge some steel wool into a small glass, moisten it, and invert it in a pan of water. There should be an air space between the steel wool in the inverted glass and the water. Within a few days, the children will be able to observe the formation of rust on the steel wool—a chemical change.

Science/Language Arts: Activities such as this one can make children more sensitive to the concept of change. Recognizing changes in the environment can serve as an important first step in writing experiences that focus on change. You may wish to have the children write poetry about the changes they observe in the world around them.

For Middle-Level Learners [PS 2]

Pendulums

Objectives
- The children will predict how changing the string length and mass of a pendulum bob affect the motion of the pendulum.
- The children will measure the effect of changing the string length and mass of the bob on the motion of the pendulum.

Science Processes Emphasized

Observing   Measuring
Predicting

Materials for Each Child or Group

Horizontal wooden support at least 1 m (about 40 in.) long
4 screw eyes fastened along the length of the support
Spool of heavy-duty twine
4 sticks of modeling clay
Stopwatch
Metric ruler

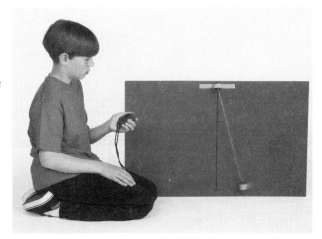

Working with pendulums gives children opportunities to make predictions and form hypotheses.

Motivation   Display the materials, and ask the children to guess what they will be learning about in this activity. Tell them that they will be making some predictions and then doing an activity to check their predictions.

Directions   1. Have one member of each group be responsible for making the pendulum bob from the clay and attaching it to string. Have another member be responsible for using the stopwatch. The children should switch roles during the activity.
2. Begin by having the children predict how changing the length of the string will affect the time it takes for the pendulum to make one complete forward-and-backward movement. Use the term *period* to represent this amount of time.
3. Explain that any object hanging from a pendulum string is call a *bob,* and ask the children to make a bob from half a stick of clay.
4. Have the children start with a 1 meter length of string and shorten it by 10 centimeters (about 4 inches) during each of the five trials. In starting the pendulum movement, always move the bob 10 centimeters (4 inches) to the left of its stationary position before releasing it.
5. The children should find the time of one back-and-forth movement by completing five such movements and then dividing by five. Once they have found the time, have them check it against their predictions.
6. Now have the children repeat this procedure using three different bobs made of one-quarter, one-half, and three-quarters of a stick of clay. Maintain the string lengths at 1 meter (about 40 inches). Each time the bob is changed, the children should predict the period and then check their predictions against their observations.

Key Discussion Questions   1. Did you predict that the length of the string would affect the period of the pendulum? *Answers will vary.*
2. What did you observe when just the length of the string was changed? *The length of the string affects the period. The longer the string, the longer the period.*
3. Did you predict that the mass of the bob would affect the period of the pendulum? *Answers will vary.*
4. What did you observe when just the mass of the bob was changed? *Changing the mass of the bob does not change the period of the pendulum.*

Science Content for the Teacher   A pendulum is a weight, or bob, suspended from a fixed point that is able to swing back and forth freely. The period of a pendulum is the time it takes for the bob to make one complete back-and-forth swing. Galileo discovered that the period of a pendulum is independent of the mass of the bob and depends only on the pendulum's length.

Extensions   *Science:* Ask the children if they think that the period of a pendulum depends on how far the bob is released from the point at which it is hanging straight down. They can then conduct an activity to check their ideas. (The period remains the same regardless of the position from which the bob is released.)

Science / Social Studies: This activity provides an excellent opportunity for children to become aware of Galileo. Read a brief biography of Galileo in a reference book, and then have children do some social studies activities that focus on him. For example, they can make a timeline and mark on it the time of Galileo's life as well as such events as the discovery of America, the American Revolution, the launching of the first space satellite, and the first moon walk. The children could also locate Italy on a world map and find the town of Pisa, where Galileo made his observations of the swinging pendulum.

For Middle-Level Learners [PS 3]

Heat and the Fizzer

Objective	■ The children will experiment to discover the relationship between temperature and the speed of a chemical reaction.
Science Processes Emphasized	Experimenting
Materials for Each Child or Group	3 Alka Seltzer tablets 3 clear plastic cups 1 ice cube Access to cool and hot water
Motivation	Review the difference between physical and chemical changes with the children. Tell the children that in this activity, they will observe the results of a chemical change and discover how heat affects chemical changes.

Directions
1. Distribute three cups and three tablets to each group. Provide access to ice cubes as well as to hot and cold water.
2. Tell the children that they are going to use their senses of sight and hearing to gauge the speed of the reaction of the tablet with water.
3. Have the children prepare the three cups of water and arrange them from cold (tap water plus an ice cube) to cool to hot. Tell the children to write their observations of bubble production and fizzing after they have dropped one tablet in each cup.

Key Discussion Questions
1. How did the temperature of the water affect the speed of each reaction? *The hotter water produced more bubbles faster.*
2. Does this experiment prove that heat speeds up a chemical reaction? *No. It only shows that more heat seems to speed up this reaction. There may be reactions that slow down if heat is added.*

Science Content for the Teacher
One of the products of the reaction of Alka Seltzer with water is carbon dioxide gas. The rate of production of carbon dioxide bubbles is one indicator of the rate at which this reaction takes place.

Extension
Science/Health: Have the students compare the ingredients in a variety of over-the-counter stomach upset remedies. After they have done this, have them research the common causes of an upset stomach and the preventive steps people can take to reduce their dependence on over-the-counter remedies.

DEMONSTRATIONS

The Toy Car in the Wagon: Pushes and Pulls

Objectives
- The children will identify one type of force as a push and another as a pull.
- The children will observe the tendency of an object to remain in one place or to remain in uniform motion.

Science Processes Emphasized
Observing
Making hypotheses

Materials
Child's wagon   Large toy car with functioning wheels

Motivation
Display the wagon, but keep the car out of sight. Tell the children that you are going to use the wagon to help them learn some interesting things about how objects move. Ask for a volunteer to assist you.

Directions
Note: Because this demonstration requires ongoing discussion, Key Discussion Questions are included in each step.

1. Ask the children why the wagon is not floating in the air. Use their responses to help them understand that the earth is pulling the wagon downward. Explain that this pull is called a *force*. Then pick up the wagon, and ask the children if you used a force. Put the wagon down, and ask your volunteer to use a force to pull the wagon. Have the volunteer demonstrate a push. Summarize by explaining that forces can be pushes or pulls.
2. Ask the children if the wagon moves in the same direction as the force. *Yes.*
3. Place the toy car in the back of the wagon so the back of the car is touching the back of the wagon. Have the children make guesses (hypotheses) about what will happen to the wagon and car if the volunteer pulls the wagon forward at a steady but high speed. Before the volunteer demonstrates this, ask how the toy car in the wagon will move during the journey and at the stop. Have the children watch the demonstration closely. They will observe that the toy car continues to move forward after an abrupt stop. Repeat this with the toy car at the front of the wagon.

Key Discussion Questions
See Directions.

Science Content for the Teacher
When the wagon is stationary, all forces acting on it balance each other. The earth's pulling force is balanced by a reacting force: the earth pushing on the cart in the opposite direction. The wagon displays forward motion if an unbalanced force acts on it. Although the term is not used, the toy car placed at the back of the wagon is used to demonstrate *inertia*. In other words, an object set in motion tends to keep moving.

Extension
Science/Physical Education: Bring a variety of athletic equipment to class, such as a baseball, baseball bat, football, field hockey stick, field hockey ball, jump rope, and so forth. Have various children demonstrate how forces are involved in using these objects.

For Young Learners [PS 2]

How Does an Earth Satellite Get Placed in Orbit?

Objectives
- The children will observe a model of the launching of a rocket and the placement of a satellite in orbit.
- The children will identify the forces at work during the launching process.
- The children will infer the causes of the forces.

Science Processes Emphasized
Observing
Inferring

Materials

Tennis ball	Globe
1 m (1 yd.) length of string	Small model rocketship
Magazine pictures of various satellites that have been placed in orbit	

Motivation
Before class, firmly attach the tennis ball to the string. When class begins, display the magazine pictures of the satellites and engage the children in a discussion of how satellites are placed in orbit. Solicit their ideas about why satellites remain in orbit after they are launched. Now display the materials, and explain to the children that you are going to use these materials to illustrate the process of launching and orbiting a satellite.

Directions
1. Hold the rocket so the children can see it. Place it on the surface of the globe. Indicate that a satellite is usually placed in the nose cone of the rocket that will launch it into orbit. Show the satellite being launched by lifting the rocket from the earth's surface. Explain that the exhaust gases are expelled from the back of the rocket and that this causes the rocket to move forward.
2. Explain that as the rocket moves upward, it must counteract the force of gravity pulling on it. Show the rocket turning as it places the satellite in orbit.
3. Use the tennis ball on the string to show how the satellite stays in orbit. Whirl the ball around your head by the string that is attached to it, and explain that the string represents the earth's pull on the satellite. The reaction force that is produced on the forward-moving satellite acts outward and counteracts the effect of gravity. Because the inward force is counterbalanced by the outside force, the satellite is weightless.

Key Discussion Questions
1. Have you ever seen a satellite launch on television? What were some of the things you noticed? *Answers will vary.*
2. Does the rocket stay attached to the satellite when the satellite is put into orbit? *No. It falls to the earth, and the satellite keeps moving ahead.*
3. What keeps pulling the satellite downward? *Gravity.*
4. Why does the satellite keep moving forward? *If you start an object moving, it keeps moving unless something slows it down. In space, there are no air particles to slow the satellite down.*

Science Content for the Teacher
A ball thrown in a perfect horizontal line from the top of a tall building follows a curved path as it falls to the earth. How far it travels from the building before it strikes the earth depends on how fast it was thrown and how high the building is.

An object thrown forward at a speed of 7,800 meters per second (about 25,600 feet per second) at a height of 160 kilometers (about 100 miles) would not return to the earth. Instead, it would follow a curved path around the earth. Inertia would carry it forward, and the attraction of the earth's gravitational field would keep it continually bending toward the earth's surface.

Satellites remain in orbit as a result of a balance between the pull of gravity inward and a reaction force outward. The scientific names for these forces are *centripetal* (inward) and *centrifugal* (outward). The satellite orbits the earth because the inward and outward forces produce a balance.

Extensions
Science: This demonstration provides a good starting point for somewhat more extensive study of rockets and space exploration. You may wish to obtain age-appropriate books from your learning center to place in your classroom. Encourage children to look for pictures of rocket launches, actual satellites, and descriptions of each satellite's use.

Science/Social Studies: Talk to the children about the financial cost of space exploration. Are the costs justified when compared with the short-term and long-term benefits? The risks involved in space travel could also be part of this discussion, given the potential for loss of lives as well as costly resources. Children can be made aware of the fact that a society's resources are limited and that difficult decisions must be made to ensure that they are used wisely.

For Middle-Level Learners [PS 5]

Teacher on Wheels: Action and Reaction Forces

Objectives
- The children will observe that an action force applied in one direction produces a reaction force in the opposite direction.
- The children will predict the direction and magnitude of reaction forces.

Science Processes Emphasized
Observing
Predicting

Materials
A pair of inline skates or a skateboard
Length of board 25 cm × 3 cm × 50 cm (about 10 in. × 1 in. × 20 in.)
12 large marbles
Old textbooks of assorted sizes (or large beanbags)

Motivation
Tell the children that you intend to get on inline skates or a skateboard to demonstrate action and reaction forces. That should be sufficient motivation!

Directions
1. Place the board on the floor. Stand on the board, and have the children predict what will happen to it when you jump off one end of it. Jump and then explain to the children that although they didn't observe anything happening to the board, your action caused a reaction force to be applied to it. The board didn't move because of the friction between the floor and the board.
2. Ask the children to predict what will happen if you repeat your jump but reduce the friction between the floor and the board. Place all of the marbles under the

board. Spread them out so that they support all parts of the board. Step on the board gently so that you do not disturb the marbles under it, and jump off one end. The children will see the board move in the opposite direction.

3. Put on the skates or step on the skateboard. Have a volunteer hand you some old textbooks or beanbags. Ask the children to predict what will happen if you throw a textbook or beanbag from your perch on wheels. Execute a rapid underhand throw of the textbook or beanbag to an awaiting container.

4. Vary the number of books or beanbags and the direction and speed with which they are thrown. Have children make predictions prior to each demonstration of action and reaction.

Key Discussion Questions

1. When I threw the book while I was standing on the skateboard (skates), what was the reaction and what was the action? *The action was the book being thrown. The reaction was your movement in the other direction.*

2. What happened when I threw the book faster? *You moved in the other direction faster.*

3. Jet and rocket engines work because of action and reaction. What is the action and what is the reaction when these engines operate? *The hot gases going out the back of the engine is the action. The plane or rocket moving forward is the reaction.*

Science Content for the Teacher

This demonstration illustrates Newton's third law of motion, although it is unnecessary to refer to it as such. This law states that for every action, there is an equal and opposite reaction. For example, when we apply a force to the earth as we try to take a step, a reaction force pushes our body forward. Similarly, any time we apply a force to an object, a reaction force is produced. This law of nature can be taken advantage of to produce motion in any direction. A jet engine causes an airplane to move forward as a reaction to the action force produced when hot gases are expelled from the rear of the engine.

Extensions

Science: Have a group of children follow up this demonstration by attempting to build a device that will launch small objects in one direction and display a reaction force in the other direction.

Many toystores sell plastic rockets that are launched as a result of the rearward movement of water out the back end. A small pump is used to fill the rocket with water. A small group of children might wish to demonstrate (under your close supervision) the launching of such a rocket on the playground.

Science/Physical Education: Some children may wish to extend their knowledge of action and reaction forces by identifying athletic events that depend on these forces. For example, the downward jump on the diving board by a diver is the action force; the reactive force is the upward propelling of the diver.

NOTE

1. This was adapted from "Change," Module 17, in *Science: A Process Approach II* (Lexington, MA: Ginn).

9A Energies and Machines

Content

How Energy Is Transferred

"Psssst. Drop your pencil at exactly 9:15. Pass it on."

A little mischief is about to take place, and a substitute's teaching day is about to take a turn for the worse. It's an old prank, but it will work once again. At precisely 9:15, 25 pencils fall from desktops to the floor, and innocent faces gaze about, waiting for the substitute's reaction.

I'll bet that the conspirators in the old drop-the-pencils-on-the-floor routine don't realize that they are demonstrating an important scientific phenomenon: the process of energy change. Imagine that the substitute teacher outsmarted the class by not reacting to the tap, tap, tap of the pencils and the class decided to try a repeat performance. Follow the energy changes as the prank is recycled.

When you pick up the pencil from the floor and place it on your desk, you do work and use energy. Your body uses some of the energy created by the chemical breakdown of the food you eat. This energy enables you to move, grasp, and lift. It may surprise you to learn that when you pick up the pencil, some of the energy that you use increases the pencil's potential energy. The pencil resting on the desk has some potential energy. When it is lifted above the desktop, it has even more. It is higher above the earth than it was before, and if you drop it again, you will hear a sound when it hits the floor. That sound is produced when the potential energy of the falling pencil is converted to the energy of motion.

Energy of motion is called *kinetic energy*. The amount of kinetic energy of an object is equal to $\frac{1}{2}mv^2$ (one-half the object's mass times its velocity squared). As the pencil falls, it moves faster and faster, continually gaining kinetic energy. When it hits the floor, its acquired kinetic energy causes the floor and itself to vibrate, producing a sound wave (a vibration that moves through the air). The pencil and the floor also heat up slightly. The original potential energy of the pencil was transformed into sound energy and heat energy.

The Conservation of Energy

The ability of energy to change its form is the basis of the *law of conservation of energy*. This important law simply states that energy is neither created nor destroyed. Whenever we use energy, we change its form, but we do not use it up. The energy we use may be changed to a less useful form, but it still exists. In the example of the pencil being picked up, placed on a table, and dropped again, some of the sun's energy was stored in food, your digestive and cellular-respiration processes released some of this energy, and you used this energy to lift the pencil. In the process, you transferred some of this energy to the pencil in the form of heat. The pencil acquired potential energy from its new position, and as it fell, it displayed increasing kinetic energy. The kinetic energy was changed to heat and sound. It is at least theoretically possible, if difficult in practice, to recapture this heat and sound energy and reuse it. All the energy you used to pick up the pencil still exists. It has just changed to other forms of energy.

According to Albert Einstein, energy and matter are related. In fact, they can be considered one and the same, since each can be converted to the other. Einstein's equation $E = mc^2$ does not contradict the law of conservation of energy because mass can be viewed as stored energy. Scientists no longer say that energy is never used up; instead, they say that the total amount of energy and mass in the universe is never used up. The interchangeability of mass and energy has resulted in the use of a more general law than either the law of conservation of energy or the law of conservation of mass. Now it is generally agreed that we should think in terms of a *law of conservation of mass and energy*.

Energy Transfer in Action: The Segway

For an extraordinary example of how cutting-edge technology is able to transfer energy from one source to another, just consider the *Segway Human Transporter (HT)* (see Figure 9A.1). This personal transportation vehicle, invented by a group of scientists led by Dean Kamen, can "read" the minute changes in muscle pressure transmitted by its rider and move accordingly: forward, backward, left, right, and so on.

In terms of energy transfer, the process begins at an electricity-generating plant, where fossil, hydroelectric, or nuclear energy causes generators to turn and produce electrical energy. That electrical energy is then sent through power wires to a variety of destinations: homes, factories, schools, and businesses.

FIGURE 9A.1   The Segway Human Transporter (HT) converts electrical energy to kinetic energy.

Structural components are thoroughly analyzed, fatigue and strength tested, and subjected to long-term durability testing.

Segway HT's on-board processors (10 in total) monitor balance and system health 100 times a second, responding instantly to the rider's movements.

Segway HT's electrical system meets or exceeds industry standards for electrical safety and interference.

Fully redundant electrical design can continue to balance and gracefully come to a stop after a component failure.

The Segway HT's design puts the weight low, resulting in a center of gravity only 10 inches above the ground.

At one such destination—say, your home—the Segway is connected to an electrical outlet and its batteries are charged. The stored chemical energy in the batteries is transformed into electrical energy once you get onboard and direct the Segway. In fact, based on what other riders have reported, you'll likely find that the Segway is so sensitive to changes in your body position that it will seem as though it's reading your mind! In any event, the wheels turn as electrical energy is converted to kinetic energy and the Segway rolls along.

Electrical Energy

The bright flash of lightning jumping across the night sky and the subdued light coming from a desk lamp are both produced by electrical energy. They are similar to each other in that the source of their energy is electrons. They are different, however, in that lightning is a form of static electricity and the light from a desk lamp is a form of current electricity.

Static Electricity

Lightning, a spark jumping from your fingertip to a metal doorknob, and the clinging together of articles of clothing when they are removed from a clothes drier are all forms of *static electricity.* In order to understand them, you will need to review your knowledge of atoms. An atom consists of protons, neutrons, and electrons. Each proton has a positive charge—one unit of positive energy. Each electron has a negative charge—one unit of negative energy. Neutrons have no charge. Because atoms normally have the same number of electrons as protons, the positive and negative charges cancel each other out. As a result, atoms usually have no charge; they are considered neutral.

If, however, an electron is removed from a neutral atom, the atom is left with a positive charge. If an electron is added to a neutral atom, the atom acquires a negative charge. When certain materials are rubbed together, electrons are transferred from one surface to the other. In other words, one surface gains electrons and acquires a negative charge. The other surface, having lost electrons, is left with a positive charge. When a surface has acquired a strong negative charge, the extra electrons may jump to a neutral or positive object. You see this jump of electrons when you see a spark. A spark is a rapid movement of a number of electrons through the air.

You may have had the exciting adolescent experience of kissing a boyfriend or girlfriend with braces and being shocked by a spark. The excitement may have come from the kiss, but the shock was the result of static electricity. Electrons were probably inadvertently rubbed from the fibers of a rug or other floor covering by the soles of the "kisser" or "kissee," giving that person's body a surplus negative charge. The extra charge was removed by the spark jumping from the negatively charged person to the neutrally charged person.

Lightning is a giant spark that sometimes occurs when clouds that have acquired a charge suddenly discharge electrons. The rapid outward movement of the air heated by the lightning causes the sound wave that reaches our ears as thunder.

Current Electricity

Sometimes, it seems that my doorbell never stops ringing, and if I am busy, I get grumpier each time it rings. If I get grumpy enough, sometimes I curse Benjamin Franklin, Thomas Edison, and my local electric company all in one breath for bringing electrical energy to my home. Even so, I know we are living at a time when electricity is a necessity, not a luxury. Occasional electrical blackouts bring activities to a grinding halt: Traffic lights don't work; elevators stop wherever they happen to be; heating and cooling equipment stops functioning; lights go out; and food in refrigerators begins to rot. Electricity has become a necessity for us because it is an excellent and convenient form of energy. It can be converted to heat, to light, and to sound. It can also be used to operate electric motors that cause objects to move.

Current electricity comes from a stream of electrons moving through a conductor. The rate at which the electrons move through the conductor is called *current*. So many electrons flow through a given point in a conductor in a short time that scientists have found it useful to have a unit to represent a large number of electrons flowing through a current. The unit for measuring electrical current is the *ampere*. It is equal to the flow of 6.25×10^{18} electrons past a point in a conductor in 1 second. Electron current that moves in just one direction is termed *direct current*. Electricity from dry cells (batteries) is direct current. Current that changes direction is known as *alternating current*. Electricity for home or industrial use is alternating current.

A *conductor* is any material that electrons can move though easily. Such a material offers little *resistance* to the flow of electrons. The amount of resistance to the flow of electrical energy is measured in *ohms*. Examples of materials that are good conductors include copper, silver, gold, and aluminum. Energy is transferred through a conductor by a process that includes high-energy electrons imparting their energy to the outermost electrons of adjacent atoms of the conductor.

Not all substances are good electrical conductors. Wood, rubber, plastic, and dry air are examples of substances that do not carry electrical energy very well. Because these materials are poor conductors, they offer high resistance to the flow of electron and are called *insulators*.

Some substances—for example, germanium, silicon, and selenium—are neither conductors nor insulators. They are *semiconductors* that can be used to make tiny electrical devices to control the flow of electrons. Semiconductors are widely used in the fabrication of computer chips.

Electrical Circuits

Figure 9A.2 (page 258) illustrates a simple electrical circuit. In an electrical circuit, electrons with a great deal of energy leave a source (in this case, a dry cell), move through a conductor (a wire), lose some energy in a load or resistance (a light bulb), and return to the source. As long as the switch is closed (the wires are connected), energy is transmitted through the circuit. The light bulb—the resistance—converts some of the electrical energy to light energy.

In the type of electrical circuit illustrated in Figure 9A.3 (page 258), chemical reactions in the dry cells provide the push that starts and keeps high-energy electrons

FIGURE 9A.2

In this electric circuit, the lamps are wired in series.

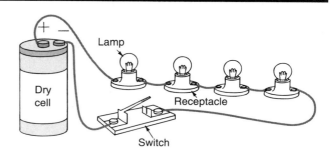

FIGURE 9A.3

When lamps are wired in parallel, as shown here, the bulbs will remain lit even if one goes out.

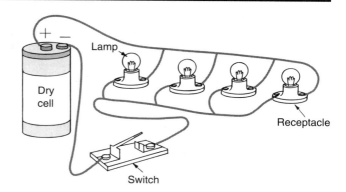

flowing into the conductor. The electrons leave the negative pole, or port, and return to the dry cell at the positive pole, or port. The amount of push that causes the electrons to move through a circuit is called the *voltage*. The voltage that a dry cell can produce can be measured by determining the amount of work that the electrons do in the circuit. The unit of measurement for voltage is *volts*.

Although there are many ways to attach sources of high-energy electrons, conductors, and loads to each other, we usually concern ourselves with two basic circuits: series circuits and parallel circuits. A *series circuit* has only one path for electrons. A circuit that has more than one path for electrons is a *parallel circuit*. Figure 9A.2 shows a series circuit. Figure 9A.3 shows a parallel circuit.

Since there is only one path, the current is the same throughout a series circuit. In a parallel circuit, however, the current is divided among many paths. If one light bulb in a series circuit burns out, all the light bulbs will go out because only one path for electrons exists. If a light bulb in one branch of a parallel circuit burns out, the bulbs in the other branches will remain lit.

Magnets, Generators, and Motors

Although chemical reactions in dry cells can start a flow of electrons through a conductor, moving a conductor through a magnetic field or moving a magnet so that the lines of force in the magnetic field cut through the conductor can also start a flow of electrons. Metals that have the ability to attract iron, steel, and some other metals are said to have a property called *magnetism*. Magnetite, or lodestone, is a naturally occurring iron ore that has such magnetic properties. Alnico, a material that contains aluminum, nickel, cobalt, and iron, can be used to make a permanent magnet, even though aluminum, nickel, cobalt, and iron are not naturally magnetic. When these substances are brought near a strong magnet, they become magnetic.

All magnets have two poles: a north pole and a south pole. A bar magnet suspended at its center by a string will rotate until one end points north. The magnet end that points north is known as the *north-seeking pole*. The other end of the magnet is the *south-seeking pole*. If two **N** poles or two **S** poles are brought near each other, they will repel. When unlike poles are brought near each other, they attract. The rotation of a freely suspended bar magnet until it is oriented north and south is evidence that the earth itself is a magnet. The earth's magnetic pole attracts the pole of a magnet.

Around all magnets is a region that we call a *magnetic field*. If we move a conductor through a magnetic field so that it cuts through the lines of force in the field, an electric current will be produced in the conductor. An electrical generator produces electrical energy either by spinning a coiled conductor between the poles of a magnet or by rotating a magnet or series of magnets around a coiled conductor. Of course, a source of energy is needed to spin the coiled conductor or rotate the magnets. For commercial electrical generators that source may be moving water; fossil fuels such as coal, gas, and oil; or nuclear fission.

An electrical generator permits us to produce electricity. An electric motor permits us to put electricity to work moving objects. A simple electric motor converts electrical energy into the energy of motion by means of a coil of wire wrapped around a metal core. This wire-wrapped core is suspended between the magnetic poles of a permanent magnet. When a current flows through the coil, it becomes a magnet. The coil's **N** and **S** poles are repelled by the **N** and **S** poles of the permanent magnet. As a result of this repulsion, the coil turns. If we change the direction of flow of electricity through the coil, the location of its **N** and **S** poles will change. The coil will continue to spin as its ends are continually repelled by the poles of the permanent magnet.

Sound Energy

Sounds affect us in many different ways. The purring of a kitten brushing against your leg may make you feel wanted. The chirping of baby birds may make you feel joyful. The uproarious and chaotic sounds of sanitation workers waking up your neighborhood with an early morning symphony of bangs, crunches, screeches, and shouts may annoy you immensely. But what causes the sounds that bring you pleasure or irritation?

What Causes Sound?

All sounds, whether they come from a garbage-can orchestra or a kitten, are produced by vibrating matter. A vibrating object receives energy from a source (a kitten or a dropped garbage can) and transfers energy to a *medium,* such as air. The medium carries the energy away from the vibrating object. Sound travels in all directions from its source. In other words, you can hear a sound whether your ears are above it, to the side of it, or below it.

A vibrating tuning fork is a good example of a source of sound. When a tuning fork is struck, its prongs move back and forth rapidly. When a prong moves in one direction, it presses together the modules in the air ahead of it. This pressed-together air is known as a *compression.* As the tuning fork moves in the opposite direction, it causes a portion of air to pull apart. This area is known as a *rarefaction.* The movement of each prong back and forth alternately produces compression and rarefaction.

The molecules in the air disturbed by the vibration of the tuning fork during compression transfer energy to adjacent molecules before returning to their original positions during rarefaction. The newly disturbed molecules pass some of their energy on to still other molecules, and the process is repeated. If you could see the molecules being disturbed, you would see areas of compression and rarefaction, or *sound waves,* being continuously created and moving away from the source of the vibration. A full sound wave consists of one compression and one rarefaction.

Sound waves require a medium for transmission. They cannot travel through a vacuum, so if you are wondering how astronauts communicate with one another in the vacuum of space, they do so using radio transmissions. Radio waves do not require a medium. Sound waves travel most rapidly through solids and least rapidly through gases. At a temperature of 0°C, sound travels at a speed of 340 meters per second (about 1,090 feet per second) in air. In water, sound travels at about 1,420 meters a second (about 4,686 feet a second).

The *wavelength* of a sound wave is the distance between the centers of two rarefactions. The amount of energy contained in a wave is interpreted by our ears as the loudness or softness of a sound. The loudness, or *intensity,* of a sound is measured in decibels. The *pitch* of a sound—how high or low the sound is—depends on the number of complete vibrations that the vibrating object makes in one second. This rate of vibration is known as the *frequency.*

Sound Can Be Absorbed or Reflected

Sound waves that strike a surface may be so strong that they travel through the object struck. However, some surfaces absorb little sound and cause the sound wave being received to bounce off the surface, or be reflected. Reflected sound waves that can be distinguished from the original sound are known as *echoes.* Although echoes are interesting to hear, they can be distracting. Therefore, many classrooms are fitted with sound-absorbing tiles or draperies.

Some of the energy carried by a sound wave causes the surface of the object it strikes to heat up slightly. Usually, the amount of heat produced cannot be detected without the use of special instruments.

Light Energy

Light energy, like sound energy, travels in waves, but a light wave is very different from a sound wave. Light waves travel at the speed of 300,000 kilometers per second (about 186,000 miles per second) and do not require a medium. Thus, light waves, unlike sound waves, can travel through a vacuum.

Light energy is produced from other types of energy. If we burn a substance, one of the products of combustion is light energy. The light is released as a result of the electrons in the substance changing energy levels as new compounds are formed. Electric light bulbs change electrical energy to light energy. The light energy that reaches us from the sun and other stars is the result of nuclear explosions. On stars, huge amounts of matter are converted to energy as a result of nuclear fusion. In nuclear fusion, hydrogen atoms are fused together to form helium atoms, a process accompanied by the release of light energy as well as other types of energy.

Light energy can be transformed into other forms of energy, such as heat or electricity. If you've ever had a sunburn, you've experienced both the conversion of light energy into heat (as your skin became warm) and the effect of light energy on the molecules of substances that make up your skin (as it turned red or blistered).

The Reflection and Refraction of Light

Light is able to pass through some materials, such as clear plastic or glass. A material that light can pass through is called *transparent*. Materials that light cannot pass through are called *opaque*. Materials that permit some, but not all, light to pass through are called *translucent*. Windows made of frosted glass are translucent.

As light passes from one medium to another, it is bent, or *refracted*. Light traveling through air bends as it enters water, glass, or clear plastic. This bending, or refraction, of light waves can be put to good use. A lens, for example, changes the appearance of objects because the image we see through the lens is produced by rays of light that have been bent. Eyeglasses, microscopes, hand lenses, and telescopes all provide images formed by light rays that have been refracted.

A *convex* lens is thicker in the middle than it is at its edges. Such a lens pulls light rays together. The point at which rays of light are brought together by the lens is called the *focal point*. The distance from the focal point to the center of the lens is the lens's *focal length*. When light is reflected from an object through a convex lens, the rays of light are brought together at the focal point and an image is formed. The size, position, and type of image formed depend on the distance of the object from the lens. If the object is more than one focal length from the lens, the image is inverted and formed on the opposite side of the lens. This type of image is called a *real image,* and it can be projected onto a screen. If the image is two focal lengths away, the image is the same size as the object.

If the object is less than one focal length from the lens, the image formed is magnified and rightside up. This type of image is called a *virtual image*. It is formed on the same side of the lens as the object and can be seen by looking through the lens toward the object, but it cannot be placed on a screen. When you use a convex lens as a magnifier, the image you see is a virtual image.

The refraction of light through a lens can be illustrated with a *ray diagram.* Look at the ray diagrams in Figure 9A.4. As you study them, note that the *principal axis* is an imaginary line passing perpendicular to the lens through its center. The *virtual focus* is the point on the axis at which the light would converge if you passed the light through the lens to the object, rather than from the object to the lens.

A lens that is thicker at its edges than at its center is a *concave lens.* A concave lens causes light rays to bend toward its edges. This type of lens can only produce virtual images that are smaller than the real objects (see Figure 9A.5).

FIGURE 9A.4

These ray diagrams for convex lenses illustrate how a convex lens focuses light. Light passing through the lens converges to form an image that can be seen on a screen.

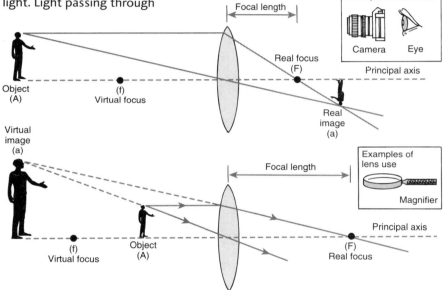

FIGURE 9A.5

As this ray diagram for a concave lens illustrates, the lens disperses light, and the image produced cannot be seen on a screen.

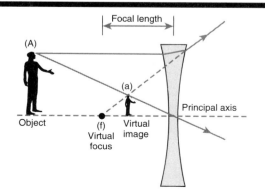

Light, Prisms, and Color

Have you ever been surprised to see an array of colors projected on a wall or ceiling as a result of sunlight passing through a crystal glass? This band of colors is called a *spectrum*. Some pieces of glass are made to separate sunlight or artificial light into a spectrum. A triangle-shaped piece of such glass is called a *prism*.

The colors of a spectrum represent the components of a light wave that enters a prism. As the light wave is refracted by the prism, the light is separated according to wave lengths. Each wavelength corresponds to a different color. The colors of a spectrum caused by the refraction of light by a prism are red, orange, yellow, green, blue, indigo, and violet.

The color of an object we see is a property of the wave length reflected from the object. *Pigments*—the chemical substances that we usually think of as the sources of color—actually produce their effects because they absorb some light waves and reflect others. Grass is green to our eyes because pigments in grass absorb the red, orange, yellow, blue, indigo, and violet waves and reflect the green.

Heat Energy

Suppose that one hot summer afternoon, you decide to buy a double-dip chocolate ice cream cone and sit in the park while you eat it. As you walk toward the park clutching your cone, you will certainly notice the effect of heat on ice cream. Heat from the hot surrounding air will flow to the colder ice cream, causing an increase in the temperature of the ice cream, a lowering of the temperature of the surrounding air, and the immediate need for a napkin as the change in the temperature of the ice cream results in a change in the ice cream's state—from solid to liquid. The phenomenon of melting can be a good starting point for understanding heat and how it brings about change.

What Is Heat?

Heat is energy that travels from a warm substance to a cool substance. Keep in mind that all substances are made of molecules, and molecules, even in solids, are in constant motion. The motion and positions of these molecules determines the internal energy of (the energy within) a substance. If the molecules in a substance move slowly, the substance has a low level of internal energy. If the molecules move rapidly, the substance has a high level of internal energy. *Temperature* is an indication of the internal energy of a substance. The higher the temperature of a substance, the greater its internal energy and the more heat it releases to a cool substance. The temperature of a substance is measured in *degrees*. There are two temperature scales in wide use: the Celsius, or centigrade, scale and the Fahrenheit scale.

A *thermometer*, which measures temperature, consists of a narrow column of mercury or tinted alcohol sealed in a glass tube. Changes in temperature cause the liquid in a thermometer to expand or contract. Since the mercury or alcohol within the thermometer expands and contracts more than the surrounding glass with each degree of temperature change, we can see changes in the mercury or alcohol level.

Two important markings on all thermometers are the freezing and boiling points of water. The Celsius thermometer shows the temperature at which water freezes as 0° and the temperature at which water boils as 100°. The Fahrenheit scale shows the temperature at which water freezes as 32° and the boiling temperature as 212°. Wherever possible, use a Celsius thermometer and Celsius measurements in the classroom.

How Is Heat Measured?

Since it is virtually impossible to add up the individual energies possessed by the millions of individual molecules found in even a very small amount of a substance, heat energy must be measured indirectly. This is done by measuring its effect on a substance. The standard unit of heat is the *calorie,* the heat required to raise the temperature of 1 gram of water 1° Celsius. Since this is a very small amount of heat, the *kilocalorie,* which equals 1,000 calories, is a more practical unit. The energy contained in foods is expressed in kilocalories.

In the English system of measurement, the British Thermal Unit (BTU) is the standard unit of heat. This is the amount of heat required to raise the temperature of 1 pound of water 1° Fahrenheit.

How Do Changes in State Occur?

When you knock on a door or kick a tire, your hand does not go through the door and your foot does not go through the tire, even though each object is made of millions of molecules that vibrate. Therefore, there must be some force that holds the molecules together. The forces that hold molecules together are known as *cohesive forces.* By adding heat to an object, we cause the individual molecules of the object to move more freely. If we add sufficient heat, the molecules of a solid will move out of their fixed positions, and the solid will melt to form a liquid. The addition of even more heat can cause the molecules in the liquid to break free of the cohesive forces. At this point, the liquid becomes a gas. These transformations are called *changes of state.*

Machines

It is our ability to harness the various types of energy discussed in the previous sections that permits us to use machines to do work. To understand how machines operate, you need to understand what a force is. In its simplest terms, a *force* is a push or a pull. Machines enable us to increase a force, increase the speed of an object, change the direction in which a force is acting, or change the place where a force is acting. Machines work by changing one form of energy to another.

Regardless of the type of machine we study, we are always concerned with two forces: the effort and the resistance. The *effort* is the force we apply. The *resistance* is the force we overcome. We are also concerned with the amount of resistance that can be overcome by the application of a given effort. In scientific terms, this quantity is known as the *mechanical advantage*. There are various ways of calculating the mechanical advantage of a machine. In many cases, we can simply divide the resistance by the effort.

When we use a machine, we put energy into it. But not all of this energy goes into moving the resistance; some is lost to friction. The *efficiency* of a machine is a comparison of the work done by the machine (the energy put out by the machine) with the work (energy) put into it.

In Chapter 8A, Newton's laws were discussed. You will recall that they are used to explain how forces can change the motion of objects. Humans discovered, through the invention of simple machines, that they could multiply the force they could apply to an object or change the direction in which an effort force is applied.

Simple Machines

You may not realize it, but the school yard seesaw is a simple machine: a *lever*. Wheelbarrows and fishing poles are also levers, as are crowbars, shovels, hammers, and oars. All levers, regardless of shape, have three parts: *a fulcrum, an effort arm,* and *a resistance arm.* As shown in Figure 9A.6, there are three types, or classes, of levers. Note the

FIGURE 9A.6

There are three classes of levers. In a first-class lever, the fulcrum falls between the resistance and the effort. In a second-class lever, the fulcrum is at one end, the effort at the other end, and the resistance at some point between the two. In a third-class lever, the effort is applied between the fulcrum and the resistance.

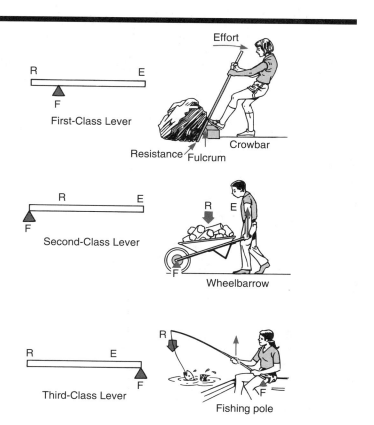

First-Class Lever

Crowbar

Resistance Fulcrum

Second-Class Lever

Wheelbarrow

Third-Class Lever

Fishing pole

location of the effort, resistance, and fulcrum in each type. It is the position of the fulcrum that determines the type of lever.

Levers are not the only simple machines. Others are the wheel and axle, the pulley, the inclined plane, the screw, and the wedge. All other machines (which are known as *compound machines*) combine at least two simple machines.

The *wheel and axle* can be thought of as two circular objects, one larger than the other. The larger one is the wheel; the smaller one is the axle. Think of the wheel as a lever that can be moved in a complete circle around its fulcrum. The axle is the wheel's fulcrum and is at the center of the wheel. Examples of the wheel and axle are the windlass, water wheel, doorknob, pencil sharpener, screwdriver, windmill, and potter's wheel. A wheel and axle increase the effort force applied to it. When an effort force is applied to the wheel, a larger force is produced at the axle. However, the wheel moves slowly because of the resistance the effort must overcome. When effort is applied to the axle, there is less resistance, and the increased force moves the wheel more quickly. To find the ideal mechanical advantage of a wheel and axle, divide the radius of the wheel by the radius of the axle.

A *pulley* is a grooved wheel that turns loosely on an axle. The grooved wheel and axle do not have to turn together. The grooved wheel is called a *sheave*. The frame in which it rotates is called the *block*. Pulleys may be either fixed or movable. Figure 9A.7 shows examples of each. A fixed pulley does not travel with the resistance, or *load;* a movable pulley does. A block and tackle is a combination of a fixed pulley and a movable pulley. The mechanical advantage of a pulley can be calculated by dividing the effort distance (the distance the load moves) by the resistance distance (the distance the

FIGURE 9A.7

A fixed pulley remains stationary, while a movable pulley travels with the object.

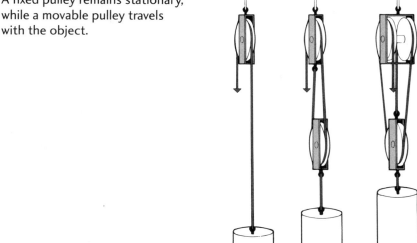

rope you pull moves) or by dividing the resistance by the effort. The ideal mechanical advantage of a pulley system can be determined simply by counting the number of supporting ropes. Figure 9A.7 shows how mechanical advantage can be achieved through an increase in the number of supporting ropes and pulleys in the system. Assuming the same effort is applied in each pulley system shown and that the pulley systems are frictionless, the three-pulley system can lift three times the weight that a single-pulley system can.

An *inclined plane* is a flat surface that is raised at one end. Ramps, slopes, and stairs are inclined planes. A resistance can be moved up an inclined plane to a desired height with less effort than it can be lifted directly to the same height. The ideal mechanical advantage of an inclined plane can be found by dividing the length of the inclined plane (the effort distance) by its height (the resistance distance).

A *screw* is a twisted or rolled-up inclined plane. Some common screws are a wood screw, a bolt, a screw jack, a brace and bit, and an auger. Screws are used to lift objects, to hold objects together, and to carry things from place to place. The rotary motion of a turning screw is changed into a straight-line motion by a lever, which is needed to turn the screw. The ideal mechanical advantage of a screw is the distance the effort moves divided by the distance the resistance moves (the distance between the threads of the screw, or its *pitch*).

A *wedge* is a double inclined plane. Some common wedges are knives, needles, axes, can openers, and cold chisels. Wedges are used to pierce, split, cut, and push apart things. Effort is needed to move the wedge into the resisting object. The ideal mechanical advantage of a wedge can be calculated by dividing its length by the thickness of its widest end.

Friction

To work, every machine, whether simple or complex, must overcome friction. *Friction* is the resistance that an object meets when the surface of the object rubs against another surface. Friction retards motion and generates heat. It is the result of the irregularities that exist in every surface. Even surfaces that seem smooth to our touch consist of bumps and grooves. To overcome the attraction of particles of the surfaces to one another and the retardation of motion caused when a bump hits a groove, some of the energy used to move an object is changed to heat where surfaces are in contact.

There are many ways to reduce friction. Ball bearings, oils, and other lubricants permit surfaces to slide across one another more easily. If you drive a car, you should know that both the condition of bearings at the junction of the axle and wheels and the quality and quantity of lubricating oil in the engine must be checked periodically. If this is not done, the metal parts that are in contact will wear excessively or break.

Although we usually think of friction as a phenomenon that must be overcome, friction also has many positive benefits. Our ability to walk, for example, is a direct result of the friction between the bottoms of our shoes and the floor. Without friction, shoes would simply slide across floors and we would not be able to move forward.

Summary Outline

I. Energy is never destroyed. It is changed from one form to another.

II. Electricity is a form of energy that results from the storage or movement of electrons.
   A. Static electricity is produced by an imbalance between the positive and negative charges on the surface of an object.
   B. Current electricity is produced when electrons flow through a conductor.
      1. A source of current, a conductor, and a load (a device that converts electricity to some other form of energy) can be combined to form an electrical circuit.
      2. Generators produce electricity by moving a conductor across a magnetic field or vice versa.
      3. Motors convert electrical energy to kinetic energy.

III. A sound wave is produced in a medium by the vibration of an object.

IV. Light travels in waves that are refracted, or bent, as they pass from one medium to another.

V. The heat energy contained by a substance is the total kinetic energy possessed by the atoms or molecules of the substance.

VI. Machines are devices that enable us to increase a force, increase the speed of an object, change the direction of a force, or change the location of a force.

9B

Energies and Machines

Attention Getters, Discovery Activities, and Demonstrations

ATTENTION GETTERS

How Do Instruments Make Sounds?

Materials	1 ruler Assortment of musical instruments: cymbals, bells, small drum, triangle, guitar, clarinet, and so on
Motivating Questions	Point to each instrument and ask: ■ Do you think this instrument will make a high or low sound? ■ What part of this instrument does the musician vibrate?
Directions	1. Ask the children what happens when you tap on your desk. Walk around the room tapping on various objects. 2. Indicate that tapping on an object causes it to move back and forth very quickly, or vibrate. Explain that there are many ways to make things vibrate. 3. Display each instrument, and have the children suggest what parts vibrate.
Science Content for the Teacher	All sounds are the result of vibrating objects. High-pitched sounds come from objects that vibrate very fast. Each musical instrument produces a sound because the musician causes some part of it to vibrate.

Do Magnets Pull on All Objects?

Materials	Assortment of objects such as a rubber band, a metal tack, a piece of chalk, paper clips Magnet
Motivating Questions	■ Which of these objects do you think will be pulled toward the magnet? ■ How are the objects that are pulled to the magnet different from objects that are not pulled?
Directions	1. Write the names of the objects on the board. 2. Display the magnet, and have the children predict which objects will be pulled toward it. Note their predictions under the names of the objects you have written on the board. 3. Have the children touch each object with the magnet. Record the results in another row on the chart, and explain that the objects that are attracted are those that contain iron (steel).
Science Content for the Teacher	A magnet has the ability to attract objects that contain iron, nickel, cobalt, and their alloys. Most common objects that are attracted to a magnet contain iron in the form of steel.

Why Do Some Machines Need Oil?

Materials	1 ice cube	Sandpaper	1 wooden block
	1 saucer	1/4 cup of sand	1 can of motor oil

Motivating Questions
- Which will move more easily: the ice cube on the plate or the block on the sandpaper?
- Why do you think a car needs oil?

Directions
1. Show the children how easily the ice cube slides across the plate, and then show them how difficult it is to move the wooden block across the sandpaper. Explain that it is difficult for car tires to stop or move forward on roads that are covered with snow or ice.
2. Ask the children for ideas about what could be done to make it easier for tires to start and stop in ice and snow.
3. Demonstrate how friction can be increased by sprinkling some sand on the plate and sliding the ice cube across the sand. Display the can of oil, and discuss its use as a liquid that permits the metal parts of an engine to slide over one another easily.

Science Content for the Teacher
The ice cube on the plate melts slightly, producing a layer of water that reduces the friction between the ice cube and the plate. Reducing the friction makes it easier to move one surface over another surface. The presence of friction converts some of the energy used to operate a machine into heat. Oil is frequently used to reduce this energy loss. The oil fills in some of the roughness on the metal surfaces so the parts ride on an oil film.

Can Sound Travel through a Solid Object?

Materials for Each Group Meterstick

Motivating Questions
- Have you ever heard sounds while you were swimming underwater?
- Have you ever heard sounds through a wall?
- Do you think sound can travel through a meterstick?

Directions
1. Have the children work in pairs. One child will stand, and one child, the listener, will be seated. The child standing will hold one end of the meterstick, and the listener will hold the other. The meterstick should be parallel to the floor and 50 centimeters (about 20 inches) away from the listener's ear.
2. Have the child who is standing gently scratch his or her end of the meterstick. The listener should say whether he or she heard the scratches.
3. Repeat the procedure with the meterstick 25 centimeters (about 10 inches) away from the listener's ear.

4. Finally, have the listener position the meterstick so that it is gently touching the jawbone joint in front of his or her ear, and have the standing student gently scratch the meterstick. The listener should hear the sounds clearly.

Science Content for the Teacher   Sound waves are disturbances that move through a medium. The medium may be a solid, liquid, or gas. A dense solid, such as the hardwood in a meterstick, carries sound waves very well. When the standing child scratches the meterstick, the sound waves travel through the meterstick and into the tissues and bones near the listener's ear, eventually reaching his or her eardrum.

For Middle-Level Learners [PS 6]

What Type of Cup Loses Heat the Fastest?

Materials   Plastic cup   Ceramic cup
Styrofoam cup   Source of hot water
Metal cup or empty soup can with label removed

Motivating Questions
- If you were going to have a cup of hot chocolate on a cold day, which of these cups do you think would keep it hot for the longest time?
- If you were going to have a cup of cold chocolate milk on a hot day, which of these cups would keep it cold for the longest time?

Directions
1. Display the cups, and have the children make predictions about their heat-retaining abilities. You may wish to have the children arrange the cups in order of their ability to retain heat.
2. Fill each cup half full of hot water. *Safety Note:* Alert the children to the dangers of working with hot water.
3. Have the children gently touch the outside of each cup as soon as the water is added and then gently touch the cup again after 1 minute and after 2 minutes.
4. Have the children discuss how their predictions matched or differed from their experiences.

Science Content for the Teacher   All solids conduct heat; however, some conduct heat better than others. Metals tend to be good conductors of heat. Thus, a cup made of metal will permit heat to pass through it easily, resulting in the cooling down of the liquid within the cup. Ceramic materials, on the other hand, are good insulators, so most china cups will retain heat. The Styrofoam cup is an excellent insulator because bubbles of air are part of the materials that make up the cup.

For Middle-Level Learners [PS 4]

Can You Move a Stream of Water without Touching It?

Materials   Access to a water faucet   Inflated balloon
Plastic or hard rubber comb   Piece of wool fabric

Motivating
Question

- Do you think it is possible to move a stream of water without touching it or blowing on it?

Directions

1. Keep the comb and balloon out of sight as you begin this activity. Turn the water faucet on so that it produces a thin stream of water, and ask the children how the stream could be moved without touching it.
2. Display the comb and the balloon. Run the comb through your hair or over the wool fabric a few times, and then move it near the stream of water. The water will bend toward the comb.
3. Repeat the demonstration using the balloon rubbed across the wool fabric.

Science Content
for the Teacher

The water has a neutral charge. The comb picks up a negative charge after it has been run through hair or over a sweater. When the comb is positioned near the water, negative ends of neutral water molecules move away from the negatively charged comb, leaving the positive ends on the portion of the molecules closest to the comb. These ends are attracted to the comb, causing the stream to bend. The same phenomenon can be observed if you use a charged balloon in place of the comb.

For Middle-Level Learners [HNS 2, 3, and 4; SPSP 9 and 11]

"I Am Alfred Nobel"

Materials

Access to the Internet   Science resource books and encyclopedias
Posterpaper and markers   Assorted art materials
Assorted fabric pieces

Motivating
Questions

- How would you feel if you invented something to blast apart rocks and help make roads, tunnels, and foundation holes for schools and hospitals and it was also used to make bombs?
- What would you do with your money if you became rich because of your invention?

Directions

1. Have the children form cooperative groups, and give each group the same challenge:
   a. Research the life and scientific work of Alfred Nobel. Find out what he did and what he invented.
   b. Discover what is meant by the term *Nobel Prize*.
   c. Find out who won the most recent Nobel Prizes for science, literature, peace, and other topics.
2. Have each group write a script in which "Alfred Nobel" tells about his life and work in a 3- or 4-minute presentation. Each group should select and prepare one of its members to play Nobel, and he or she may use primitive costume pieces and simple props. The presentation must begin with "I am Alfred Nobel."

Science Content
for the Teacher

Alfred Bernhard Nobel (1833–1896) was a Swedish scientist who experimented with nitroglycerin and eventually invented dynamite. His sale of explosives made him wealthy. Some of his fortune was used to create a fund for prizes that are awarded each year for outstanding work in fields that benefit humanity, such as medicine and literature.

DISCOVERY ACTIVITIES

Move Those Loads: Making and Using a Simple Lever

Objectives
- The children will identify the effort force, load, and fulcrum of a lever.
- The children will construct a lever and make and test hypotheses about the effect of changing the fulcrum's position.

Science Processes Emphasized

Making hypotheses
Experimenting

Materials for Each Child or Group

30 cm (12 in.) wooden ruler   Masking tape
Flat-sided pencil   Marking pen
2 paper cups
8 to 10 objects of equal mass, such as washers
Small objects to serve as loads: chalk sticks, boxes of paper clips, chunks of clay

Motivation

On the day of the activity, take to class a block of wood with a nail partially embedded in it and a claw hammer. Before beginning the activity, demonstrate how to remove the nail using the claw end of the hammer. Tell the children that the hammer is a lever. Without pointing to the apparatus, review the meaning of effort force, load, and fulcrum (turning point). Then ask if they can locate the effort force, load, and fulcrum. Leave this as an open question, and begin the activity.

Directions

1. Distribute the cups, rulers, tape, flat-sided pencil, washers, and objects used as loads to each group.
2. Have the children make one label reading *Effort Force* and attach it to one cup. Have them make another label reading *Load* and attach it to the second cup. Have them tape a cup to each end of the ruler.
3. Tell the children to place a load in the Load cup and center the ruler on the flat-sided pencil. Have them determine how much effort force is needed to move the load by adding washers to the Effort Force cup.
4. Have the children make and test hypotheses about the effect of moving the fulcrum closer to or further from the load.

Key Discussion Questions

1. Where is the load, fulcrum, and effort force in your lever? *The load is the weight of the objects in the Load cup, the fulcrum is the top of the pencil, and the effort force is the weight of the washers in the Effort Force cup.*
2. When did you use the least amount of force to move the load? The most? *The least force was needed when the fulcrum was near the Load cup. The most was needed when the fulcrum was close to the Effort Force cup.*
3. When you moved the load with a small force, what moved the greatest distance—the load or the effort force? *The effort force.*

Science Content for the Teacher
The lever constructed by the children is a lever of the first class. This lever multiplies the effect of an effort force. A small effort force moving a large distance can move a large load a small distance.

Extension
Science/Art: Some children may enjoy discovering that mobiles are really levers. They can use thread, plastic straws, paper cutouts of birds, and other objects to assemble mobiles.

For Young Learners [S&T 1]

Can You Build a No-Frills Telephone?

Objectives
- The children will construct a telephone-like device that allows them to communicate with one another.
- From their experimentation, the children will infer that a vibration moving through a thread is the basis for how their devices work.

Science Processes Emphasized
Communicating
Inferring

Materials for Each Child or Group
2 paper cups
2 toothpicks or buttons
2 m (about 7 ft.) or longer length of strong sewing thread or dental floss
Additional thread, buttons, and cups for those children who wish to invent more complicated phone circuits

Motivation
Display the materials. Ask the children if they can guess what they will be making with them. After they have made some guesses, tell them that they will be making telephones that will actually work.

Directions
1. Before distributing the cups, punch a small hole in the center of the bottom of each one. You can use scissors or a pencil to make the holes.
2. Distribute two toothpicks or buttons, two cups, and a length of thread to each group. Have the children thread the string through the prepunched hole in the bottom of the cup and knot one end of the thread around the center of the toothpick or through the button. You may need to assist some children with this. They should then do the same with the other cup.
3. When the thread between the cups is stretched, the toothpick will keep the thread end in the cup. If the thread is taut, the sound of one child speaking directly into a cup will be transmitted along the thread to the cup held to a listener's ear.
4. Encourage the children to try their telephones. Some groups may want to construct more complicated telephone circuits.

Key Discussion Questions
1. Which cup is used like the bottom part of a telephone? *The speaker's cup.*
2. Which cup is used like the top part of a telephone? *The listener's cup.*
3. How could you make a telephone that will let one person speak and two people listen? *Answers will vary. Have children try an experiment to test out their ideas. Some will find that tying a second cup somewhere along the string will permit the second listener to hear the sounds made by the speaker.*

Science Content for the Teacher	When we speak, our vocal cords vibrate and produce sound waves that travel through the air. When the children use their string telephones, sound waves vibrate the bottom of the speaker's cup. These vibrations move through the string and cause the bottom of the listener's cup to vibrate and reproduce the sound waves in the air inside the listener's cup. These sound waves strike the listener's eardrum and cause it to vibrate. In a real telephone, the vibrations produced by the speaker are converted to variations in electrical impulses that travel through wires.
Extension	*Science/Art:* Have the children design and then draw various arrangements of thread and cups for more complex telephone systems prior to further experimentation.

For Middle-Level Learners [S&T 4]

Simple Circuits

Objectives	■ The children will assemble a simple series circuit and a simple parallel circuit. ■ The children will describe the similarities and differences between a series circuit and a parallel circuit.
Science Processes Emphasized	Observing Communicating Experimenting
Materials for Each Child or Group	3 bulbs 2 dry cells, size "D" 3 bulb sockets Switch 8 pieces of insulated bell wire, each 2.5 cm (about 1 in.) long and stripped at the ends
Motivation	This activity should follow a class discussion about the nature of simple circuits and the functions of various circuit components. Display the materials, and make schematic drawings on the chalkboard of a three-lamp series circuit and a three-lamp parallel circuit (like the ones shown on the facing page). Have a general discussion of how the circuit diagrams are alike and different. Keep the discussion open ended, and begin the activity at an appropriate point in the discussion.
Directions	1. You may wish to have half of the groups construct series circuits and the other half construct parallel circuits. If you happen to have double the amount of equipment listed, each group can construct both circuits. 2. Have the children light the bulbs to demonstrate how their circuits operate. Suggest that they make observations of what occurs when one bulb is removed from each type of circuit. 3. Allow the children time to make observations, and then have a class discussion about how the circuits are the same and different.
Key Discussion Questions	1. What do the symbols in the circuit diagrams stand for? 2. How is the path of the electrons different in the two circuits? *In the series circuit, all the electrons go through all the bulbs. In the parallel circuit, they split up: Some go to each bulb.*

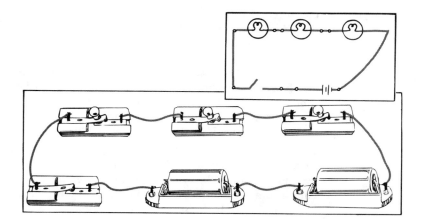

A series circuit

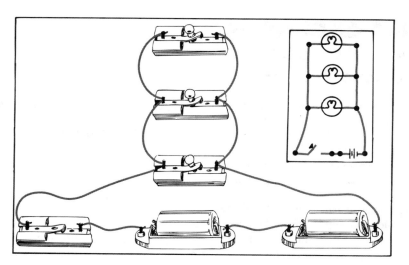

A parallel circuit

3. What happened when you took one lamp out of each type of circuit? Why? *In the series circuit, the other bulbs went out. In the parallel circuit, the other bulbs got a little brighter. The series circuit bulbs went out because there was a gap (a break) in the circuit, so the current stopped. In the parallel circuit, the electrons stopped going through one path and joined the electrons going through the other paths. The bulbs got brighter because they had extra current going through them.*

Science Content for the Teacher

Circuits can be represented by diagrams and symbols like those shown above. In a series circuit, all the electrons go through all the bulbs (or other resistances) in the circuit. A gap, or break, at any place in the circuit will stop the flow of current through the entire circuit. A defective bulb, a loose connection, or a break in the wire will stop the flow of current. If the voltage is large enough, electrons may jump across gaps in the circuit, a phenomenon evidenced as a spark. In a parallel circuit, the current divides. Some of it flows through each resistance. If a resistance is removed from a parallel circuit, the current that would normally have flowed through it is distributed to the remaining resistances.

Extensions   *Science:* If you have access to a small electric motor, have a group substitute it for a bulb in the series circuit and in the parallel circuit to determine the effect of a running motor on the brightness of the bulbs.

You may wish to challenge one or two groups to combine their resources and make a circuit that is partly parallel and partly series.

Science / Social Studies: Some children might enjoy studying one of the bulbs more closely to see if they can find the path that the electrons take. This could be the beginning of some library research on the scientist who invented the incandescent bulb: Thomas Edison. Have the children focus their attention on how everyday life has been affected by Edison's many inventions.

For Middle-Level Learners [S&T 4]

Electrical Conductors and Nonconductors

Objectives
- The children will distinguish between materials that conduct electricity and materials that do not.
- The children will make hypotheses about characteristics of conductors.

Science Processes Emphasized
Experimenting
Making hypotheses

Materials for Each Child or Group

Dry cell, size "D"	Box of paper clips
Dry-cell holder	Sharpened pencils
Flashlight bulb	Box of toothpicks
Flashlight-bulb holder	Box of crayons
Strips of aluminum foil	Box of steel nails

3 pieces of insulated bell wire, each about 25 cm (10 in.) long and stripped at the ends
Assortment of 2.5 cm (1 in.) lengths of bell wire of various thicknesses

Motivation   This activity should follow activities or class discussions about the characteristics of simple circuits. Ask the children to describe the function of the wire used in circuits. They will indicate that the wire serves as the path for electrons. Then display the materials, and indicate that the children will be finding out whether the electrons can pass through them.

Directions   1. Have each child or group assemble a simple circuit using two of the pieces of wire, a dry cell, and a bulb. After the bulb lights, detach the wire attached to the negative end of the battery and attach the third wire in its place. The exposed ends of the two wires (one from the dry cell and one from the bulb holder) will serve as probes to be touched to the materials tested.

2. Ask the children to check that their testers work by briefly touching the exposed ends together. If the dry cell is fresh, the bulb is in working condition, and all the connections have been properly made, the bulb will light.

3. When all the circuits are working, have the children test the various materials by touching both exposed wires to the materials at the same time. If the material is a conductor, the circuit will be completed and the bulb will light. Have the children note which materials are good conductors of electricity. They should manipulate each material to see if those that are conductors share similar characteristics.

4. When this has been accomplished, have the children make hypotheses that distinguish electrical conductors from nonconductors.

Key Discussion Questions

1. Which of the materials were good conductors of electricity? *Aluminum foil, paper clips, wire pieces.*
2. Which of the materials did not conduct electricity? *Toothpicks, crayons.*
3. Was there anything that conducted electricity but conducted it poorly? *The lead (graphite) in the pencil.*
4. What are some hypotheses that you made? *Metals conduct electricity.*
5. What other activities could you do to test your hypotheses? *Answers will vary.*

Science Content for the Teacher

Substances that allow the movement of electrons with relatively little resistance are known as conductors. Materials that do not allow electrons to pass through them are insulators. There are no perfect conductors, since all materials offer some resistance to the flow of charges. Metals are better conductors than nonmetals. Metals differ in conductivity. The following metals are arranged from highest to lowest conductivity:

Silver
Copper
Aluminum
Tungsten
Platinum
Tin
Steel
Lead

Extensions

Science: Some children may wish to invent activities that will reveal whether good electrical conductors are also good conductors of heat. Others may wish to modify their tester circuit so that the entire apparatus can be packaged in a small cardboard box. The tester should have two probes extending from the side and the light bulb extending from the top.

Science/Social Studies: Some children may be interested in discovering what areas of the world are sources of the various metals used in this activity. To identify these regions, the children can use an encyclopedia and look under headings such as "Copper" and "Aluminum."

For Middle-Level Learners [PS 6]

The Ink-Lined Plane

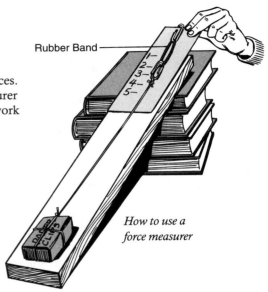

Rubber Band

How to use a force measurer

Objectives	■ The children will construct a simple device that can be used to measure forces. ■ The children will use their force measurer to find how an inclined plane makes work easier.
Science Processes Emphasized	Experimenting Measuring
Materials for Each Child or Group	Piece of cardboard 25 × 12 cm (about 10 × 5 in.) 3 paper clips Rubber band 1 m (40 in.) length of board String Small box of paper clips, crayons, or chalk 5 books Wood wax and cloth for polishing the board

Motivation Start this activity with some humorous word play. Do not display any of the materials. Tell the children that today they are going to work with an "ink-lined plane." When you say the phrase, space the words as shown and do not write the words on the chalkboard. Tell the children that one year you had a student who thought you wanted him to build an "ink-lined plane" (say it exactly as you said it before). The children should be a little puzzled. Now show the children what the imaginary child built by making a paper airplane and drawing some lines across it. Explain that the child was really confused until you wrote the phrase on the chalkboard. Ask the children to guess what you wrote on the board.

When they have done this, write the words *inclined plane* on the chalkboard, bring out the materials, and discuss the characteristics of an inclined plane. Tell the children that in this activity, they are going to make a device that measures forces and then use it to see how an inclined plane makes work easier.

Directions 1. Have each child or group of children make a force measurer by clipping one paper clip to the cardboard, attaching a rubber band to the paper clip, and clipping another paper clip to the end of the rubber band. Now have the children make their own scale divisions on the cardboard. The scale divisions shown in the illustration above are arbitrary, but the first division should began at the bottom of the rubber band.

2. Tell the children to assemble the inclined plane by elevating one end of the board and placing three books under it. The children should wax the board until its surface is smooth.

3. Have the children determine how much force is needed to lift the box of paper clips from the tabletop straight up to the high end of the board using their force measurers. To do this, they will need to tie a string around the box and attach the string to the paper clip hanging from the bottom of the rubber band on the force measurer. Have them note the amount of force required.

4. Now have them measure the force needed to move the paper-clip box to the same height by means of the inclined plane. They should pull the box up the length of the board, parallel to the surface of the board.

5. Have the children compare the amounts of force required and experiment with various loads and inclined-plane heights. Then hold a class discussion of the results.

Key Discussion Questions

1. Which required less force, pulling the load straight up or moving it along the sloping board? *Moving it along the board.*

2. Why do you think people use inclined planes? *You can move heavy objects up without applying a lot of force.*

3. Show the children that the distance the load moves vertically is the load distance, or resistance distance, and that the distance along the sloping board is the effort distance. Now ask the children how the effort distance compares with the load distance. *The effort distance is longer.* (This question helps the children see that inclined planes require that the small effort force moves over a long distance.)

Science Content for the Teacher

The inclined plane is a simple machine used to move heavy objects to heights. Ramps used to load boxes on a truck and roads that slope upward are inclined planes. An inclined plane multiplies force at the expense of distance, since the effort force must move farther than the distance the load is raised. Steep inclined planes require more effort force than less steep planes.

Extensions

Science: Have two or three groups of children assemble inclined planes of various slopes and move the same load up all of them to observe the increased force needed on the steeper machines. If possible, secure a toy truck with wheels that roll easily and have the groups compare the effort forces required to move it up the various slopes.

Science/Math: Have some children measure the effort distance and load distance of an inclined plane and compare them. Then have the children make the inclined plane steeper and repeat their measurements of effort and load distance. They can then repeat their measurements with the inclined plane in more steep and less steep positions.

DEMONSTRATIONS

How Does Heating and Cooling Change a Balloon?

Objective	▪ The children will predict and then observe how balloons are affected by heating and cooling.

Science Processes Emphasized	Observing	Communicating
	Predicting	

Materials	2 or 3 round balloons	Saucepan 1/4 full of water
	Hot plate	Access to a refrigerator

Motivation   Display the balloons. Then inflate each one to about one-half its capacity and tie a knot in the neck. If the balloons are new, stretch them a few times before inflating to make them more elastic. Ask the children to predict what will happen to the sizes of the balloons as they are heated and cooled.

Directions   1. Have a volunteer draw the balloons at their exact sizes on the chalkboard.
2. Place one balloon on the saucepan so it is held above the surface of the water by the sides of the pan. Have another volunteer take the other balloon to the school kitchen to be stored in a refrigerator. Turn on the hot plate, and set the heat indicator to low or warm.
3. Have the children note changes in each balloon every half hour for the next 2 hours. After they have made their observations, have them try to explain what caused the changes.

Key Discussion Questions   1. Why do you think the heated balloon became larger? *The molecules of the gases in the air in the heated balloon started to move faster. They started to bounce into each other and the sides of the balloon more.*
2. Why do you think the cooled balloon became smaller? *It lost energy. The molecules of the gas slowed down and didn't bounce into each other or the sides as much. They moved closer together.*

Science Content for the Teacher   The heat energy of an object is the total energy of motion of all atoms the object has. An object gains energy if it is placed in an environment that has more heat energy than it and loses heat energy if it is placed in an environment that has less heat energy than it.

Extension   *Science/Health:* Discuss how the loss of heat from an object can be diminished. This will offer the children an opportunity to talk about the need to wear particular types of clothing to decrease or increase heat loss.

Tuning Forks Feed Food for Thought

Objectives
- The children will observe that the source of the sound produced by a tuning fork is the vibration of the tines.
- The children will predict various effects that will occur when the tuning fork is struck vigorously.

Science Processes Emphasized
Observing
Predicting

Materials
2 tuning forks that produce sounds of different pitches
Rubber striker (rubber tuning fork hammer)

Motivation
Display the tuning forks, and ask the children if they have ever seen any objects like them before. Ask the children if they have any ideas about what these objects are used for.

Directions
1. Without striking the fork, have the children sit quietly and listen to the natural sounds of the classroom and school. After a minute or two, gently strike one of the forks with the rubber hammer and have the children listen to the sound produced. Ask volunteers to touch, very gently, one of the tines after you have struck the fork. Have them tell the class what they feel.
2. Strike the tuning fork harder, and have the children listen to the change in the sound.
3. Ask the children to predict how the sounds produced by the two forks will differ. Strike one fork, stop its vibration, strike the other fork, and ask the children how correct their predictions were. If you happen to have a larger selection of tuning forks available, ask the children to place them in order from the highest pitch to lowest pitch. Check the children's ideas by striking each fork in turn.

Key Discussion Questions
1. Can you guess why the tuning fork is called a *fork? Answers will vary. Some children will note the resemblance between a tuning fork and a fork used for eating.*
2. How do you think the sound will change if I hit the tuning fork harder? *Answers will vary. Some children will say that the sound will be louder.*

Science Content for the Teacher
When you strike a tuning fork, the tines vibrate back and forth. This vibration produces sound waves in the air. Although tuning forks are used for experimentations with sound, they are also used by piano tuners and others who need to hear sounds at exact pitches.

Extension
Science/Music: Some children may be interested in how musical instruments amplify sounds. Display various musical instruments, and for each, have the children identify the part that vibrates and the part or parts that make sounds louder—for example, the wooden structure of the guitar amplifies the sound of the vibrating string.

For Middle-Level Learners [PS 6]

You Could Hear a Pin Drop: The Conduction of Heat[1]

Objectives
- The children will observe the ability of various materials to conduct heat.
- The children will make a hypothesis concerning the nature of objects that conduct heat.
- The children will predict which of three objects will conduct heat the fastest.

Science Processes Emphasized

Observing   Predicting

Making hypotheses

Materials

Candle   5 steel pins
Safety matches   Chalk stick
Old metal fork   Long, narrow chip of pottery
Support stamp and burette clamp   Watch with second hand
Container of water to extinguish matches
Glass, steel, and brass (or aluminum) rods of equal thickness

Motivation

This demonstration should follow a class discussion about energy and heat as a form of energy. *Safety Note:* The demonstration requires the lighting of a candle by you and manipulation of the candle flame by you. Appropriate safety measures should be observed.

Display all the materials, and indicate that you are going to do a demonstration that will help the children discover how well various materials conduct heat. Explain that you are going to attach a pin near one end of each rod with a dab of wax, heat the end of each rod, and measure the time for the wax to melt and the pin to fall. Select a responsible child to measure the length of time it takes the wax to melt.

Directions

1. Fasten a steel pin to a dab of wax placed 4 centimeters (about 1.5 inches) from the end of each of the three rods. Do this by lighting the candle, allowing it to burn for 2 minutes, and then rolling the rod in the pool of wax beneath the candle flame. Briefly heat the head of a pin in the flame and press it into the wax. Repeat this procedure for the fork, the piece of pottery, and the chalk.
2. Place one of the rods in the burette clamp, and lower the clamp so that the end of the rod is about 1 centimeter from the tip of the flame (see illustration).
3. Ask your assistant to time how long it takes for the pin to drop.
4. Repeat steps 2 and 3 for the other two rods, and ask the class to make a hypothesis about the type of material that is a good conductor of heat.
5. Display the test objects, and have the children use their hypothesis to predict which will be the best heat conductor. Repeat steps 2 and 3 with each object.

Key Discussion Questions

1. Which rod was the poorest conductor? *Glass.*
2. What conclusion can you make about heat conducting? *Metals are good conductors of heat.*
3. What are some objects that are good conductors of heat? *Pots and pans.*
4. What test object did you predict to be the best conductor of heat? *The metal fork.*

Science Content for the Teacher

The carrying of heat by a solid is called *conduction.* Heat energy is transferred through a conductor as a result of the increased movement of molecules at the point on the object where heat is applied. The increased motion of these molecules causes adjacent molecules to increase their energy.

In this activity, the glass rod will be the poorest conductor. The best heat conductor among the metal rods will be the aluminum one, followed by the brass, and then the steel.

Extensions *Science:* Have some children find out how the transfer of heat takes place in air. They should focus their investigation on the term *convection*.

Have some children bring in samples of kitchen utensils that are both conductors and insulators (e.g., a stirring spoon with a metal end and a wooden handle).

Science/Math: You can extend this demonstration by fastening pins at regular intervals along each rod. The children can time how long it takes the heat to travel down the rods to release each pin. This data can then be graphed, with "Time for Pin to Drop" on the vertical axis and "Distance from Heat Source" on the horizontal axis.

For Middle-Level Learners [S&T 4]

Making Work Easier: Using Fixed and Movable Pulleys

Objectives
- The children will predict how a fixed pulley and a movable pulley can be used to make work easier.
- The children will observe the effect of using various pulley arrangements to move loads.
- The children will compare the required effort force and the direction of the effort force used in various pulley arrangements.

Science Processes Emphasized

Observing
Measuring

Predicting

Materials

Spring scale
String
Rock that has about 100 grams of mass
Single fixed pulley

Single movable pulley
2 screw hooks
Supported horizontal wooden board

Motivation Prior to the demonstration, insert the screw hooks into the wooden support. Display the pulleys, and ask the children if they have ever seen one being used. Discuss various uses of pulleys, and then display the rock. Tell the children that pulleys make work easier and that they will observe this during the demonstration. Have a volunteer come forward to assist you.

Directions 1. Have your assistant weigh the rock by tying a piece of string around it and attaching it to the spring scale. Write the weight on the board. Be sure that the children understand that the rock is the load to be moved with the pulleys. Attach the fixed pulley to the screw hook on the horizontal board, tie one end of a piece of string around the rock, and run the string through the pulley.

2. Ask the children to predict what the effect of using a fixed pulley will be. Have your volunteer carry out the demonstration, and ask the children to compare their predictions with the actual result.
3. Attach a string to the other screw hook, run one end of it through the pulley, and attach the rock to the pulley with another piece of string. Have your volunteer carry out the demonstration.
4. Now use the fixed pulley and the movable pulley together. Attach the string to he eye of the fixed pulley, and run the string through the bottom of the sheave of the movable pulley and up through the top of the sheave of the fixed pulley. Have your assistant repeat the demonstration.
5. Have the children compare the distance moved by the effort in step 4 with the distance moved by the load.

Key Discussion Questions

1. How does using a fixed pulley make work easier? *You can apply the effort force in a different location.*
2. How does using a movable pulley make work easier? *You use less force to move the load.*
3. About how much less effort do you need to raise a load with a movable pulley? Why? *You need about half as much. The load is held up by the hook and by the person holding the other end of the string.*
4. How does using a movable pulley and a fixed pulley together make work easier? *You use less force than the load's weight. The fixed pulley lets you change the direction of the effort force.*

Science Content for the Teacher

Pulleys are simple machines that enable us to multiply the effect of an effort force or change the direction in which the effort force is applied. A fixed pulley performs the latter function. For example, a fixed pulley at the top of a flagpole makes it possible to move a flag upward by pulling down on the rope attached to the flag. A movable pulley attached to a load can ideally halve the effort needed to move the load. Friction, of course, diminishes the pulley's efficiency. When a movable pulley is used to lift a load, the effort force must move farther than the distance the load is lifted.

Extensions

Science: If you can acquire additional pulleys, children may enjoy assembling more elaborate machines. A movable-and-fixed pulley arrangement (block and tackle) can be used to show how loads can be moved by quite small effort forces.

Science/Math: You can help children understand the amount of energy lost to overcoming of friction by comparing the actual mechanical advantage of the pulley (found by dividing the load by the effort) with the ideal mechanical advantage (found by dividing the load by the number of strands supporting the movable pulley).

NOTE

1. This demonstration is an adaptation of a portion of "Conduction and Non-Conduction," Module 70, *Science: A Process Approach II* (Lexington, MA: Ginn).

For the Teacher's Desk

Position Statements of the National Science Teachers Association (NSTA)*

Women in Science Education

The continuing policy within NSTA is, and has been, to involve and encourage all teachers and members of the scientific community, regardless of sex, to participate in all organizational activities.

As teachers, however, our responsibility for contributing to the development of the science skills and interests of women lies principally in the classroom. Three elements within the educational system have subtle but significant roles in supporting or negating our efforts in this regard. They are (1) the development and use of criteria for the selection of student-used materials, e.g., textbooks, films, filmstrips, to insure the equitable portrayal of girls and boys, women and men involved in science; (2) the support of guidance departments that encourage students to develop to their full potential and to advise them of the course options available to them in school and the career options available to them after school; (3) the encouragement and guidance provided by the teacher regarding student achievement and careers in science; and (4) the inclusion of appropriate role models.

Because of the importance of these three elements, NSTA takes the following positions:

I. Any teacher whose charge includes the responsibility of evaluating or selecting instructional materials should demand that the materials (a) eliminate sex role stereotyping and (b) reflect a realistic female/male ratio in relation to the total number of people portrayed. Materials should be rejected by the teacher if they do not meet the above two criteria.

II. Science teachers must exert their influence to encourage guidance counselors to treat female students identically to male students relative to career opportunities and program planning. Science teachers can assist guidance counselors in this endeavor by providing them with detailed updated information and data on the interests and abilities of specific female students.

III. Science teachers must consciously strive to overcome the barriers created by society which discourage women from pursuing science for its career opportunities and for the enjoyment it brings to involved students.

—Adopted by the NSTA Board of Directors, July 1985

Multicultural Science Education

Science educators value the contributions and uniqueness of children from all backgrounds. Members of the National Science Teachers Association (NSTA) are aware that a country's welfare is ultimately dependent upon the productivity of all of its people. Many institutions and organizations in our global, multicultural society play major roles in establishing environments in which unity in diversity flourishes. Members of the NSTA believe science literacy must be a major goal of science education institutions and agencies. We believe that ALL children can learn and be successful in science and our nation must cultivate and harvest the minds of all children and provide the resources to do so.

Rationale

If our nation is to maintain a position of international leadership in science education, NSTA must work with other professional organizations, institutions, corporations, and agencies to seek the resources required to ensure science teaching for all learners.

Declarations

For this to be achieved, NSTA adheres to the following tenets:

- Schools are to provide science education programs that nurture all children academically, physically, and in development of a positive self-concept;
- Children from all cultures are to have equitable access to quality science education experiences that enhance success and provide the knowledge and opportunities required for them to become successful participants in our democratic society;
- Curricular content must incorporate the contributions of many cultures to our knowledge of science;
- Science teachers are knowledgeable about and use culturally-related ways of learning and instructional practices;
- Science teachers have the responsibility to involve culturally-diverse children in science, technology and engineering career opportunities; and
- Instructional strategies selected for use with all children must recognize and respect differences students bring based on their cultures.

—Adopted by the NSTA Board of Directors, July 2000

Substance Use and Abuse

Rationale

There is abundant evidence that the general public considers substance abuse a major problem. Students have revealed the same concern in surveys conducted nationwide. NSTA endorses the efforts of many school systems to conduct programs to help students understand the problem.

NSTA proposes the following guidelines for the development and implementation of such programs:

- The science education curriculum should include information about the effects of substance use and abuse.
- The thrust of such programs should be to promote healthful living.
- The programs should include information to help students make rational judgments regarding the consumption of commonly accepted over-the-counter drugs such as nicotine, alcohol, caffeine, and aspirin.
- The fact that the use of tobacco or tobacco products in any form is harmful to good health should be clearly documented.
- Student should be informed of the research which demonstrates clearly that marijuana, cocaine, and other illegal substances does cause physiological harm.
- Facts concerning the effects of the use of substances that may be abused should be presented, rather than counter-productive detailed discussion and explanation of the substances themselves.
- The programs should make available to students medical evidence that will help them to understand the inherent dangers of substance use and abuse.
- The ultimate goal of substance use/abuse awareness programs should be to eliminate substance abuse by giving students the up-to-date scientific knowledge they must have in order to make informed decisions.

—Adopted by the NSTA Board of Directors, January 2000

Science Competitions

The National Science Teachers Association recognizes that many kinds of learning experiences, including science competitions, can contribute significantly to the education of students of science. With respect to science competitions such as science fairs, science leagues, symposia, Olympiads, and talent searches, the Association takes the position that participation should be guided by the following principles:

I. Student and staff participation in science competition should be voluntary.
II. Emphasis should be placed on the learning experience rather than on the competition.
III. Science competitions should supplement and enhance other educational experiences.
IV. The emphasis should be on scientific process, content, and/or application.
V. Projects and presentations must be the work of the student with proper credit to others for their contributions.

—Adopted by the NSTA Board of Directors, July 1986

Keeping Living Things . . . Alive

Living Materials in the Classroom*

Animals

Before introducing animals into the classroom, check the policy of your local school district. When animals are in the classroom, care should be taken to ensure that neither the students nor the animals are harmed. Mammals protect themselves and their young by biting, scratching, and kicking. Pets such as cats, dogs, rabbits, and guinea pigs should be handled properly and should not be disturbed when eating. Consider the following guidelines for possible adoption in your science classroom.

1. Do not allow students to bring live or deceased wild animals, snapping turtles, snakes, insects, or arachnids (ticks, mites) into the classroom, as they are capable of carrying disease.
2. Provide proper living quarters. Animals are to be kept clean and free from contamination. They must remain in a securely closed cage. Provision for their care during weekends and holidays must be made.
3. Obtain all animals from a reputable supply house. Fish should be purchased from tanks in which all fish appear healthy.
4. Discourage students from bringing personal pets into school. If pets are brought into the classroom, they should be handled only by their owners. Provision should be made for their care during the day—give them plenty of fresh water and a place to rest.
5. When observing unfamiliar animals, students should avoid picking them up or touching them.
6. Caution students never to tease animals or insert fingers, pens, or pencils into wire mesh cages. Report animal bites and scratches to the school's medical authority immediately. Provide basic first aid.
7. Rats, rabbits, hamsters, and mice are best picked up by the scruff of the neck, with a hand placed under the body for support. If young are to be handled, the mother should be removed to another cage—by nature she will be fiercely protective.
8. Use heavy gloves for handling animals; have students wash their hands before and after they handle animals.
9. Personnel at the local humane society or zoo can help teachers create a wholesome animal environment in the classroom.

Plants

Create a classroom environment where there are plants for students to observe, compare, and possibly classify as a part of their understanding of the plant world. Plants that are used for such purposes should be well-known to you. Plants that produce harmful substances should not be used.

*From "Living Materials in the Classroom," *Science Scope* 13, no. 3 (November/December 1989), p. 517. Used with permission of the National Science Teachers Association.

Since many plants have not been thoroughly researched for their toxicity, it is important for students and teachers to keep in mind some common-sense rules:

1. Never place any part of a plant in your mouth. (*Note:* Emphasize the distinction between nonedible plants and edible plants, fruits, and vegetables.)
2. Never allow any sap or fruit juice to set into your skin.
3. Never inhale or expose your skin or eyes to the smoke of any burning plant.
4. Never pick any unfamiliar wildflowers, seeds, berries, or cultivated plants.
5. Never eat food after handling plants without first scrubbing your hands.

The reason for these precautions is that any part of a plant can be relatively toxic, even to the point of fatality. Following is a list of some specific examples of toxic plants. This list is only partial; include additional poisonous (toxic) plants for your specific geographical area.

A. Plants that are poisonous to the touch due to exuded oils are:

Poison ivy (often found on school grounds)	Poison oak
Poison sumac	(other)

B. Plants that are poisonous when eaten include:

Many fungi	Belladonna	Pokeweed	Indian tobacco
(mushrooms)	Wake robin	Tansy	Jimson weed
Aconite	Henbane	Foxglove	(other)

C. The saps of the following plants are toxic:

Oleander	Trumpet vine	Poinsettia	(other)

Note: Also be aware that many common houseplants are toxic.

The Plant Picker

Plants That Will Survive with Little Sunlight

African Violet	Corn Plant	Peperomia	Spider Plant
Asparagus Fern	English Ivy	Philodendron	Spiderwort
Begonia	Ficus	Piggyback (Tolmeia)	(Tradescantia)
Boston Fern	Hen and Chickens	Snake Plant	Staghorn Fern
Chinese Evergreen	Parlor Palm		

Plants That Need a Great Deal of Sunlight

Agave	Echeveria	Mimosa (Acacia)	Spirea
Aloe	Geranium	Oxalis	Swedish Ivy
Blood Leaf	Hibiscus	Sedum	(filtered sunlight)
Cactus	Jade Plant		Yucca
Coleus	(filtered sunlight)		

Safety Management Helper

Safety Checklist*

The following general safety practices should be followed in your science teaching situation:

_____ Obtain a copy of the federal, state, and local regulations which relate to school safety, as well as a copy of your school district's policies and procedures. Pay special attention to guidelines for overcrowding, goggle legislation and "right to know" legislation.

_____ Know your school's policy and procedure in case of accidents.

_____ Check your classroom on a regular basis to insure that all possible safety precautions are being taken. Equipment and materials should be properly stored; hazardous materials should not be left exposed in the classroom.

_____ Before handling equipment and materials, familiarize yourself with their possible hazards.

_____ Be extra cautious when dealing with fire, and instruct your students to take appropriate precautions. Be certain fire extinguishers and fire blankets are nearby.

_____ Be familiar with your school's fire regulations, evacuation procedures, and the location and use of fire-fighting equipment.

_____ At the start of each science activity, instruct students regarding potential hazards and the precautions to be taken.

_____ The group size of students working on an experiment should be limited to a number that can safely perform the experiment without confusion and accidents.

_____ Plan enough time for students to perform the experiments, then clean up and properly store the equipment and materials.

_____ Students should be instructed never to taste or touch substances in the science classroom without first obtaining specific instructions from the teacher.

_____ Instruct students that all accidents or injuries—no matter how small—should be reported to you immediately.

_____ Instruct students that it is unsafe to touch their faces, mouths, eyes, and other parts of their bodies while they are working with plants, animals, or chemical substances and afterwards, until they have washed their hands and cleaned their nails.

*Reprinted with permission from *Safety in the Elementary Science Classroom.* Copyright © 1978, 1993 by the National Science Teachers Association, 1840 Wilson Boulevard, Arlington, VA 22201-3000.

SAFETY MANAGEMENT HELPER

When working with chemicals:

_____ Teach students that chemicals must not be mixed just to see what happens.

_____ Students should be instructed never to taste chemicals and to wash their hands after using chemicals.

_____ Elementary school students should not be allowed to mix acid and water.

_____ Keep combustible materials in a metal cabinet equipped with a lock.

_____ Chemicals should be stored under separate lock in a cool, dry place, but not in a refrigerator.

_____ Only minimum amounts of chemicals should be stored in the classroom. Any materials not used in a given period should be carefully discarded, particularly if they could become unstable.

Glassware is dangerous. Whenever possible, plastic should be substituted. However, when glassware is used, follow these precautions:

_____ Hard glass test tubes should not be heated from the bottom. They should be tipped slightly, but not in the direction of another student.

_____ Sharp edges on mirrors or glassware should be reported to the teacher. A whisk broom and dustpan should be available for sweeping up pieces of broken glass.

_____ Warn students not to drink from glassware used for science experiments.

_____ Thermometers for use in the elementary classroom should be filled with alcohol, not mercury.

Teachers and students should be constantly alert to the following safety precautions while working with electricity:

_____ Students should be taught to use electricity safely in everyday situations.

_____ At the start of any unit on electricity, students should be told not to experiment with the electric current of home circuits.

_____ Check your school building code about temporary wiring for devices to be used continuously in one location.

_____ Electrical cords should be short, in good condition, and plugged in at the nearest outlet.

_____ Tap water is a conductor of electricity. Students' hands should be dry when touching electrical cords, switches, or appliances.

Materials to Keep in Your Science Closet

Primary Grades

Depending on the maturity of your students, you may wish to keep some
or most of these items in a secure location in the room:

aluminum foil
aluminum foil pie plates
aquarium
baking soda
balance and standard
    masses
basic rock and mineral
    collection
beans, lima
camera and supplies
cardboard tubes from
    paper towel rolls
clipboard
cooking oil
corks
dishes, paper

dishes, plastic
egg cartons
feathers
first aid kit
flashlight
food coloring
globe
hand lenses
hot plate
iron filings
latex gloves
lemon juice
lunch bags, paper
magnets, various sizes
    and shapes
masking tape

measuring cups
measuring spoons
meterstick
microscope
mirrors
modeling clay
peas, dried
plastic bucket
plastic jugs
plastic spoons
plastic wrap
potholder
potting soil
rain gauge
rubber balls of various
    sizes

salt
sandwich bags, plastic
scales and masses
seeds, assorted
shell collection
shoe boxes
small plastic animals
small plastic trays
sponges
string
sugar
tape measure
terrarium
vinegar
yeast, dry

Middle Grades

Depending on the maturity of your students, you may wish to keep some
or most of these items in a secure location in the room:

aluminum foil
assorted nuts and bolts
balance and standard
    masses
balloons
barometer
batteries
beakers
binoculars
cafeteria trays
calculator
candles
cans, clean, assorted,
    empty
cellophane, various
    colors
chart of regional birds
chart of regional rocks
    and minerals
clothespins, spring-
    variety

compass, directional
compass, drawing
desk lamp
extensive rock and
    mineral collection
eyedroppers
first aid kit
flashlight
flashlight bulbs
forceps or tweezers
glass jars
graduated cylinders
graph paper
hammer
hand lenses
hot glue gun*
hot plate*
hydrogen peroxide (3%)*
incubator
iron filings
isopropyl alcohol*

latex gloves
lenses
litmus paper
map of region, with
    contour lines
map of country, with
    climate regions
map of world
marbles
microscope slides and
    coverslips
mirrors
net for scooping material
    from streams and/or
    ponds
petroleum jelly
plastic bucket
plastic containers, wide-
    mouth, 1 and 2 L
plastic straws
plastic tubing

plastic wrap
pliers
prisms
pulleys
safety goggles
screwdriver
seeds, assorted vegetable
sponge, natural
steel wool
stop watch
sugar cubes
switches for circuits
tape, electrical
telescope
test tubes (Pyrex or
    equivalent)
thermometers
toothpicks
washers, assorted
wire for making circuits
wood scraps

*Keep these items in a locked closet.

The Metric Helper

Length

1 centimeter (cm) = 10 millimeters (mm)

1 decimeter (dm) = 10 centimeters

1 meter (m) = 10 decimeters

1 kilometer (km) = 1,000 meters

Liquid Volume

1,000 (mL) = 1 liter (L)

Dry Volume

1,000 cubic millimeters (mm3) = 1 cubic centimeter (cm3)

Mass

1,000 milligrams (mg) = 1 gram (g)

1,000 grams (g) = 1 kilogram (kg)

Some Important Metric Prefixes

kilo = one thousand

deci = one-tenth

centi = one-hundredth

milli = one-thousandth

micro = one-millionth

Temperature

Water freezes at 0° Celsius

Normal body temperature is 37° Celsius

Water boils at 100° Celsius

Approximate Sizes

millimeter = diameter of the wire in a paper clip

centimeter = slightly more than the width of a paper clip at its narrowest point

meter = slightly more than 1 yard

kilometer = slightly more than ½ mile

gram = slightly more than the mass of a paper clip

kilogram = slightly more than 2 pounds

milliliter = 5 milliters equal 1 teaspoon

liter = slightly more than 1 quart

Content Coverage Checklists

The following content checklists can be used to evaluate various elementary science textbooks, curriculum materials, audiovisual materials, software packages, and other resource materials for use in your classroom. Obviously, these lists do not include every concept, but they will provide a framework for analysis.

The Earth/Space Sciences and Technology

_____ The universe is 8 to 20 billion years old.

_____ The earth is about 5 billion years old.

_____ The earth is composed of rocks and minerals.

_____ Evidence of the many physical changes that have occurred over the earth's history is found in rocks and rock layers.

_____ The study of fossils can tell us a great deal about the life forms that have existed on the earth.

_____ Many species of animals and plants have become extinct.

_____ Our knowledge of earlier life forms comes from the study of fossils.

_____ Such forces as weathering, erosion, volcanic upheavals, and the shifting of crustal plates, as well as human activity, change the earth's surface.

_____ Natural phenomena and human activity also affect the earth's atmosphere and oceans.

_____ The climate of the earth has changed many times over its history.

_____ *Weather* is a description of the conditions of our atmosphere at any given time.

_____ The energy we receive from the sun affects our weather.

_____ The water cycle, a continuous change in the form and location of water, affects the weather and life on our planet.

_____ Weather instruments are used to assess and predict the weather.

_____ The natural resources of our planet are limited.

_____ The quality of the earth's water, air, and soil is affected by human activity.

_____ Water, air, and soil must be conserved, or life as we know it will not be able to continue on the earth.

_____ The responsibility for preserving the environment rests with individuals, governments, and industries.

_____ Our solar system includes the sun, the moon, and nine planets.

_____ The sun is one of many billions of stars in the Milky Way galaxy.

_____ Rockets, artificial satellites, and space shuttles are devices that enable humans to explore the characteristics of planets in our solar system.

_____ Data gathered about the earth, oceans, atmosphere, solar system, and universe may be expressed in the form of words, numbers, charts, or graphs.

The Life Sciences
and Technology

_____ Living things are different from nonliving things.

_____ Plants and animals are living things.

_____ Living things can be classified according to their unique characteristics.

_____ The basic structural unit of all living things is the cell.

_____ All living things proceed through stages of development and maturation.

_____ Living things reproduce in a number of different ways.

_____ Animals and plants inherit and transmit the characteristics of their ancestors.

_____ Species of living things adapt and change over long periods of time or become extinct.

_____ Living things depend upon the earth, its atmosphere, and the sun for their existence.

_____ Living things affect their environment, and their environment affects living things.

_____ Different areas of the earth support different life forms, which are adapted to the unique characteristics of the area in which they live.

_____ Animals and plants affect one another.

_____ Plants are food producers.

_____ Animals are food consumers.

_____ Animals get their food by eating plants or other animals that eat plants.

_____ The human body consists of groups of organs (systems) that work together to perform a particular function.

_____ The human body can be affected by a variety of diseases, including sexually transmitted diseases.

_____ Human life processes are affected by food, exercise, drugs, air quality, and water quality.

_____ Medical technologies can be used to enhance the functioning of the human body and to diagnose, monitor, and treat diseases.

The Physical Sciences
and Technology

_____ *Matter* is anything that takes up space and has weight.

_____ Matter is found in three forms: solid, liquid, and gas.

_____ All matter in the universe attracts all other matter in the universe with a force that depends on the mass of the objects and the distance between them.

_____ Matter can be classified on the basis of readily observable characteristics, such as color, odor, taste, and solubility. These characteristics are known as *physical properties of matter.*

_____ Matter can undergo chemical change to form new substances.

_____ Substances consist of small particles known as *molecules.*

_____ Molecules are made of smaller particles known as *atoms.*

_____ Atoms are composed of three smaller particles called *protons, neutrons,* and *electrons.* (Protons and neutrons are composed of yet smaller particles known as *quarks.*)

_____ Atoms differ from one another in the number of protons, neutrons, and electrons they have.

_____ Some substances are composed of only one type of atom. These substances are known as *elements.*

_____ In chemical reactions between substances, matter is neither created nor destroyed but only changed in form. This is the law of conservation of matter.

_____ An object at rest or moving at a constant speed will remain in that state unless acted upon by an unbalanced external force.

_____ *Acceleration* is the rate at which an object's velocity changes.

_____ The amount of acceleration that an object displays varies with the force acting on the object and its mass.

_____ Whenever a force acts on an object, an equal and opposite reacting force occurs.

_____ The flight of an airplane results from the interaction of four forces: weight, lift, thrust, and drag.

_____ *Energy*—the capacity to do work—manifests itself in a variety of forms, including light, heat, sound, electricity, motion, and nuclear energy.

_____ Energy may be stored in matter by virtue of an object's position or condition. Such energy is known as *potential energy.*

_____ Under ordinary circumstances, energy can neither be created nor destroyed. This is the law of conservation of energy.

_____ The law of conservation of matter and the law of conservation of energy have been combined to form the law of conservation of matter plus energy, which states that under certain conditions, matter can be changed into energy and energy can be changed into matter.

_____ The basic concepts of matter, energy, force, and motion can be used to explain natural phenomena in the life, earth/space, and physical sciences.

_____ The diminishing supply of fossil fuels may be compensated for by the increased utilization of alternate energy sources, including wind, water, and synthetic fuels, and by energy conservation measures.

CONTENT COVERAGE CHECKLISTS

Your Science Survival Bookshelf

The Bookshelf

Abruscato, Joseph. *Whizbangers and Wonderments: Science Activities for Young People*. Boston: Allyn and Bacon, 2000.

Abruscato, Joseph, and Jack Hassard. *The Whole Cosmos Catalog of Science Activities*. Glenview, IL: Scott Foresman/ Goodyear Publishers, 1991.

Blough, Glenn, and Julius Schwartz. *Elementary School Science and How to Teach It*. Fort Worth, TX: Holt Rinehart & Winston, 1990.

Carin, Arthur A. *Teaching Science through Discovery*. Columbus, OH: Merrill, 1996.

Esler, William K., and Mary K. Esler. *Teaching Elementary School Science*. Belmont, CA: Wadsworth, 1996.

Friedl, Alfred E. *Teaching Science to Children*. New York: Random House, 1991.

Hassard, Jack. *Science Experiences: Cooperative Learning and the Teaching of Science*. Menlo Park, CA: Addison-Wesley, 1990.

Jacobson, Willard J., and Abby B. Bergman. *Science for Children*. Englewood Cliffs, NJ: Prentice-Hall, 1991.

Lorbeer, George C., and Leslie W. Nelson. *Science Activities for Children*. Dubuque, IA: W. C. Brown, 1996.

Neuman, Donald B. *Experiencing Elementary Science*. Belmont, CA: Wadsworth, 1993.

Tolman, Marvin H., and Gary R. Hardy. *Discovering Elementary Science*. Boston: Allyn and Bacon, 1999.

Van Cleave, Janice Pratt. *Chemistry for Every Kid*. New York: Wiley, 1989.

Victor, Edward, and Richard E. Kellough. *Science for the Elementary School*. New York: Macmillan, 1997.

The Magazine Rack

For Teachers

Audubon Magazine
National Audubon Society
1130 Fifth Avenue
New York, NY 10028

Natural History
The American Museum of
    Natural History
Central Park West at Seventy-Ninth Street
New York, NY 10024

Science Activities
Heldref Publications
1319 Eighteenth Street, NW
Washington, DC 20036

Science and Children
National Science Teachers Association
1840 Wilson Boulevard
Arlington, VA 22201-3000

Science Scope
National Science Teachers Association
1840 Wilson Boulevard
Arlington, VA 22201-3000

Science Teacher
National Science Teachers Association
National Education Association
1742 Connecticut Avenue, NW
Washington, DC 20088-0154

For Children

Chickadee
Young Naturalist Foundation
P.O. Box 11314
Des Moines, IA 50340

The Curious Naturalist
Massachusetts Audubon Society
208 South Great Road
South Lincoln, MA 01773

Current Science
Xerox Education Publications
5555 Parkcenter Circle Suite 300
Dublin, OH 43017

Junior Astronomer
Benjamin Adelman
4211 Colie Drive
Silver Springs, MD 20906

Junior Natural History
American Museum of Natural History
Central Park West at Seventy-Ninth Street
New York, NY 10024

Ladybug
Cricket Country Lane
Box 50284
Boulder, CO 80321-0284

National Geographic World
National Geographic Society
Seventeenth and M Streets, NW
Washington, DC 20036

Odyssey
Kalmbach Publishing Company
1027 North Seventh Street
Milwaukee, WI 53233

Owl
Young Naturalist Foundation
P.O. Box 11314
Des Moines, IA 50304

Ranger Rick
National Wildlife Federation
1412 Sixteenth Street, NW
Washington, DC 20036-2266

Science Weekly
Subscription Department
P.O. Box 70154
Washington, DC 20088-0154

Science World
Scholastic Magazines, Inc.
50 West Forty-Fourth Street
New York, NY 10036

SuperScience
Scholastic Magazines, Inc.
50 West Forty-Fourth Street
New York, NY 10036

WonderScience
American Chemical Society
1155 Sixteenth Street, NW
Washington, DC 20036

Free and Inexpensive Materials

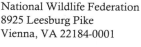

American Solar Energy Society
2400 Central Avenue, Suite G–1
Boulder, CO 80301

American Wind Energy Association
777 North Capitol Street, NE, Suite 805
Washington, DC 20002

Environmental Protection Agency Public
  Information Center and Library
401 M Street, SW
Washington, DC 20460

Environmental Sciences Services Administration
Office of Public Information
Washington Science Center, Building 5
Rockville, MD 20852

Fish and Wildlife Service
U.S. Department of the Interior
1849 C Street, NW
Mail Stop 304 Web Building
Washington, DC 20240

Jet Propulsion Laboratory (JPL)
Teacher Resource Center
4900 Oak Grove Drive
Mail Stop CS–530
Pasadena, CA 91109

National Aeronautics and Space
  Administration (NASA)
NASA Education Division
NASA Headquarters
300 E Street, SW
Washington, DC 20546

National Park Service
U.S. Department of the Interior
1849 C Street, NW
Washington, DC 20240

National Science Foundation
Division of Pre-College Education
1800 G Street, NW
Washington, DC 20550

National Wildlife Federation
8925 Leesburg Pike
Vienna, VA 22184-0001

Superintendent of Documents
U.S. Government Printing Office
732 North Capital Street, NW
Washington, D.C. 20401

U.S. Bureau of Mines
Office of Mineral Information
U.S. Department of the Interior
1849 C Street, NW
Washington, DC 20240

U.S. Department of Education
555 New Jersey Avenue, NW
Washington, DC 20208

U.S. Department of Energy
Conservation and Renewable Energy
  Inquiry and Referral Service
P.O. Box 8900
Silver Spring, MD 20907

U.S. Department of the Interior
Earth Science Information Center
1849 C Street, NW, Room 2650
Washington, DC 20240

U.S. Forest Service
Division of Information and Education
Fourteenth Street and Independence Avenue, SW
Washington, DC 20250

U.S. Geological Survey
Public Inquiries Office
U.S. Department of the Interior
Eighteenth and F Streets, NW
Washington, DC 20240

U.S. Public Health Service
Department of Health and Human Services
66 Canal Center Plaza, Suite 200
Alexandria, VA 22314

The "Wish Book" Companies

AIMS Education Foundation
P.O. Box 7766
Fresno, CA 93747

Carolina Biological Supply Co.
2700 York Road
Burlington, NC 27215

Central Scientific Company (CENCO)
3300 CENCO Parkway
Franklin, Park, IL 60131

Connecticut Valley Biological
    Supply Co., Inc.
82 Valley Road
Southhampton, MA 01073

Delta Education, Inc.
P.O. Box 915
Hudson, NH 03051-0915

Exploratorium Store
3601 Lyon Street
San Francisco, CA 94123

Flinn Scientific, Inc.
131 Flinn Street
P.O. Box 291
Batavia, IL 60510

Frey Scientific
905 Hickory Lane
Mansfield, OH 44905

Hubbard Scientific
3101 Iris Avenue, Suite 215
Boulder, CO 80301

Learning Things, Inc.
68A Broadway
P.O. Box 436
Arlington, MA 02174

LEGO Systems, Inc.
555 Taylor Road
Enfield, CT 06802

NASCO West, Inc.
P.O. Box 3837
Modesto, CA 95352

Ohaus Scale Corp.
29 Hanover Road
Florham Park, NJ 07932

Science Kit and Boreal Labs
777 East Park Drive
Tonawanda, NY 14150

Ward's Natural Science
    Establishment, Inc.
5100 West Henrietta Road
P.O. Box 92912
Rochester, NY 14692

Wind and Weather
P.O. Box 2320-ST
Mendocino, CA 95460

Young Naturalist Co.
614 East Fifth Street
Newton, KN 67114

Bilingual Child Resources

Alabama, Florida, Georgia, Kentucky, Mississippi, South Carolina, Tennessee

Bilingual Education South Eastern Support Center [BESES]
Florida International University
Tamiami Campus, TRM03
Miami, FL 33199

Alaska, Idaho, Montana, Oregon, Washington, Wyoming

Interface Education Network
7080 SW Fir Loop, Suite 200
Portland, OR 97223

American Samoa, Hawaii

Hawaii/American Samoa Multifunctional Support Center
1150 South King Street, #203
Honolulu, HI 97814

Arizona, California (Imperial, Orange, Riverside, San Bernardino, San Diego Counties)

SDSU-Multifunctional Support Center
6363 Alvarado Court, Suite 200
San Diego, CA 92120

Arkansas, Louisiana, Oklahoma, Texas Education Service Regions V–XIX

Bilingual Education Training and Technical Assistance Network [BETTA]
University of Texas at El Paso
College of Education
El Paso, TX 79968

California (all counties north of and including San Luis Obispo, Kern, and Inyo), Nevada

Bilingual Education Multifunctional Support Center
National Hispanic University
255 East Fourteenth Street
Oakland, CA 94606

California (Los Angeles, Santa Barbara, Ventura Counties), Nevada

Bilingual Education Multifunctional Support Center
California State University at Los Angeles
School of Education
5151 State University Drive
Los Angeles, CA 90032

Colorado, Kansas, Nebraska, New Mexico, Utah

BUENO Bilingual Education Multifunctional Support Center
University of Colorado
Bueno Center of Multicultural Education
Campus Box 249
Boulder, CO 80309

Commonwealth of Northern Mariana Islands, Guam, Trust Territory of the Pacific Islands

Project BEAM [Bilingual Education Assistance in Micronesia]
University of Guam
College of Education
UOG Station,
Mangilao, GU 96923

Commonwealth of Puerto Rico, Virgin Islands

Bilingual Education Multifunctional Support Center
Colegio Universitario Metropolitano
P.O. Box CUM
Rio Piedras, PR 00928

Connecticut, Maine, Massachusetts, New Hampshire, Rhode Island, Vermont

New England Bilingual Education Multifunctional Center
Brown University, Weld Building
345 Blackstone Boulevard
Providence, RI 02906

Delaware, District of Columbia, Maryland, New Jersey, North Carolina, Ohio, Pennsylvania, Virginia, West Virginia

Georgetown University Bilingual Education Service Center
Georgetown University
2139 Wisconsin Avenue, NW, Suite 100
Washington, DC 20007

Illinois, Indiana, Iowa, Michigan, Minnesota, Missouri, North Dakota, South Dakota, Wisconsin

Midwest Bilingual Educational Multifunctional Resource Center
2360 East Devon Avenue, Suite 3011
Campus Box 136
Des Plaines, IL 60018

New York

New York State Bilingual Education Multifunctional
Support Center
Hunter College of CUNY
695 Park Avenue, Box 367
New York, NY 10021

*Texas Education Service Center, Regions
I through IV, XX*

Region Multifunctional Support Center
Texas A&I University
Kingsville, TX 78363
Native American Programs

*Alaska, Arizona, California, Michigan,
Minnesota, Montana, New Mexico,
North Carolina, Oklahoma, South Dakota,
Utah, Washington, Wyoming*

National Indian Bilingual Center
Arizona State University
Community Services Building
Tempe, AZ 85287

Special-Needs Resources

Alexander Graham Bell Association for the Deaf
3417 Volta Place, NW
Washington, D.C. 20007

American Foundation for the Blind
15 West Sixteenth Street
New York, NY 10011

American Printing House for the Blind
1839 Frankforth Avenue, Box A
Louisville, KY 40206

American Speech, Language, and Hearing
Association
10801 Rockville Pike
Rockville, MD 20852

Center for Multisensory Learning
University of California at Berkeley
Lawrence Hall of Science
Berkeley, CA 94720

Council for Exceptional Children
1920 Association Drive
Reston, VA 22091

ERIC Clearinghouse on Handicapped and
Gifted Children
1920 Association Drive
Reston, VA 22091

The Lighthouse for the Blind and
Visually Impaired
1155 Mission Street
San Francisco, CA 94103

National Technical Institute for the Deaf
One Lomb Memorial Drive
Rochester, NY 14623

The Project on the Handicapped in Science
American Association for the Advancement
of Science
1776 Massachusetts Avenue, NW
Washington, DC 20036

Recording for the Blind
20 Roszel Road
Princeton, NJ 08540

Sensory Aids Foundation
399 Sherman Avenue
Palo Alto, CA 94304

Science Teachers Associations

The major association for teachers with an interest in science is the National Science Teachers Association (NSTA). For information on membership, write to this address:

National Science Teachers Association
1840 Wilson Boulevard
Arlington, VA 22201-3000

This affiliated organization may also be reached through the NSTA address:

Council for Elementary Science International

Other science-related associations that may be of interest include the following:

American Association of Physics Teachers
c/o American Institute of Physics
335 E. 45th Street
New York, NY 10017

American Chemical Society
1155 Sixteenth Street, NW
Washington, DC 20006

National Association of Biology Teachers
1420 N. Street, NW
Washington, DC 20005

National Earth Science Teachers Association
P.O. Box 2194
Liverpool, NY 13089-2194

School Science and Mathematics Association
16734 Hamilton Court
Strongsville, OH 44149-5701

NASA Teacher Resource Centers

NASA Teacher Resource Centers provide teachers with NASA-related materials for use in classrooms. Contact the center that serves your state for materials or additional information.

Alabama, Arkansas, Iowa, Louisiana, Missouri, Tennessee

NASA Marshall Space Flight Center
Teacher Resource Center at the U.S. Space and
   Rocket Center
P.O. Box 070015
Huntsville, AL 35807

Alaska, Arizona, California, Hawaii, Idaho, Montana, Nevada, Oregon, Utah, Washington, Wyoming

NASA Ames Research Center
Teacher Resource Center
Mail Stop 253-2
Moffett Field, CA 94035

California (cities near Dryden Flight Research Facility)

NASA Dryden Flight Research Facility
Teacher Resource Center
Lancaster, CA 93535

Colorado, Kansas, Nebraska, New Mexico, North Dakota, Oklahoma, South Dakota, Texas

NASA Johnson Space Center
Education Resource Center
1601 NASA Road #1
Houston, TX 77058

Connecticut, Delaware, District of Columbia, Maine, Maryland, Massachusetts, New Hampshire, New Jersey, New York, Pennsylvania, Rhode Island, Vermont

NASA Goddard Space Flight Center
Teacher Resource Laboratory
Mail Code 130.3
Greenbelt, MD 20771

Florida, Georgia, Puerto Rico, Virgin Islands

NASA Kennedy Space Center
Educators Resource Laboratory
Mail Code ERL
Kennedy Space Center, FL 32899

Kentucky, North Carolina, South Carolina, Virginia, West Virginia

NASA Langley Research Center
Teacher Resource Center at the Virginia Air and
   Space Center
600 Settlers Landing Road
Hampton, VA 23669

Illinois, Indiana, Michigan, Minnesota, Ohio, Wisconsin

NASA Lewis Research Center
Teacher Resource Center
21000 Brookpark Road
Mail Stop 8-1
Cleveland, OH 44135

Mississippi

NASA Stennis Space Center
Teacher Resource Center
Building 1200
Stennis Space Center, MS 39529-6000

Virginia and Maryland Eastern Shore

NASA Wallops Flight Facility
Education Complex-Visitor Center
Building J-17
Wallops Island, VA 23337

General inquiries related to space science and planetary exploration may be addressed to:

Jet Propulsion Laboratory
NASA Teacher Resource Center
Attn: JPL Educational Outreach
Mail Stop CS-530
Pasadena, CA 91109

For catalogue and order forms for audiovisual material, send request on school letterhead to:

NASA CORE
Lorain County Joint Vocational School
15181 Route 58 South
Oberlin, OH 44074

Index

Note: Page numbers in bold type indicate activities/demonstrations.

Photo, Figure, and Text Credits